D1439128

cientific

B15989

THE GROWING BOY

The author, aged 14

THE GROWING BOY

Being the first book of an Autobiography

1892–1908

by

CECIL ROBERTS

HODDER AND STOUGHTON

Printed in Great Britain for Hodder and Stoughton Limited,
St. Paul's House, Warwick Lane, London, E.C.4,
by The Camelot Press Ltd., London and Southampton

CONTENTS

ACKNOWLEDGEMENTS

IN the course of *la recherche du temps perdu* I am greatly indebted to many who have suffered my inquisition so patiently and given me much assistance. Among them: Mr. Trevor Allen; the Rev. A. Ash, of Church Langton; the Rev. E. R. Boston, M.A., of Cadeby Rectory; Mr. William Burgess, of Sutton Cheney Hall-Farm, Leics.; Mr. Richard Church, C.B.E.; Mr. E. Gerard, B.A., Chief Librarian, Nottingham Public Libraries; Miss A. Forneris and Mr. M. F. Holloway, of the British Council Library, Rome; Professor Denys Hay; Lord and Lady Hazlerigg, of Noseley, Leics.; Mr. D. Matthews, of the London Library; Mr. M. D. Moody, B.A., of Mundella School; the Rev. G. C. Oakley, Willesden Vicarage; the late Mr. Chance Quarrell, M.A.; Mr. John W. Roberts, of Richmond, Virginia, U.S.A.; Mr. Robert Spencer, East Langton Hall, Leics.; Mr. H. G. Swinburn, Editor, *Guardian Journal*, Nottingham; Marchesa Stella Vitelleschi; Mr. Seymour Wright, Old Rectory, Rempstone; the Royal Historical Society, and Professor Denys Hay for permission to quote from his translation of Polydore Vergil's *Anglica Historia* (Camden Series); Rupert Hart-Davis, for a quotation from *George Moore: Letters*; the Vatican Library, Rome, which permitted me to examine the original manuscript of *Anglica Historia*, and to reproduce two facsimile pages.

Above all, I wish to thank my cousin, Mr. Walter Roberts, of Neuilly-sur-Seine, for his painstaking and percipient reading of my manuscript. Also, I wish to thank many others, unnamed, involved in what Nancy Cunard called "the time-devouring correspondence which is inseparable from the writing of books".

Rome, 1965–6–7.   C. R.

ILLUSTRATIONS

PREFACE

WHEN I was thirty-five I wrote an autobiography called *Half Way*. It told the story of some of my life up to that age. The *Daily Telegraph* said: "In thirty-five years of life he has crowded experience and delight that would enrich three lives. It would be easier to consider what he has not seen and done than to attempt to summarise the astonishing volume which he names *Half Way*."

A gratifying reception; but as the book passed through impression after impression, it sold over one hundred thousand copies, it threw an ever-lengthening shadow. There was a suggestion that, by the grace of God, a day would come when I should write about the second half of my life. I shivered a little. No young man quite believes he will live to be seventy. At twenty old age is a myth, at fifty, a thought to be avoided. Now, well past the second half, shall I be justified in opening my mouth, or say, with Hamlet—"The rest is silence"? Many a promising play has collapsed in the last act.

I have a precedent. Goldoni, the author of more than a hundred plays, began his *Memoirs* at the age of seventy-seven and finished them at eighty, in 1787. They are still very readable. There is a difficulty in writing one's life, since the spotlight is continuously on the centre figure that occupies the stage. The light magnifies the egotism of the performer. And how much truth, how much suppression, maintaining the decencies of human behaviour, should one indulge in? As an art form the autobiography is the most difficult of all. Well, I will make the effort, and this time I shall start at the very beginning. I was too impatient, too ambitious at thirty-five, too forward-looking, to wish to look back. Hesiod wrote, around 700 B.C.—"The half is greater than the whole." That is not my experience, and here is my attempt to prove it. I have found the whole way exciting and rewarding.

9

CHAPTER ONE

The Infant Years

I

I WAS BORN in Nottingham on May 18th, 1892, at four o'clock in the morning. In the improbable event that someone should seek to mark my birthplace with a plaque, it cannot be done. Soon afterwards it became a vast hole in the ground, and in this sixty-foot hole the Great Central Railway built the Victoria Station, naming it after the reigning Queen. In turn this station is to give place to an underground garage and a skyscraper block of offices, following the curtailment of the British Railways.

I have no idea what the street of my birthplace was like, but I surmise it was grim. I had arrived, unwanted, at a low ebb in the family's affairs. My father's disapproval of me was based on two disconcerting facts. I had been born in Nottingham instead of Leicestershire, in which the family had its roots, and I was a boy, the second, whereas he longed for a daughter. Consequently his first comment when I was shown to him was unflattering—"He has eyes like burnt holes in a blanket," he said.

Happily his disapproval did not last long. My first memory of him was that he was more gentle than my mother when it came to the order of the bath, taken in a round tin in front of the kitchen fire, that he had fascinating whiskers with which he tickled me, and that he was incredibly tall. For years I was convinced he was the tallest man in the world. Much later I learned the truth with some disappointment. He delighted me with rhyming verses written specially for me in his bold beautiful handwriting. These were signed "Longfellow, six-feet-one in his socks". To this day I remember one of his productions. It told in couplets the adventurous life-story of "The Fly that wouldn't die." Each verse was accompanied by the terrific whack of a folded newspaper demonstrating the agility of that evasive fly. I recall also his patience and artfulness when the time came to wean me from a baby's rubber 'comforter'. It was pink with a ring through which a blue ribbon was threaded and hung about my neck. My mother had decided that I should relinquish this childish delight, but all her attempts provoked storms of tears. My father was more artful. He offered to share it with me, and let me put it in his mouth, to my great delight. I repeatedly forced it upon him, sensing the comic. He would sit with it in his mouth, reading a paper. Little by little I surrendered all my rights. Then it disappeared completely.

He was wonderful at making a rabbit out of a handkerchief and causing it to jump up his arm and over his shoulder. I learned the trick later and to this day can keep an infant wide-eyed with rabbit antics. As the years grew I discovered he had endless little skills. There was a tin money-bank in the form of a scarlet pillar-box with *V.R.* over its slit and posting times underneath. Into this I was encouraged to insert my pennies, an early lesson in thrift. But sometimes I grew impatient about this hoarded wealth. I shook the pillar-box vigorously. It rattled loudly but never would a penny come out. Then one day, seeing my frustration, he took a table knife, inserted the blade, reversed the bank, and gently withdrew it. A penny lay on it. How simple! Too simple in the eyes of my disapproving mother. Yet the trick had its domestic uses. We had a penny-in-the-slot gas meter and, suddenly plunged into darkness, there would be urgent need of a penny. When this was not forthcoming Queen Victoria's pillar-box was raided. The knife-blade delivered us from darkness.

II

The first two things I remember are related to smells, one of tar, one of bark tan. I recall being held, wrapped in a shawl, at about the age of two, by my mother, over an iron vehicle filled with boiling tar. I suppose this was one of those vats used by road repairers. I had whooping cough and the fumes of tar were supposed to have curative properties. The second odour is that of brown flakes of bark which had been used by the leather tanners. This was bought and laid down on cobbled roads to lessen the noise of passing solid-wheeled traffic when a person was dangerously ill. To this day I linger by boiling tar, it evokes the first memory of my childhood. The bark tan is never seen these days. Pneumatic tyres and asphalted roads have abolished its use as a noise-deadener.

I was about four when the first tragedy in my life swept down upon me. The horror of it is still vivid. I was ravished from the bosom of my family. I had scarlet fever and was carried off in a horse van, a strange woman in attendance, to an isolation hospital. There I found myself in a ward of hateful children. I was put into a strange coarse nightgown, and worse, my fair curls were ruthlessly cut away. It was the first blow to my vanity. I howled when I saw myself in a mirror. I do not know how long I was in durance vile, but at last came Visitors' Day. What a mockery of a visit! Since we were infectious the visiting parents were only allowed to stand on a gravel path outside the high windows of the long ward, to which we were carried by the nurses, wrapped up in blankets. There was a mad scramble of parents searching for their particular urchin. I had no difficulty in identifying my parents in that bustling mob. My father stood high above them all. I gave out a wild scream of recognition. And then it was I saw my mother. I see her today, over seventy years later. She blew kisses at me with a dark gloved hand. In turn the nurse took my hand and waved it at her. I had my first sensation of pride. She wore a large grey hat with a rose in it, and a spotted veil. My infantile consciousness knew no word to match the impression she made. She was somehow very distinct from all the other frantic mothers. Years later I knew the word she embodied. She was elegant.

For about ten minutes we were exhibited. In vain the parents below shouted up to their offspring. The thick window panes shut off all sound. After this frustrated meeting, we were withdrawn from view. It was an unsettling experience for everybody. For half an hour afterwards there was a ward of wailing children.

My return home was something of a disaster. There was a complete change in me. Crop-headed, violent, I had picked up, in the common mêlée, frightful words and an appalling accent. I screamed, I swore, I kicked. A quiet-mannered angel had been transformed into a rampant demon. It took my despairing parents a month to tame me and eradicate all traces of that corrupting sojourn in hospital.

I was a very delicate child, highly strung and apprehensive. I caught everything, scarlet fever, German measles, mumps, whooping cough, tonsilitis, chicken-pox, bronchitis, shingles. When an epidemic of smallpox broke out in Liverpool and cases were reported in Nottingham my parents lived in a state of acute apprehension. It seemed inevitable that with my gregarious gift for infection I should contract the disease. This I escaped, but throughout my early childhood I was so delicate that it was thought I would not survive. All kinds of remedies were tried on me. I went from cotton wool to cold baths. I swallowed Dr. Collis Brown's Chlorodyne, Dr. Parrish's Chemical Food, Scott's Emulsion of Cod Liver Oil, Virol, and Liebig's Extract of Meat. At least I was a good taker. I could swallow anything without reluctance and I always had a pink and white complexion and a flawless skin. The pimples and boils of boyhood and adolescence never touched me. "You were so delicate we feared you would be blown out like a candle. Sometimes you had a transparent look that frightened us," said my mother.

In those years I knew nothing of my parents' desperate struggle to keep their heads above water. Happily childhood is scarcely aware of poverty or the successive blows of fate. Like animals and birds, children have an easy confidence that the next meal will be there, that sufficient for the day are the supplies thereof. They have a Christian confidence, without being Christians or expecting the beneficence of God, Who to them is more often a Holy Spy invoking all manner of punishments rather than a Benign Presence. My mother being devout lost no opportunity of introducing me to God, a Deity Who seemed interested only in the Church of England. Every night before I got into bed I would kneel at my mother's knees, my small feet sticking out of a flannelette nightgown, my hands devoutly folded, my eyes shut, and pronounce the Lord's Prayer. After this came my category of requests, extended from my father and mother to a beloved pink-eyed white rabbit kept behind galvanised wire in the narrow backyard. Yet all this was only a preliminary to the business of the evening that really mattered. My mother read me to sleep. The books she read were mostly of an 'improving' nature. There was *Line upon Line*, culled from the Scriptures, with coloured illustrations, some of bearded old men in long white nightgowns who always seemed to be denouncing someone for doing something. I was troubled by angels with wings—how did they get their nightshirts on and how did they balance those plates behind their heads? In due time I came to take them for granted, much as the Anglicans take the Thirty-Nine Articles, that the Church of England hides away in small print in its Prayer Book. But there was lighter entertainment in that evening performance. *Home Chat* had an enchanting pictorial serial depicting the adventures of a pig in trousers, a hen in a bonnet, a mouse in a tailcoat and a flirtatious pussy that wore a pleated skirt and had the eyelashes of a musical comedy actress.

The author in 1894, aged 2

My mother in 1894, aged 39

Home Chat went out of publication when I was about sixty years of age. It was like the loss of a piece of the British Empire.

There was also more emotional fare. I was reduced to floods of tears by the harrowing story of *Christy's Old Organ*. Later, not at bedtime but on my father's knee, I was introduced to Edward Lear —*The Owl and the Pussy-Cat, The Dong with the Luminous Nose*. My father read with such dramatic emphasis that I squealed with delight. I did not realise then that he had a wonderful sense of words and that my young ears were being trained to the richness of the English language. On the sideboard of that kitchen-living-room there was a heavy volume. It was Dr. Annandale's Dictionary. "That's his Bible," said my mother sorrowfully. It was to play a momentous part in my life.

For me Sunday was not the day of a clean frock, white socks and shiny black shoes with straps. It was the day of the Frock Coat. My father appeared in all majesty, attired to take my mother for a walk. She was lovely and dainty in a 'picture' hat, a grey veil with white spots, buttoned-up suede gloves, a grey feather boa across her shoulders, and tiny feet twinkling from the flounced bottom of a trailing skirt. She was in the early forties then, my father three years her junior. Being of medium height—all her life she cherished the illusion that she was a tall woman—my father towered up above her. His black tightly buttoned frock coat emphasised the height of his slim, martially erect figure. He added to their disparity by a shining top hat that had been polished with a velvet pad. Under his frock coat he wore a white double-breasted waistcoat which had been laundered and pressed by my mother. Lavender gloves, an ebony walking stick, and long, slipper-light shoes that looked as if they had never been walked in, completed my father's attire.

In those days I was dressed in a white frock and sailor blouse, with a large round straw hat from which hung a streamer. I, too, wore a pair of fawn kid gloves with one button. A contemporary photograph of the young Cecil has a revealing fact. Incongruously, the little sailor is holding a hunting stock and has a symbolic horse. That was the Leicestershire touch, supplied by my father. I surmise it identified me with the Robertses whose breed, in marble effigies, is to be found in Leicestershire churches, of which I was to become aware later.

This whole Sunday parade was their make-believe. It proclaimed a prosperity that did not exist, though I was blissfully unaware of the flimsy props behind this resplendent façade. Bankruptcy, bailiffs, exiguous living and the successive blows of vindictive Fate lurked in the shadowy past.

We were a singularly restricted family. To this day I look with amazement and some envy on families with endless ramifications, sisters, brothers, cousins, aunts, uncles, great-aunts, great-uncles, grandmothers and grandfathers, that are the inheritance of many children. I never cease to be amazed by the fecund nature of Jewish and Italian families, where birth-control imposes no limitations, where the herd instinct and matriarchy are supreme. My own small family consisting of my father, mother and an elder brother, seemed to be without living relations. I had no grandparents, maternal or paternal. My mother had no living brothers or sisters, aunts, uncles or cousins. My father had one younger brother and a spinster sister who married late in life. My uncle Vincent, who lived in another town, I only saw twice in my life for a few minutes. He bore no resemblance to my father. He was trimly bearded and energetic. He came and vanished like a comet. I could not have identified him in any cluster of human beings. The spinster aunt, Susan (the girls for generations appear to have been called Susan), kind, genial, I remembered better because she fitted into the Leicestershire frame. As a very small boy I was taken by my father to visit her and was deeply impressed. She lived in a large Georgian house near Melton Mowbray. It had a stately entrance hall, a wide marble stair-case, a fine leathery library. A long drawing-room was covered down in dust-sheets. Its French windows opened on a balustraded terrace and a great lawn with flower beds and massive trees. There was a range of stables surmounted by a clock, but there were no horses in the stables and no hounds in the kennels. The whole house was strangely empty and silent. It looked as if my aunt was about to leave or had just arrived. Having made the tour of the house, she gave us tea in a small sitting-room bright with chintz. There was a large scarlet parrot in a cage that I fed with sugar. The bird and my aunt seemed to be the only living creatures in that large silent house.

Passing through the hall as we left, my father paused to look at two full-length oil portraits. The man was in hunting kit, as also the lady.

"Is that your aunt and uncle?" I asked my aunt.

She laughed gaily. "No, darling. That's Captain Melville and Lady Eva, his wife," she explained.

This was a hunting-box. The family was absent, it being out of season. My aunt was the housekeeper.

A lonely child. No holidays with grandparents, aunts or uncles. No playing with cousins, no seasonal reunions. We were alone in the world. But for a cruel fate I should have had another brother and a sister. These two had died, the boy aged seven months, the girl aged one year. This left a gap of eleven years between my elder brother and myself. My parents had returned one evening to find the little girl suffocated in her cot. The neighbour who had volunteered to look after her had left the house after putting her to bed. The boy had mysteriously died of pneumonia within twenty-four hours. The mystery was solved on the way to the cemetery. "Oh, mummy, I told Minnie (the nursemaid) not to put Vincent on the grass," said my brother. It transpired that in the arboretum she had taken the baby out of the pram and gone off to flirt with a soldier. As soon as my mother returned from the funeral she called the maid, gave her her wages and had her out of the house within an hour. She never spoke of these two lost children. I was grown up before I learned about them, but how deeply their loss had bitten into her soul I realised when, after her death, I opened the cash box in which she had stored small things, among them two printed black-edged mourning cards, setting forth their ages and dates of death, a tiny handkerchief embroidered with little Susan's name, and a pair of white baby socks with blue tassels that surely had been Vincent's.

I had no idea what my father's business then was. He went out early, always kissing my mother, and came in late, again kissing her. I did not know then that I dwelt in a nest lined with love. Later I learned with amazement of homes in which the husband and wife quarrelled, the women were sometimes beaten, the men drank. In the somewhat Nonconformist-Puritan surroundings of the district in which we lived, divorce was unheard of. The poor could not escape each other in this manner. They were bound together for better or worse. Moreover, divorce carried the stigma of disgrace. Whatever the cause, a divorced woman was 'finished'. She might go and live with another man but, divorced, she was beyond the pale. It never occurred to me until early manhood that there was such a thing as domestic unhappiness, unfaithfulness, quarrels, violence.

My father, a yeoman farmer's son, had fallen in love with another farmer's daughter. Every Saturday he walked twelve miles to Kirkby Green, from Lincoln, where he was apprenticed in a grain business,

to court my mother. He married her when he was twenty-two in her
tiny village church. She was twenty-five. The wedding breakfast
was given by a well-to-do county family called Byron, related to the
poet. One of the wedding presents, a tea service, came from dashing
Henry Chaplin, the local squire. I still own that Georgian Sheffield-
plate tea service.

My father and mother were married in 1881. The vicar was a
pluralist, a drunkard and a passionate rider to hounds. My mother
told me how, as a girl, she had seen him conduct a burial service
with his riding boots and spurs showing beneath his surplice, being
in such a hurry to leave for the hunt. He was once so drunk that he
fell flat on his face coming down from the pulpit. My parents were
apprehensive on the wedding day, but happily he was on his best
behaviour and made a charming little speech at the wedding breakfast.

I think they must have been a handsome pair. My mother had
merry blue eyes, abundant chestnut tresses, a slim figure and, to the
day of her death, forty-five years later, a marvellous complexion and
skin. I recall as a boy the pleasure of nestling close to her, lured by
the satin quality of her flesh and the rose-coloured cheeks that never
knew or needed a touch of cosmetics or powder. My father also was
blond, pink-and-white. He carried his height like a young guards-
man, and in this respect he was a martinet with me. He would never
allow me to slump in a chair at table, and if I walked in the street,
stooping, he would bring his cane smartly across my shoulders. I
am grateful to him for that early discipline. My posture has caused
me to be mistaken at times for an ex-army officer. One day, indig-
nantly shaking a newspaper that contained a picture of a young
royalty, he exclaimed: "Good God! Why doesn't his tutor go after
that hippocampus!" Not knowing what a hippocampus was, I went
to Dr. Annandale's Dictionary. "Hippocampus—a kind of small fish:
sea-horse." There was an illustration and the curve justified the
simile.

In later years my mother, under my prompting, would talk about
her early life, but the narration always took on an air of sadness, and
she would suddenly stop, get up and find something to do. She had a
happy childhood, there were two brothers. Her father, delicate and
not suited to farming, died soon after she was married, and her
brothers carried on the farm. Of her brothers, the younger died of
consumption, the other took to drink, and eventually the farm was

sold. He became a misanthrope, and in old age a miser. Despite her affection for him he drove her off, aware of my father's contempt, and finally refused to have any contact with her. Past fifty, he married a neat little widow but treated her so badly that finally she had to leave him. He was found, unattended and dying, in a room piled high with furniture. Carried off to the public hospital, he loudly protested that he had no money. He died in hospital, and it was found that he had hoarded eight hundred pounds in gold sovereigns in a coal scuttle. He had willed everything to a local charity, so the wife he had starved and driven out got nothing. Happily she had well-to-do connections. Despite all she put fresh flowers on his grave every week. Her brother's fate saddened my mother until she died. For some reason she had a deep affection for him.

All her life she never ceased to be interested in the Squire of Blankney, Henry Chaplin, a rip-roaring young Victorian who in old age portly, monocled, became the patriarch of the House of Commons, and was always a favourite in Court and Turf circles. In the public eye he epitomised the squirearchy. He was a crony of Edward, Prince of Wales, with whom he was at Christ Church, Oxford. They drank, hunted and wenched together. On one occasion they met a fat old peasant woman in a lane on the Blankney estate. They tied her skirts up over her head, stuck a five-pound note in her bloomers and left her, blindfolded, to find her way home. There was no scandal. It was still an age when the tenantry didn't quarrel with the Squire. On another occasion, wildly driving home in a four-in-hand after a midnight revel, with the Prince of Wales and other friends, Chaplin forgot all about the closed iron gates of Blankney Hall and drove the team headlong into them. The two leading horses were killed outright and a third had to be shot.

Chaplin's obsession was horses. At Oxford he hunted six days a week. When Queen Victoria's ponies had 'pink-eye' it was to Chaplin she turned for advice. He was the beau-ideal of the hunting country squire. He was a good landlord and very popular. There was much sympathy for him when he was jilted in 1864 by Lady Florence Paget. A few weeks before the announced wedding she went to the opera with her fiancé and the Marquess of Hastings, a wealthy young rake of twenty-two. The next day she married Hastings, providing Society with a sensational scandal. Chaplin behaved with great chivalry towards Hastings. Rivals on the Turf, he was associated with the Marquess's downfall. They both entered horses for the 1867

Derby. Chaplin's horse was 'Hermit', bought for a thousand guineas two years before. It entered the race with odds of 66 to 1 against it. Hastings heavily backed 'Vauban', with odds of 6 to 4. The favourite was 'The Rake'. On the morning of the race Chaplin's 'Hermit' had not found a jockey. A lad of twenty, Darley, was put in the saddle an hour before the race. The Derby was run in a snowstorm. 'Hermit' defeated the 'Rake' by a neck. 'Vauban' was third. On this race Hastings lost £120,000. To meet debts of £300,000 he had to sell his Scottish estates. He owed £20,000 to Chaplin who generously postponed payment. "Who will dare to say that racing is a sinful arrangement?" asked *Punch*. "Think, £120,000 carried off from a Rake by a Hermit for the benefit of a Chaplin!" Within eighteen months Hastings was dead of Bright's disease, caused by excessive drinking, bankrupt, aged twenty-six, the last marquess. A few weeks before his death, sitting in the library of his ancestral home, Donington Hall, irritated by a portrait of Chaplin hanging on the wall, he picked up a revolver and shot out its eyes.

III

My father and mother, newly wed, made their home in Lincoln. With a legacy he had bought a small grain business. Unhappily he had not the slightest business ability. He allowed bills which he failed to collect to be run up by customers. Within two years the crash came. The bailiff, a heavy beer-soddened man, walked into the house and refused to move. He was there to prevent the disposal of any assets while the bankruptcy proceedings took their course. My father could not turn to his own father for help. He had suffered a dire stroke of Fate. Following two desolate harvests, there was an epidemic of foot-and-mouth disease rampant over the land. It leaped two farms and, at Scalford, settled on his. Government inspectors came and condemned the herd. They dug trenches and shot ninety-four pedigree Friesian cows and buried them. This was before the days of compensation. I heard my father describe all this—how he had seen his own father stand up and in a loud voice curse the Government. A second blow followed. He had stood bond for a friend whose business failed. Ruined, he had to sell the farm. He left my motherless father, a boy of seventeen, to look after the younger brother, three sisters and the farm until he secured a position as factor. In his own distress my father therefore had no one to whom he could turn. He was stunned and bewildered. He had no knowledge, and would have scorned to use it, of how artful bankrupts salted away assets. There was nothing in his wife's name and she had to sit there, nursing my infant brother, knowing that any day all the household belongings would be taken and sold at auction. Meanwhile that hateful beer-soddened bailiff spat, smoked and tried to ingratiate himself with a heavy geniality that was worse than silence. From the auction of their possessions my parents succeeded in retaining some silver and family portraits. They were also left, as laid down by law, with a bed, a table and a chest of drawers. My brother told me how when they moved to Sheffield, homeless, he was put to bed in the bottom drawer of that chest. All this was suffered for a deficit of three hundred and eighty pounds, that, in six years, my father wiped out. He was a saddened man for the rest of his life. I think he lamented most the loss of his small library. There were often wistful references to it.

There were various wanderings following this catastrophe. My father had a gift for figures. He could memorise large groups of numerals, add, subtract, divide and multiply, all in his head. His collection of figure-games seemed inexhaustible. He puzzled and astonished people with them. Once he came home from the public library with a book on trigonometry. I had no idea what the word stood for until I had consulted our beloved Dr. Annandale. He would become engrossed with sheets of strange signs and figures. After intense silence and industry he would suddenly exclaim—"I've got it!"

I came home from school one day, having had a lesson in elementary arithmetic. I had been given some simple multiplication tables to memorise. My father looked at my exercise book, laughed and said, "Haven't they ever heard of the Table of Pythagoras?" He took my exercise book and drew a large square. This he divided into one hundred and forty-four small squares by drawing vertical and horizontal lines, numbered 1 to 12, down; 1 to 12, across. He then taught me how to work it. I was fascinated. It made multiplication quite a game.

Who was this Pythagoras? My father said he was a wise old Greek who lived over five hundred years before Christ. Pythagoras believed that after death we went into other bodies, and were reincarnated as man, animal or plant, and he tried to explain the world through the theory of numbers. Some believed he invented the decimal dot. "I find that rather singular," said my father, "because the Greeks had no numbers, they had to use letters of the alphabet. Nations behave in very odd ways over figures. We still go on discussing the adoption of the decimal system, but the trades that operate with 'dozens', like the wine, egg and bakery, will have nothing to do with it. Tens throw them out of gear. Those Romans, too, could build great roads and temples but they never discovered how to write 2, 3, 4, 6, 7, 8, 9, as individual symbols. When they put up a monument in the Roman Forum to celebrate a victory over the Carthaginians in 260 B.C., and wanted to express the numeral 2,300,000, they repeated C̱, which stood for 100,000, twenty-three times. But all nations show oddity over numbers. The French can write 80 but they can't say it. They have to say 'four-times-twenty'—'quatre-vingts' to get it! As for the Egyptians. They could build pyramids but they couldn't count. They were worse than the Greeks and the Romans. They had only two number-symbols, 1 and 0. They had nothing for 2, 3, 4, 5, 6, 7, 8, 9. To express 2352 they wrote 1000 + 1000 + 100 + 100 + 100 + 10 + 10 + 10 + 10 + 10 + 11.

One day in a Shakespeare class, I came across Pythagoras again. He appeared in *Twelfth Night*, associated with crazed Malvolio.

Clown: What is the opinion of Pythagoras concerning wild fowl?
Malvolio: That the soul of our grandam might haply inhabit a bird.
Clown: What thinkest thou of his opinion?
Malvolio: I think nobly of the soul, and no way approve his opinion.

When, forty years later, I lived in Italy, I discovered, printed at the back of every Italian schoolboy's exercise book, the *Tavola Pitagorica*. He begins his education in arithmetic with it.

To-day I think wistfully how my father would have found a niche in this age of technology in the drawing-offices of the Rolls-Royce Company, or with numerous companies of chartered accountants, a modern profession of tremendous growth. In my own time I have seen the despised 'book-keeper' become an 'accountant', the accountant a 'chartered accountant', the chartered accountant a Peer of the Realm, a Field-Marshal of figures, heading battalions of clerks battling with armies of Government clerks over taxation assessments. Somewhere in this remunerative field my father would have found gainful employment.

His skill with figures served him, however, though a mere book-keeper in those days was in an ill-paid category. A friend who was buying a business in Sheffield wished to have its books checked. So to Sheffield, with its black blanket of smoke, the family went. But the gloom and the steady infiltration of soot began to affect my mother, physically and mentally. After eighteen months they moved to one of the cleanest towns in the kingdom, Nottingham. Its fame then rested on its manufacture of lace curtains, exported all over the world. The Victorian age witnessed a firm conjunction of the lace curtain and the aspidistra in every window. As the industrial revolution, bringing factories and railways, ate up the green fields with a leprosy of dismal small houses, the lace curtain, symbol of respectability, decorated the parlour windows of England.

Nottingham rose to wealth and fame on the proliferation of this symbol. It was essentially a clean industry, since lace was white and fragile. Hundreds of neatly attired young women tended the machines. In one large factory in the Lace Market the day's work was preceded by prayers. It had its own chapel and parson. A large Wesleyan chapel flourished in the centre of this so-called Lace Market. How many oratorios, *The Creation, Elijah, Messiah,* etc., have broken the Sunday silence of the factories and sent hundred-voiced blasts of the *Hallelujah Chorus,* etc., against the tiered windows! It was in a street not far distant from this centre of lace and Nonconformity, almost within hearing of these oratorial echoes, that I was born.

One shadow had hung over our new home, present before my birth. My grandfather, a widower, deprived of his farm, became nomadic. In what I write of him I may be unjust for I rely on hearsay, and this came from my mother who did not like him. I suspect that her first charge against him was the coat-of-arms, a patent of gentility to which he clung. She felt herself smothered by the Robertses of Thorpe Langton and Sutton Cheney, those long-dead knights and squires who, in stone and marble, accompanied by their spouses, now lie on their backs, hands prayerfully upraised, in the churches of Leicestershire. "I'd sell the whole lot for sixpence," she said one day, shifting the framed coat-of-arms during a spring cleaning. But she restrained her contempt in the presence of my father, aware of his veneration of this object. For she, too, was under the spell of the family ju-ju. I think she felt also that I sided with him. She had witnessed my inoculation. My brother, who was utterly devoid of any historical or family sense, shared her derisive view. In after years when I questioned him he remembered little and cared little about family history. My father dying when I was young, I had to rely on what he had told me, a mere boy blessed with a retentive memory, also on a few books and documents and a momentous 'Visitation' that I had made with him to the scenes of family origins.

In his last days my grandfather was a defeated man, but I was told he kept up a gallant façade, fastidious in his dress, *grand seigneur* in his manner. He seems to have just missed fame. He had two happy marriages but lost both wives before he was fifty. He was an eloquent public speaker, in much request on public platforms where he was a passionate advocate of the Reform measures, being known to Gladstone's radical group. He was a type that would have entered Parliament but lacked the financial independence essential in those days. He chafed at being tied to his farm, which my father said he neglected, going off on speaking engagements. He shocked the family by becoming a Wesleyan 'local preacher', which did not go with the Roberts tradition, for the family had provided a long line of clergymen to occupy the family 'livings'. "He wasn't really a Wesleyan, but he just couldn't resist a platform or a pulpit, and it went with his Radical views," said my mother. "Did you ever hear him?" I asked. "Yes, I must say he was very good," she admitted.

I surmise that my mother was a little unjust. She only knew him in his last years, when he was hard-pressed. She was irritated by his habit of asking my father for small loans, at recurrent crises, which he could ill afford. He came intermittently and stayed for long periods, another strain on the household. He would ask for a silk shirt to be laundered. He wore expensive clothes. His shoes had to be hand-made. He was an excellent conversationalist and monopolised any company. Such was the picture of him I was given. He died quite suddenly. I think my mother felt a little remorse, knowing my father's affection for him. "He had beautiful manners, was always very courteous to me, and he was certainly good company—when he had the centre of the stage—but he was full of wind," she added, with a twinkle in her eye.

Those handmade shoes. I wonder if that was the origin of my father's fetish. His shoes were rarely hand-made but they were always of the highest quality. They were among his proudest possessions, ranking after the coat-of-arms, to which he now succeeded as head of the line. What mocking Fate ordained that he should pass his last years in a shoe shop?

I cannot remember when I was first initiated in the reverent care for shoes but I know it will never leave me, so ingrained is the habit. That my father was vain about his feet there can be no question. It was one of the many lovable traits of that dear man. He had slender feet of which he was justly proud, and he felt that the wearing of shoes was as important as the wearing of gloves, to which he was also addicted. His idiosyncrasies—he had plenty of them—were harmless and sometimes amusing. There was the rite of newspaper-reading for instance. He read *The Daily News*, often disapproving of its politics, for he was a staunch Conservative, but was lured by the literary page which he thought one of the best in the country. He had two extra papers. On Wednesday he treated himself to *The Morning Post*. It was from one of its advertisements that he taught me what a 'left-handed footman' and a 'tiger' were. On Saturday he bought *The Times*.

One day, going with my father on a train excursion, I beheld the newspaper ritual in its most impressive form. My father sat in a corner seat, *The Times* across his knees, myself occupied with *Comic Cuts*.* He drew off his yellow chamois gloves and put on a pair of black cotton ones. He then took out a slim pocket knife. It had a thin ivory haft and a short sharp blade. Holding up *The Times* with one black gloved hand, he raised the open knife with the other. This was watched with some apprehension by the occupants of the carriage. Their fear subsided when they saw him insert the blade at the top of the paper and then slit it down the spine. This done, he closed the knife, replaced it in his pocket, and proceeded to read each detached sheet, one by one. When he finished each sheet he crumpled it, lowered the window and threw it out. When the whole paper was consumed he replaced the cotton gloves with the yellow chamois ones. As he explained, nothing was more awkward and annoying than a fellow trying to open and turn a newspaper in a crowded compartment, or more difficult in a wind. Also, newspaper ink came off on one's hands or dirtied delicate gloves. And how untidy carriages became with crumpled newspapers lying around!

The shoe formula as I came to know it was equally ceremonial.

* *Comic Cuts* and *Chips* were weeklies, forerunners of the American strip cartoons, with a great vogue. They produced an illustrator of genius, Tom Browne, who invented two famous 'bum' characters, Weary Willie and Tired Tim. Browne was born in Nottingham in 1870. He became a contributor to *Punch* and famous as an illustrator of low life, ranking with Phil May. He died of overwork, aged thirty-nine.

Every night our shoes were put on to lasts. My father never wore the same pair consecutively. Each had to be given a day's rest. A special shelf was put up in the scullery. On it there was a box with cleaning rags, chamois leathers, pieces of linen cloth, velvet and flannel, brushes and bottles, and trees and polish. In one side of the box were the things for cleaning brown shoes and in the other, for black. They were never to be mixed, There was also a pair of gardener's gloves. The polishing cloths were boiled once a year, the brushes cleaned with methylated spirits. The polishes were of brands called Cherry Blossom Shoe Polish, Nugget, and Propert's Saddle Soap.

When my father died he had twelve pairs of shoes and only three suits. All the shoes were in excellent condition and of the highest quality. He would never allow them to be half-soled, which broke down the arches. They had to be soled through from heel to toe, and hand-sewn. After walking in the rain the undersides were dried and dressed with coltsfoot oil. Once a month the upper leathers were cleaned with saddle soap. The shoes stood along the shelf, toes forward, like exhibits in a shoe shop, shining and creaseless. No one but himself was ever allowed to touch them. He cleaned my mother's shoes, but at an early age I was taught to do my own. Woe to me if I took a wrong cloth or left a visible spot on a toecap. He inspected my footwear with an eagle eye. I never shook off that lesson. Throughout my life in what houses, hotels, ships, villas, *châteaux* and *palazzi* have I battled with astonished servants, stewards, valets, butlers, and that depressed creature called The Boots. Failing to find my footwear outside the bedroom door, they come in, lynx-eyed, and search the room. Often they are thwarted, for I hide my shoes in the wardrobe. I warn off the valets and butlers and pre-tip The Boots so that he shall not worry about his perquisite. There was a gentle scout in All Soul's College, where I was sometimes a guest. I saw he felt aggrieved until one morning I told him the story of my father. His kind old face lit up. "What a wonderful father, sir!" he exclaimed. I have a feeling that he went away thinking all the Fellows should have had fathers like mine. When, in my middle fifties, I bought a villa in Italy, my maid Angela was shocked when deprived of cleaning my shoes. "But, *signore*, in Italy all we girls clean our fathers' and brothers' shoes!"*

* In 1965, a Labour Prime Minister, living at 10 Downing St., asserted that he always cleaned his own shoes. The absence of servants has now made this a commonplace. Fifty years ago it was taboo among the middle classes.

There is one country—the U.S.A., where no one troubles about one's shoes. They are never put outside the bedroom door. If you want your shoes cleaned you must go to a 'shoe-shine parlour', ridiculously named. An American friend explained. "In our pioneer days if you left your shoes outside the bedroom door you lost them, and the safety-first habit's continued."

Some forty years later, when writing *And So To Bath*, I investigated Chiswick. Hidden away, I came upon Hogarth's house, preserved as a national monument. When I went into the garden there I saw the old mulberry tree under which the artist used to sit with his dog Trump, chatting with Mr. Garrick or Mr. Fielding the novelist. Over the garden wall I saw a modern adjunct, the Cherry Blossom Shoe Polish factory. When cutting the new wide west motorway out of London I feared for Hogarth's villa and 'Cherry Blossom', but there they are, all the surrounding slums demolished, fronting the new road. The huge Cherry Blossom Shoe Polish factory now dominates the scene.

I was about five when first initiated in the shoe-cleaning rite. There was little my father did not know about leather. When towards the end of his life he kept the accounts of a select and prosperous foot-wear shop, they were amazed at his knowledge, and he was often brought from his account books to pronounce on the quality of the leathers they were handling.

I had a battle with my father. I saw no reason why he should be the only Beau Brummell of the family. I wanted shoes with pointed toes. He forbade these and insisted on blunt footwear. "If you have pointed shoes your feet will develop hammer-toes, and then you won't get into the Navy. Colonel Sherbrooke's boy was turned down for Dartmouth because he had hammer-toes." It was news to me that I was destined for Dartmouth Naval College! I lost another battle. In winter I wore boots that buttoned up at the side. My mother said they were very smart, as she fastened them up for me with a button-hook, but at my first school I was odd man out and they drew derisive remarks. How little boys are made to suffer by their parents' whims, as we regard them!

At the age of eleven there was the matter of my summer suits which caused me mortal shame. I suppose it was economic necessity that drove my hard-worked mother to make them. She bought a length of white-striped blue linen and out of this made me two suits. Each consisted of shorts and a blouse gathered in at the waist by an elastic.

The blouse had an open neck. It went on over my head and then, with hooks and eyes, a white sailor collar was attached. These suits were cut out and run up on a sewing-machine. They had the virtue of being washable. A great grievance was that the shorts had only one pocket. With this outfit I wore black woollen stockings, and black button boots.

There was an ordeal to which these print suits subjected me. My master would come and sit on the form beside me. While helping me with a sum he inserted his hand under the elastic waistband of my shorts and slid it up and down my thigh, calling me Count Plushskin. Worse, he gave my thigh and buttock sharp pinches. Every time I squirmed and cried out he laughed. I did not know then whether he was sadistic or something else, Freudian complexes being beyond my ken. This apart, I liked him. He was kind, and was a favourite among the boys. One night when I was having a bath, my mother noticed the pink blotches on my right thigh and buttock. I said I had been bitten by an insect, being too shy to explain, although I felt those awful print suits had facilitated the pinching. Happily I was soon to have a boy's ordinary shop suit.

The buttonhook for my shoes. That article has now almost disappeared or been amalgamated with a metal shoe-horn. When sometimes I see one I am overwhelmed by a flood of memories in which all a mother's endless care comes to mind. At about six or seven I had my first tailored overcoat. It was very smart, worn only on Sundays and holidays. It was made of a fawn Melton box-cloth, double-breasted, with six large pearl buttons, a deep collar and a flap at the back. With this I wore long brown cloth gaiters with under-straps. I clearly recall, when being dressed for an outing, how I would sit on a chair while my mother took one of my legs in her lap, slipped the strap under the shoe and then with a long buttonhook, buttoned up my gaiters. I would squirm and say she was pinching me, but I really enjoyed the ceremony, as also the way she thrust my awkward fingers into tight leather gloves.

I had no Nannie, but I was well-cared for. Both my parents were punctilious over the little things. I rebelled then, I am grateful now. I was never allowed to leave things around. Every night I had to fold my clothes and put them away in the drawers, my shoes neatly together under a chair, the books I read, squared, on the side table. When I wore suits my father taught me how to fold them to avoid creases. My first exciting long trousers went into his press, a walnut affair with two boards bound by heavy steel turnscrews. My mother saved white tissue paper, and in packing a portmanteau everything had its separate sheet. She made two linen bags with draw-tapes for my shoes. These habits of neatness are with me still.

My hostesses often remark with a smile "Your room looks as if it had never been slept in!" These servantless days, I usually make my bed. "Do you write there?" asks someone, looking at my desk, which gives no signs of labour. I cannot sit in a room with a door ajar. I was always made to shut it quietly behind me. My father taught me how to 'feel' the door in, to avoid any bang. American homes, with their doorless sitting-rooms, possibly because there are no draughts in their over-heated houses, always worry me. I feel there are doors somewhere that should be shut.

IV

As I grew older my father succeeded my mother, not as a reader, but as a teller of bedtime stories. He was a born raconteur. My mother had introduced me to the delights of Hans Andersen's classic, *The Princess and the Pea*. It was to my father I owed an early acquaintance with La Fontaine's *Fables*. He had found a book of these, enchantingly illustrated, with the French on one side and the English text opposite. He read to me the French text first, "to get the proper music of the verse", and then the English. He did not so much read the fables as act them. He became a crow and a fox and a grasshopper. My mother had to censure some of these bedtime readings as they made me too excited to sleep. I learned *La Cigale et la Fourmi* off by heart. When I had my first French lesson at school I astonished the French mistress, a swarthy old spinster with a wart on her face and a whisker in it, by reciting this poem without really knowing a word of French. In 1959, motoring back to England from Italy, I found myself in Château Thierry. They had just turned the house in which La Fontaine had been born and lived into a memorial museum. There were his manuscripts, his books, the original editions, the illustrations, some of his clothes. The sheer joy of seeing my old friend in his native haunt!

But even better than La Fontaine and Hans Andersen were the stories of my father's own invention. There were special verses, composed by himself, like "The Fly that wouldn't die", "Mr. and

29

Mrs. Mince-Pie, and all the little Mince-Pies", but the *chef d'œuvre*, this in prose, was "The Cat that lost its way."

Marmaduke was a big black tom cat, very spoilt, with a wonderful home. He was allowed to sleep in his mistress's tippet. Despite this luxurious nest, he never wanted to stay at home at night. He had appointments with a large number of young ladies among whom he was greatly admired as a baritone singer.

Now, one night, after considerable success, and the moon getting very low, Marmaduke turned homewards. Horror! He had a lapse of memory. He couldn't remember the way! He went over hundreds of tiles and got lost in a wilderness of chimney pots. He tried and tried, but couldn't find the right track. Despairing, tired and hungry, he rested on a windowsill, when suddenly, up went the window and there stood an old lady in a shawl. She smiled and invited him in. There was a most appetising smell. The old lady had just cooked a kipper, so he stayed to breakfast. She lived all alone in one room at the top of an old house. She was so kind that he stayed there all day, but at night he felt he must make an attempt to get home. Alas, she did not open her window, so he was a prisoner all night. The next morning she opened it to water her geraniums. He slipped out. There was a long broad guttering, and from this he got on to the roof. The sun was blazing in the sky. Marmaduke could never see very well in the daylight as he suffered from what was called *astigmatism*. He was seeing two chimney pots where there was only one, or, more correctly, two hundred chimney pots where there were only one hundred. Marmaduke walked very carefully over the tiles and round the chimney stacks. And then he really had a scare. A nasty black thing popped out of a chimney pot, gibbered at him and popped back again. He didn't know what a ghost was, but it had all the effect of one. His fur rose. He was petrified with fear. He did not move for a long time. Then cautiously he went to the gutter and peered down into the street. From the house below he saw a black-faced man come out with a sack on his shoulder and some rods and brushes which he put into a hand-cart, and then he went off.

By this time Marmaduke's one desire was to get back to the room he had come from. How terrible if he had forgotten the way! Happily he found the window and it was open. "Why, Tommy, where have you been, your milk's waiting for you!" said the old lady. She meant well, but it irritated him to be given a common name like Tommy. He was a well-bred, well-brought-up cat and his name was—his name was—oh, dear, what was his name? He just couldn't remember! Well, perhaps one day his memory would come back and he would go home.

So he stayed for almost a year. Then a terrible thing happened. The old lady died. They came with a coffin, put her into it and carried her downstairs and out to a hearse. She had been very kind, so Marmaduke thought it only right that he should go to her funeral.

He was properly dressed in black and he followed one of the men, walking at the corner of the hearse, who had a black crêpe ribbon hanging from his top hat. The hearse moved slowly through the streets and people took off their hats. Then something happened. The hearse turned into another street and, suddenly, he saw Mr. Haddock's fish-shop, and that fish-shop was at the corner of the street in which he lived! In his excitement he forgot all about the funeral. He rushed up the street, down the garden-path and in the open door of his home. A little girl was there having her hair combed by her mother. "Marmaduke!" she exclaimed. "Where have you been?" He jumped into her lap. He was so overcome he could only mew. He was home and his name was Marmaduke!

But he had learned his lesson. And although his memory slowly came back he never went on the tiles again. Moreover, he never quite recovered his voice after the shocks he had had. So Marmaduke stayed home, and lived to a happy old age.

This was such a success there had to be other Marmaduke stories. At Christmas I received a large imitation cat, black and soft. Of course he was named Marmaduke.

There was another story my father told, a ghost story. This was very much in request even with the elders. It had been told by my grandfather in the first person singular from whom my father had acquired it. When, in after years, I asked my mother whether it was true, she said: "It may have been, but with your grandfather everything was always twice as large as life." True or not, as told by my father it was hair-raising.

"My father," he began, "had had a good day's hunting. They had run the fox to earth and turned homeward. He was a considerable distance from home when his horse went lame. The wintry afternoon was beginning to fade. He had to walk his horse and they were both tired. He decided, therefore, to stay the night in a nearby village, where he knew there was an inn. But when he arrived at the inn he was surprised to learn that there was not a bed to be had, or anywhere else in the village. It transpired that the Wesleyan Methodist Connexion was holding a Quarterly Meeting and they had gathered from all over. 'But surely,' said my father, 'you can find me a bed somewhere! I don't mind where it is. It's impossible for me to go on with my lame horse.'

"The inkeeper shook his head. Standing by him was a pleasant young woman, his daughter, who served in the dining-room. She spoke. 'If the gentleman wouldn't mind, couldn't we put him in the . . .' she stopped and didn't say where it was. 'Anywhere!' cried my father, emphatically. The innkeeper looked at his daughter, somewhat embarrassed. Then he turned to my father. 'Well, sir, I'll be frank with you. We have a room but guests have complained about it, and for some years we haven't used it. They said it's haunted.'

"'A ghost?' asked my father. 'My good fellow, there's nothing I'd like better! I don't believe in such nonsense, and I'd like to meet one. I'll sleep there with pleasure.'

"'Very well, sir, you can have the room, if you will not hold me responsible,' said the innkeeper. He turned to his daughter, and said, 'Mary, show the gentleman the room and have the bed made up.'

"The room proved to be a large, pleasant one with windows overlooking the church and churchyard.

"The guests were a little curious about the gentleman in the hunting kit. Among them were half a dozen ministers in clerical garb. They invited him to join them at their long table, and during dinner he soon became on excellent terms with them. They were very much intrigued by the fact that he was going to sleep in a haunted room, for somehow the news had got round.

"The time came to retire. They were all given lighted candles. Just as he was about to mount the staircase, a venerable old minister with snow-white hair approached my father, held out his hand, and said: 'Sir, I wish you a good night's repose in the Lord's keeping. I shall pray for you.'

"'Thank you,' said my father, touched by the old man's concern.

"He went up to his room. It looked very large in the dim candle-light, but there was a full moon when my father drew a curtain to look out on the night. A beautiful old church was silhouetted against the moonlight, which lit the churchyard with its tombstones. and mossy graves. Then he drew the curtain and proceeded to undress. There was a large four-poster bed. On a side table he placed the candlestick and his watch. My father had been lent one of the landlord's nightgowns. After kneeling and saying his prayers he drew back the casement curtains to have the pleasure of seeing the moonlight flood the room. For a time he lay still, thinking over the day's events, but, feeling drowsy, he blew out the candle and fell asleep.

"He did not know why he woke, but in the middle of the night he opened his eyes. There was a deep silence in the moonlit room, and then, as he lay there, he was astonished to see the door opening as if of its own accord. He had an impulse to sit up, but he kept still, his eyes on the slowly opening door. Presently, when it was wide open, he saw a figure move out of the darkness into the moonlight. It glimmered on the white nightdress of a young woman with hair hanging loosely down over her shoulders. Noiselessly she seemed to glide across the room towards the casement, where she stood and looked out over the graveyard. For some moments she did not move, and then she buried her face in her hands as if in a paroxysm of grief. After a while she turned, and to my father's amazement she came and sat on his bed. He could see her face quite clearly now, and it looked as if she was in a trance. My father hardly dared to breathe. A hand of the ghostly figure now rested on the side of the bed, and he observed on one finger a ring with a stone that caught a ray of moonlight. Very gently he drew the ring off her finger. Presently, after a deep sigh, the ghostly figure got up from the bed, moved softly across the room and went out of the open door.

"My father lay for a few moments, his heart thumping. He felt the solid ring in his hand. He lit the candle, and getting out of bed, he examined the ring. It was a thin gold circle with a small diamond mounted on it. He took a handkerchief out of his coat pocket, wrapped up the ring and placed the knotted handkerchief under his pillow. Then he went over to the door and out on to the landing. No one, not a sound in the night, except for the slow measured ticking of a grandfather clock at the foot of the stairs. He closed the door and looked at his watch. It was twenty minutes past three. He got into bed, blew out the candle, and presently slept.

"He slept late, tired from the previous day. When he awoke it was bright daylight. For a few moments he lay looking at the strange bedroom and then suddenly he recollected the nocturnal visit of the woman in white, from whose hand he had taken a ring. Had he dreamed it all? He slid his hand under the pillow searching for the handkerchief he thought he had placed there. Yes, it was there, knotted. He untied it and in the centre was the gold ring.

"He rang for hot water. It was brought to him by the landlord. 'Have you slept all right, sir ?' he asked, placing the flannel-covered can on the washstand.

"'Perfectly. Your bed is very comfortable,' responded my father.

"'Thank you, sir,' said the landlord, obviously very relieved, and withdrew.

"When my father came downstairs the dining-room was empty. The guests had already departed on their business. A log fire blazed in the open grate. A girl in a mobcap took his order. He made an excellent breakfast. As he went out into the hall a maid was about to mount the stairs. The innkeeper's daughter came out of a little office and called, 'Emily, when you make my bed, will you look round— I've lost my ring somewhere.'

"My father turned to the young woman. Removing a ring from his waistcoat pocket, he held it out and said, "Is this your ring, young lady ?' She picked it up, looked at it, and said, 'Oh, yes—it is! Oh, thank you! Where did you find it, sir ?'

"'You came to my room last night. You sat on my bed. I took it off your finger.'

"The young woman reddened, and looked at him in astonishment.

"Here my father used to pause and draw on his pipe, enjoying the tensity of his listeners. The explanation of it all was quite simple. Some years back the innkeeper's daughter had been engaged to a young man who had returned from America to marry her in the church a few yards away. He slept on the eve of the wedding in the room overlooking the churchyard. Next morning, his wedding morning, the young bridegroom being late coming down, the inn-keeper went up to his room, knocked on his door, and getting no answer, entered the room. The young man was still in bed. The inn-keeper went to rouse him, and found he had died in his sleep.

"This tragedy so deranged the poor young bride, the scene of her loss pressing so heavily upon her, that she was sent away to stay with an aunt in Wales. Then she came home. The bridegroom's bedroom, kept empty for some time, was brought back into use, but there were complaints that it was haunted by the ghost of a young woman, so it fell out of use. The 'ghost' of course was the innkeeper's daughter, a sleep-walker. Haunted by her broken romance, she visited the death-chamber and looked out at the church where she was never to marry her young lover.

"'I know it would be a fitting end to this story if I added that I fell in love with the pretty innkeeper's daughter and married her. But I was already married,' said my father, and, turning to me, added, 'And you, my boy, were already born.' "

Such was my grandfather's story, related with a sense of drama by my father. I was twelve when I first heard it, and he turned my flesh goosey, especially in describing the churchyard in the moonlight.

In telling the ghost story my father, when he came to the part where his own father had placed his watch on the bedside table in the haunted room, paused dramatically and, taking a gold hunter watch out of his pocket, said "It was this very watch!" I knew it well. Sitting on his knee I had been allowed to hold the watch. By pressing a button the lid flew open revealing the white enamel face with gold numerals and two hands. I was fascinated by the long seconds-hand that flew round the dial. He wore the watch with a 'dog-chain', or Albert, a large-linked gold chain, shown on the only photograph I have of him, taken in 1894.

Twenty-nine years later, dining in Leicester with Winston Churchill, I noticed that he wore an identical watch-chain. For a moment he thought I was staring at his stomach. I explained that my father had worn such a chain. He lifted it on his finger—"And this was worn by *my* father," he said. It is clearly shown in Sir William Orpen's portrait, painted in 1916, and in the photograph that Karsh took in Ottawa in 1941.

Among the papers left by Sir Winston, his son, Randolph, found a short story, an admirable piece of imaginative work. In this Churchill narrated how one day when painting in his chalet studio at Chartwell he suddenly saw his father, Lord Randolph, sitting in a chair. Amused at his son's daubing, he asked him what he had made of his life. Winston informed his father, saying he had been Prime Minister and had survived two World Wars, of which Lord Randolph had never heard. Then taking out of his vest pocket a lighter on an Albert chain, Lord Randolph sought to light a cigar. The flash dispelled the spectral image. The chair was empty again.

I asked Randolph Churchill if he had inherited the watch-chain. "Indeed I have," he replied, "and I would like to think that my son will inherit it from me. Unfortunately young men don't seem to wear waistcoats these days!"

V

As the years passed I began to learn not only of my father's idiosyncrasies but also of his defects, though nothing ever diminished the glow that surrounds his memory. I was too young when I lost him to form any critical estimate or to understand how he had sometimes exasperated my mother. He was devoid of any ambition, a characteristic he passed on to my elder brother, but certainly not to me. No such urge touched my tall, placid father. He allowed nothing to worry him. He never raised his voice. He sailed smoothly as a swan over the pond of Life. The ill-luck that dogged him, the disappointments he suffered, were all submerged, at what cost God only knows. His unhurried gait had a hidden cause. He never ran upstairs, rushed for a tram or train. I suffered agonies when out with him, certain that he would miss the essential connection. He would arrive at the station and take his seat in the carriage just as the guard blew his whistle. A highly nervous little boy, burdened by a lively imagination allied to a fundamentally pessimistic nature, I suffered agonies of apprehension as when, a train halting at the station, he would stroll over to a newspaper stand to buy a paper. I saw myself, all alone, carried off to an unknown destination as I fidgeted in my seat. "Your daddy's coming back!" would say an old lady to comfort me. But was he? Well, he always did come, he never missed anything, with an infuriating regularity.

Before these excursions my mother and I would be sitting, all dressed, waiting for him to come downstairs, fretting at his non-appearance. Then he would appear, always only just in time. This cool precision developed in me a reflex action. To this day I always arrive at a station half an hour ahead. If I order a taxi I am on tenterhooks that it will not appear at the time ordered. But how justified he was in his calm unhurried demeanour! I did not know that he had a heart condition so critical that he lived under a threat of death. As a very young man he had strained his heart, it was thought from lifting a sack of grain. His slow, measured walk, his calmness, were due to this threat. He suffered, intermittently, from terrifying nose-bleedings. He would lie prostrate for two or three days while the weakening drip, drip, went on and the doctor was baffled. Once, during one of his attacks, my mother, waking at his side, said, "Well, you've had a good night. It's stopped." He replied quietly, "No, my dear, I've been swallowing all night. I didn't

36

want to disturb you." When he recovered he was his old cheerful self.

I don't think that at any time of his life he was free from money problems, but he never showed worry. He did not drink, gamble, go to football or cricket matches, but he loved his pipe and a cigar. Sometimes my mother would notice he was not smoking and comment on the fact. "I think it will do me good to lay off a little," he would say. But she knew it was because he had no money for tobacco. When he had prosperous spells he was most generous. Fruit, flowers, books and toys would appear. Soon after my birth my mother developed a chronic gastric condition. From the age of forty until her death thirty-one years later she was unable to eat any solid food, not even a piece of bread and butter. She lived all those years entirely on a monotonous diet of Benger's Food, weak porridge, slippery elm and bread and milk. Even the bread had to be two or three days old. This milk diet had two virtues: it kept her strong, and her complexion like a rose-leaf. But it destroyed much of her social life, since she could never stay for meals anywhere or eat in restaurants. It was possible, however, for her to eat a little ripe fruit. My father would bring home half a dozen pears that he had selected carefully, put in a drawer, and inspected each day until they reached maturity. Then he would peel one and watch her eat it. "It's a beauty!" she would exclaim, and his face would light with pleasure. He liked bringing home flowers, particularly roses, especially Maréchal Niel. They would stand on the supper table. Impatient to follow my own interests, I would leave my parents sitting there, his hand put out to cover hers at the side of the rose bowl as he smoked a cigar.

Calm, a procrastinator, my father proved a martinet from time to time. He was very alert about some things. There was a scene one evening at table. I asked for the butter. My father's sharp ear pounced on my pronunciation. "What did you say?" he asked. I repeated the request.

"This awful Nottingham accent! It's butter, not batter, my boy! Say 'butter'."

"Butter," I said.

"Do you hear the difference?"

"Yes, daddy."

"In Nottingham you must mind not your p's and q's but your a's and u's. Now say 'Please pass me the butter'."

I said it. I had to say it at every meal for a week but at school I suffered as a consequence. I said 'parss' instead of 'pass', to howls of derision.

Allied with this watch on my pronunciation was what I might call 'The Dr. Annandale Game'. My father made me read aloud. I went through the whole of Kingsley's *The Water Babies* with him. He often pulled me up. Once in a rash moment, as it transpired, he said he would give me a penny for every three words correctly pronounced that he did not know. They were to be used in a sentence. Thus the Annandale Game began. I lived in that dictionary. I learned the oddest words, with their meanings. "She carried a phanerogam to her room." "An ophidian creature bit him." "He saved his money in a scalene box." I won threepence with three tries in five days. The next week I won fourpence. The pace was too hot. My father called off the game. He said I was learning a lot of useless words. But he had started he knew not what. I lived with Dr. Annandale. I became word-intoxicated.

My father was not only something of a schoolmaster, he had endless facets of character that surprised and delighted me. He was very knowledgeable and deft in a dozen practical ways. For instance, he was an expert replacer of incandescent gas mantles. Those were the days of the gas mantle. It was made of stiffened gauze, cylindrical in shape, that hung on a rod above the gas jet. In this manner two-thirds of the households of Great Britain were illuminated. It was an advance from the blue and white fan-flame that often hissed and gave a restricted light. The incandescent mantle burned with great brilliance but its life was apt to be short for it was extremely fragile and the slightest jar of the bracket, often with the putting on and off of the chimney, would demolish it. The new stiff mantle had to be 'burned off' before it could be used. Replacement was a delicate operation. My father never failed and his services were in such demand. He could also turn locks that had jammed, and many a clock resumed its service after he had dealt with it. I recall most vividly his triumph with the family cashbox. My mother had misplaced the key. It was supposed to be a very strong and intricate lock, operable by no ordinary key. My father went to work with a toothpick and two pieces of wire. In some miraculous fashion he turned the lock. "You've missed your vocation. You should have been a burglar!" said my mother, admiringly.

That cashbox held for me a great surprise one day. My mother was methodical and accounted for every penny in a Household Book kept in the box. She took charge of all documents, which were placed in the bottom of the black japanned-gilt cashbox with the strong brass handle and a divided tray-top for cash. I was always fascinated when the moment came to open the box for it meant serious business and as a child I was allowed to unlock it. I felt as important as a banker with access to a strong-room. The contents fascinated me. There was an imposing document, the Prudential Life Insurance Policy, faced with a picture of the Rock of Gibraltar. There was my mother's marriage certificate, and also my birth certificate. I looked at the latter with special interest. Why, born on May 18th, was I not registered until June 18th? I might have died between those dates. My mother explained. "Your father delayed going to the Registrar's until he was warned one day that he would be fined if you were not registered within one month. He got there just in time."

When I examined the long form I was surprised to find that my father was described as 'Sewing-machine Agent'. "Was father ever a sewing-machine agent, and what sort of sewing-machine—like the Singer one we have?" I asked my mother. "Ah, that was an unfortunate adventure," she replied. "We had saved a little money —he was a book-keeper with an insurance company—when he met a plausible rascal who said he owned a district concession for Singer Sewing Machines. It was an American firm doing quite a big business. The man produced his books. They showed a good return. He said he was selling because he wished to join a brother with a business in Canada. Your father examined the books and, satisfied, paid one hundred pounds for the business. The man went off to Canada or somewhere. In a little while your father discovered that the books had been faked. Worse, other agents were working his ground. On complaining to the Head Office he learned that no exclusive concession had ever been granted to the former owner of the business. Within two years the agency closed down. We lost our savings and your father had to seek another post. This was around the time you were born."

How tragi-comic life can be! When, a young man, I first discovered Venice and spent long periods there, I came to know a Princess de Polignac. She lived in a beautiful palace with a large garden just above the Accademia Bridge, where the Grand Canal widens. The widowed Princess was elegant, extremely musical and gave delightful parties in her long salon with its Venetian-gothic windows overlooking the Canal. It was for the death of her young daughter that Ravel composed *Pavane pour une enfante défunte*. As she was rich she not only entertained lavishly but was able to command the best artistes. Paderewski, Jan Kubelik, Kreisler, Tetrazzini, Melba, Caruso, Pachmann, and many other stars played or sang for her. It was there I first heard the young Artur Rubinstein.

Our hostess, Princess de Polignac, was an American by birth, Winnaretta Singer. Her wealth came from the Singer Sewing Machine Company. Isaac Singer, her father, a New York mechanic, invented in 1850, in twelve days, an improved sewing machine at a cost of $40. He left a fortune of $13,000,000. She married in 1893 Prince Edmond de Polignac, an elderly and scholarly aristocrat, of a distinguished French family, who was an excellent musician and composer. "He looked like a castle-tower converted into a library," said Marcel Proust who frequented their salon in Paris. When it was announced that they were to be married, a friend observed—"So the lute is going to marry the sewing-machine!" To prove that he was not too old for such a venture the Prince jumped over a chair. He adored his wife who possessed the means for him to engage orchestras and artistes to perform his compositions in their Paris salon.

The sister of the Princess had married the Duc Decase. When Edmond de Polignac died a few years after his marriage, the Princess's brother, Paris Singer, a blond millionaire giant, met Isadora Duncan, the dancer, at the Prince's funeral. It was the beginning of a famous romance. He spent vast sums on her, financed her productions, and was the 'Lohengrin' of her sensational autobiography.

As I sat in the Princess de Polignac's Venetian salon, watching the play of light on the ceiling from the restless waters of the Grand Canal, listening to the music of Mozart, Beethoven, Chopin, Brahms, Wagner and Verdi, I thought of my dead father and his unfortunate adventure with Singer Sewing Machines.

I had noticed as my mother handled the papers in the cashbox, with its two-compartment tray, that some of them seemed very brown and brittle, as if they had been badly charred. Yes, they had been nearly burnt up. The cashbox was a kind of safe. In it were placed documents, bits of jewellery and money. The kitchen parlour grate had a hot-water boiler on one side and an oven on the other. Going away for a few days, my mother hid the cashbox in the back of the oven. On returning she lit the fire to get hot water and roast a joint. Opening the oven to put in the joint, there, to her horror, was the cashbox, untouchably hot. When it had cooled off and was opened some of the contents were badly charred. My mother's marriage certificate almost collapsed into powder. Fortunately in those days there were no paper pounds and ten-shilling notes or the disaster would have been greater.

CHAPTER TWO

The World Unfolds

I

WHEN I was about eleven and the question of my education began to worry my parents, my mother, as usual, took the initiative. She saw in the local evening paper that the High School offered scholarships. She interviewed the Headmaster and came back with the necessary forms. We were dismayed to find that one of the examination subjects was Latin. I had no Latin. It was not taught in elementary schools. My father knew Latin, he had been at Southwell Grammar School, in the shade of the Cathedral.* He was something of a scholar. Among his books was a pocket Horace which he treasured. But he was hard-pressed and had no time to teach me. There was a curate in the new parish to which we had moved. My mother arranged that he should teach me Latin for a shilling an hour. A scholarship to the High School had been awarded some five years earlier to a boy from Eastwood, Nottinghamshire, the son of a miner, called D. H. Lawrence; it had no significance then.

But nothing came of my mother's planning. Before the lessons had run a month—I was distracted by the Adam's apple of the curate —I had won a scholarship for Mundella Grammar School, a newly built secondary school. This scholarship brought a problem with it. It came at a low tide in the family affairs. My parents had to give an undertaking that they would keep me at school until I was fifteen, a year beyond the usual leaving age. I can see them now with serious faces, figuring whether they could undertake this, for they had just made a second move to a better house.

* It was in Southwell that young Byron had lived with his mother. They had moved from Nottingham in 1804, to a house on The Green. A Miss Pigot, who lived until 1866, remembered him, "A bashful boy with hair combed straight over his forehead."

The rent was now twelve shillings a week and rates. It had a hall and a bow-windowed front drawing-room, a dining-room, three bedrooms, an attic bedroom, a bathroom, an indoor lavatory, and kitchen. It also had a small walled-in garden and stood in a street called Wilford Grove because of its trees. The house we had lived in had proved unendurable, with no entrance hall, no bathroom and an outside closet. This was bad enough but the neighbourhood was worse. I was not too young even then to be unaware of the drab environment. We kept aloof from the neighbours. They thought we were 'stuck-up'. We were. The men sat around in their shirt sleeves, the women were bedraggled, the children had untidy hair, dirty faces and rundown stockings. The youths had an awful hair style, a forelock heavily pomaded and brushed up. They preferred scarves to collars. The girls were loudly dressed and smelt of cheap scent. On Sundays the family moved into the front parlour, which was un-occupied all the week and had newspapers on the floor. Those who called at the front door were peered at from between lace curtains as if they were suspicious characters or debt-collectors, and the knock was not answered, since all communications were by the back door during the week. On front-parlour days the family drummed *The Maiden's Prayer* or Sousa's *Washington Post March* on a tinny piano, or wailed, out of tune, *What are the Wild Waves Saying?*, *The Lost Chord*, a favouite among chapel-goers, and *I Dreamt That I Dwelt in Marble Halls*. The piano, on hire-purchase, was a status symbol, much as the motor car is to-day. On Saturday afternoons all the men, in cloth caps, went off to the football match, where, in community singing, they bawled *Annie Laurie* and *Abide With Me* before the kick-off.

In that dismal environment there were a few notable exceptions. There was a Scots family that consisted of the husband, a van driver, his bright-faced wife, and two children, a boy and girl aged seven and eight. We became playmates, and Milly, the daughter, was my special friend. She was gawky, with a freckled face and red hair. She had enormous vitality and could beat us at any games, especially at 'Stick and goose'.* Her brother John's speciality was shove-ha'penny and

---

* How old is that game? Sixty years later I watched some Italian urchins playing it by the arches of the Theatre of Marcellus in Rome. I asked them what they called the game. *Bastóne all'oca*, they replied. So the name was the same! I wondered if it had been brought to England by Julius Caesar's legionaries, whose children played it in Londinium and other Roman camps.

43

boxing. He was strong and could take on much bigger boys than himself. He taught me to box. "You're a featherweight!" he said. I did not know what this was and the next day asked the corner grocer to show me a featherweight. We were in and out of one another's houses. Their mother was an excellent cook but the thing I liked most of hers was the thin brown bread and butter she made with demerara sugar in between. She was also a good dressmaker and our mothers held long conferences over Weldon's paper dress designs. Their house was always spotless and neat. On Sundays John wore a tartan box-pleat kilt made by his mother. I envied him the leather purse on a belt he wore in front of it. His father used to join us in games of Ludo, Snakes and Ladders. The excitement of this was unbearable and the noise tremendous.

II

It was John and Milly who had taken me on my first visit to Sherwood Forest. I did not belong to the Sunday School Treat (they were Presbyterians) that was to be held at Edwinstowe in The Dukeries. The name was given to the section of the Sherwood Forest where lay the great houses of the dukes—Bestwood Park (the Duke of St. Albans), Welbeck Abbey (Duke of Portland), Thoresby (Duke of Kingston), Clumber (Duke of Newcastle), Worksop (Duke of Norfolk) and, though not ducal, Newstead, Lord Byron's ancestral home and Rufford Abbey, Lord Savile's. Now the dukes had gone, save Portland and Newcastle, but the great houses were there with other owners.

For every Nottingham boy Sherwood Forest was a magical name. We all knew the characters in that great legend. There was the gallant Robin Hood, the robber-chief dressed in green doublet and hose with a cock's feather hat, who took from the rich to give to the poor. He led his merry men up and down the avenues and glades of the great forest. There was jovial Friar Tuck, tubby, a roysterer, no better than he should be; buxom Maid Marian, and a company of skilled horsemen and archers. And there was the unfortunate Sheriff of Nottingham, who cut a sorry figure, for he was always outwitted.

Strange how that legend has gone round the world and delighted millions of children. Robin Hood is more popular and longer established than Robinson Crusoe, Gulliver, Puck and Peter Pan. On a lecture tour of the U.S.A. in 1920 I put my head in a hornet's nest when I said there had never been such a person as Robin Hood, that he was a mythical figure in an ancient legend. The Press attacked me, dozens of indignant letters, some of them insulting, were sent to me. I was greeted in the Press of one city when I arrived with *English Poet Roberts K.O.s Robin Hood*. A professor of English Literature exposed my lamentable ignorance with a long genealogical table. He supported the American version that Robin Hood was an aristocrat with 'a democratic spirit', a favourite term in American social appraisals. The noble Earl of Huntingdon, indignant at the oppression of the people by his fellow aristocrats, had rebelled against the king, taken to the woods, and, in a 'true democratic spirit', robbed the rich to assist the poor. In vain I pointed out that no such person had ever appeared in Burke or Debrett's *Peerage* or in any reputable history book. Robin Hood was the 'democratic' Lord Huntingdon in all American schoolbooks, and that was that.*

The prospect of the Sunday School Treat upset my sleep on the eve of the great adventure. John and Milly had persuaded the School superintendent to let me join the party. At nine o'clock on a bright June morning we set out in four horse-drawn charabancs nearly a hundred strong, guarded by a dozen voluntary teachers. With tremendous good luck Milly, John and I got seats beside the driver, our legs dangling above the foot-board. It was my first trip in a charabanc and the height from the ground frightened me, although they had tied a rope across us. We set off at a smart pace, everybody on our charabanc singing *Onward Christian Soldiers*, though we were going to anything but a war. Edwinstowe, the town on the edge of the forest, was ten miles distant. Presently, out of Nottingham, we came to a noble wide avenue of trees and our charabanc turned off through gates that had been opened for us. We were visiting Newstead Abbey, a great ruined church and part-Gothic mansion, the former home of Lord Byron. On the dissolution of the monasteries Henry VIII had presented the priory of Newstead (*de Novo Loco*) to 'Sir John Byron the Little, with the great beard'. He was the grandson of the Sir John who had fought at Bosworth Field in 1485.

---

* Robin Hood's name first appears in *Piers Plowman* (1377). The Elizabethan playwright Anthony Munday made him the exiled Earl of Huntingdon. At the end of the fifteenth century he and his retinue, Maid Marian, Little John, Friar Tuck, and the Merry Men, with the accompanying Morris dancers, were inseparable from the May Day Revels. Henry VIII enjoyed one of these in which he was entertained to a feast of venison in a bower.

The abbey or priory had been built as a penance for the murder of Thomas à Becket.

I had already heard a little about the romantic Lord Byron, a great poet who had died fighting for liberty in Greece, wherever that was. He had loved a dog called Boatswain and had put up a monument engraved with verses to its memory. We descended from our chara-bancs, walked round a large lake and were allowed to file through the high rafted hall of the great house and were shown a painting of Lord Byron, a handsome young man with fiery eyes, dark curls and an open collar. "He was not really a nice man, but a great poet. He drank wine out of a skull," said one of the teachers when we asked about him. (No glimpse of his association with Teresa Guiccioli, which would have conveyed nothing to us.)

There was a grim story about this house. The fifth Lord Byron had lived there. At a club dinner in London of Nottinghamshire gentlemen he had quarrelled with his cousin, Mr. Chaworth, his neighbour. They retired to a back room and in a rapier duel Lord Byron killed him. He was tried by the House of Lords, found guilty of manslaughter, but as a peer claimed exemption. He lived in seclusion at Newstead, a grim violent man who ill-treated his wife and frightened everybody. We were told about this 'wicked Lord Byron' and our flesh went goosey. We learned also that in this house Dr. Livingstone, the missionary-explorer, had stayed. He had been found 'in darkest Africa' by another explorer, H. M. Stanley, sent out to find him. Stanley's first words of greeting were: "Dr. Livingstone, I presume?", which had become something of a joke.

We were taken through the gardens to look at the pedestal monument raised to Boatswain, and someone read the lines to us. Evidently Byron had a poor opinion of his fellow men when their characteristics were compared with those of a dog:

> Ye! who perchance behold this simple urn,
> Pass on—it honours none you wish to mourn;
> To mark a friend's remains these stones arise;
> I never knew but one—and here he lies.

When I got home I asked my father why Byron was not considered to be a nice man. "Ah, if I told you," he replied, "you would not understand. He didn't mince matters." I did not find that enlightening. For some years my curiosity went unabated until I learned about

46

the liaison with Teresa Guiccioli, the murky business with his half-sister Augusta Leigh, and his behaviour to his wife. Even so, I thought I would rather spend an evening in his company than in that of anybody else.*

From Newstead we drove on through great avenues of noble trees, bordered with grass. The forest began to close in on us. Presently we came to a village with a large open green and an inn where later we were to have lunch at long tables set in a garden. It was already quite hot. We were led across the grass into the forest. A path brought us to a vast tree, supported by iron chains. It was called the Major Oak, so large and hollow that ten persons could stand inside it. It was reputed to be over fourteen hundred years old. Solemnly we entered in groups. Had Robin Hood been in it? Well, he might have been. It was there when he was. After that we went into the woods, warned not to get lost. Our environs made the story of The Babes in the Wood seem quite true. Milly, ever adventurous, took my hand and led me off deep into a wilderness of ferns and bracken shoulder-high. The great trees spread their leafy branches over us, shutting out the sky. In the deep silence of the wood we could hear the whirring of hundreds of insects. The beauty, the majesty, the voiceless romance that seemed to pervade this summer morning of childhood! I recall now, pressing through the bracken in that leaf-shady morning, the inexpressible enchantment of the scene, the eternal hours about us, the first dim unvoiced apprehension of the mystery and beauty of life. I heard 'the horns of elfland faintly blowing', and when in due course I first saw *Twelfth Night*, with the Clown singing

> When that I was and a little tiny boy,
> With hey, ho, the wind and the rain

I knew that Shakespeare, too, had been a little boy, and stood perhaps in the Forest of Arden, and brought from that experience, immutable,

* Newstead Abbey was bought from Lord Byron by a Harrow school friend. Livingstone, while staying there in 1864–5, wrote *The Zambesi and its tributaries*. The Abbey is now the well-kept property of the City of Nottingham. I like to think I was the cause of its acquisition. In the 1920's I was sometimes the guest of Sir Julien Cahn at Stanford Hall. He was a tremendous cricket enthusiast, and kept a private eleven. He also built a charming little theatre at the Hall. He was a wealthy man and public-spirited. One day I suggested that he should purchase the Newstead Abbey estate and present it to the City, which he did. The house is embellished with Byron relics, the gift of H. Roe.

47

the wonder and pathos of childhood on the verge of the unknown world.

III

One day, when I went to her house to look for Milly I was told she was ill in bed. A week later we were shocked to hear she was dead. On the eve of the funeral my mother called with a wreath, taking me with her. I was left in the room with John while my mother went into the front room where Milly lay. Presently my mother came out, took my hand and led me into the room. The blinds were down and in the dim light I saw a coffin on trestles. Milly lay there, in a white frock, her hands folded over a posy of flowers. It was difficult to believe she was dead. I had never seen a dead person before or an open coffin. I said "Milly" in a strangled voice, and my mother drew me to her. We walked home and it all seemed quite unreal.

My father was home and my mother told him where we had been. Suddenly I flung myself on her and sobbed. She nursed me in her lap and tried to comfort me. I could not eat any supper, and my father took me up to bed and undressed me. After I had said my prayers he tucked me in and sat by my bed until I fell asleep. I woke in the early morning light. The moment my eyes were open and the memory of the previous evening returned I was possessed by a terrible fear. Death meant the persons you loved were taken away from you and hidden forever in the ground. Death did not mind who you were. It could come suddenly to anyone. It might come to my father and mother and take them away. I trembled all over at the thought. It might have taken them already, it was in the neighbourhood. My heart beating, I got out of bed and went on to the landing, and in the darkness I fumbled my way downstairs. Quietly I opened their bedroom door. It was light and my mother and father lay there very still. With terrible fear I went to the bedside and touched my mother's face. She was warm and soft. It was all right. She was there, alive, with my father. I turned to leave the room. She woke and saw me in my nightgown, barefooted. "Cecil, what is it? What do you want?" she asked, sitting up. "Nothing, mummy, nothing," I answered, and hurried out of the room, up the stairs and back to bed, a great weight off my heart. Presently the door opened, my mother in her nightdress came in. She said nothing, tucked me in and kissed me. "Now go to sleep, darling, it's only six o'clock." She smoothed my hair, smiled, and after a few moments left the room. I fell asleep.

IV

When we moved to Wilford Grove I was about nine. We lost touch with John, and his parents. Then, in the first year of the Great War, he came with his mother to see us and say goodbye. He had joined the London Scottish and looked very gallant and sturdy in his hodden-grey kilt and khaki bonnet saucily placed over his blond hair. He flung his arms round my mother and kissed her and gave me a great hug. He was killed later at Beaumont Hamel.

As it chanced, the house to which we had moved was only a few minutes' walk from the school I was destined to attend. The district we lived in was called The Meadows, and was low-lying near the banks of the River Trent. The name, Wilford Grove, was appropriate then. Subsequently all the fields were eaten up by the sporadic building of rows of new houses, a working-class villadom. It had before that a certain charm. Wilford Grove was a wide avenue lined with elm trees, and the houses, many of them detached, had gardens in front. It ran from Kirke White Street, named after a local poet of brief fame and briefer life, and lay parallel with the main thoroughfare to Trent Bridge named after the inventor of the spinning frame, Sir Richard Arkwright.* Along Arkwright Street ran the horse trams. The meadows that opened at the end of the Grove lay in the half-circle of the smooth-gliding Trent, between Wilford Bridge and Trent Bridge. In those days the former was a half-penny toll bridge replacing a ferry. Many times as a boy, coming from a renowned sylvan haunt, Clifton Grove, high above the river, I had to make a long detour by Trent Bridge because I lacked a half-penny for the toll. Once, very tired, with a friend, I tried a trick. I stood by the toll gate, cap in hand, the picture of a miserable beggar boy, and a man gave me a threepenny bit. Spending a penny to go through, we had twopence in hand, and we went off jubilantly to buy ice-creams. When I narrated this to my mother I was severely scolded.

Those fields on the verge of the Trent, where we paddled, fished and bathed, were covered with masses of yellow and purple crocuses. There were also masses of buttercups and daisies, from which we made flower chains. We spent long happy hours in these meadows,

* He set up his spinning frame in Nottingham in 1768, a revolutionary invention later driven by Watt's steam engine. His mills began the factory system, and the great stocking industry.

D   49

going home with our handkerchiefs heavy with the crocuses we had culled.

Long before I had grown up those pleasant fields had disappeared and the name The Meadows became a travesty. Happily there was some intelligent planning. A wide leafy embankment with lawns, trees and a carriage road, was made in the mile crescent between the bridges. The adjacent fields were levelled, turfed and turned into playing grounds with a cricket pavilion in the centre. Along one part of the embankment, stepped-down to the water, a local Mæcenas, Sir Jesse Boot, founder of the great chain of chemists' shops, created later a War Memorial park. At the very hub of this river-bordered *plaisance* the new Mundella School was built.

Little by little I explored the terrain. Over the Trent Bridge lay the famous cricket-ground by a road that went southwards towards Loughborough and the blue-vistaed Charnwood Forest, but this was unknown to me in childhood. In early boyhood I became familiar with Clifton Grove high above the 'race' of the Trent. It was a cathedral-like grove of trees mounting to a plateau on which stood the thatched cottages of Clifton village, and the Hall, a stately Georgian mansion, visible from the adjacent churchyard, the ancestral home of the Cliftons. The terraced front of the Hall commanded a vista of the winding Trent far below. In the grounds peacocks paraded and called. It was all very Sir Roger de Coverley. Many of the cottagers in this still feudal village were allowed to sell teas to visitors who had walked up the Grove. My first memory of tea at one of these cottages was when I was attacked by a gander. My screams brought my father running out of the cottage. The gander had me by the end of the sash round my frock and was pulling me away.

Just after one crossed the toll bridge there was a picturesque village called Wilford, with an old square-towered church whose wall on one side banked the Trent. Nearby was a large Georgian vicarage. It had to be large. The vicar was said to have twelve children. Alas, the view from this 'Gray's Elegy' churchyard had been ruined by two gaunt derricks, topped by winding wheels, and by a chimney belching smoke. These were part of Clifton Colliery, a blot on the verdant landscape. Sir Robert Clifton, a mid-nineteenth-century rake, having squandered his fortune on the Turf, opened the colliery, hoping to recover his wealth. The district behind the colliery, an eczema of mean-terraced houses, devoid of all sanitation, was inhabited by the miners and their families. The miners were a rough, swearing, heavy-drinking community, hard driven, underpaid, living like animals and treated like helots. The result was that this district was shunned as a blot on the landscape. Since it adjoined The Meadows, indeed was a part of it, there was a dividing line between chapel-going respectability on one side, and coal-grimy heathendom on the other. The dividing line was called Queen's Walk, a wide avenue of dejected trees that ran from Arkwright Street to Wilford Bridge. No queen had ever walked down it. It had been opened in 1850 and named in honour of Queen Victoria. At the top of it stood a frightful statue of Sir Robert Clifton, the last male and ninth baronet of the ancient family that had fought at Bosworth Field, been friendly with Queen Elizabeth and had entertained Charles I. He had been Member of Parliament for Nottingham. The statue had the ugliest pair of trousers ever sculptured, and Sir Robert stood with his hand on a piece of coal. It was the work of an amateur sculptor. After some sixty years it was evicted and hidden in a shrubbery on the Trent Embankment.

I was strictly forbidden to cross the boundary and enter this no-man's-land. When in 1950 I was writing my Nottingham novel, *A Terrace in the Sun*, I went back to look at this mining district. It had been transformed. Alas, a huge electric-power station raised its ugly block by the river, but sanitation had been brought to the houses, and the prosperity of the miners was visible in the automobiles standing outside their homes. The public houses now had well-furnished saloons, the people were well-dressed. Gone, forgotten were the Sunday night 'drunks' who fought in the streets, the oaths, the screams blanketed by the braying band of the Salvation Army trying to rescue souls in hell. Once, disobeying the parental veto, I went into the forbidden territory. I saw outside The Crocus two women pull out each other's hair in a fight encouraged by beer-soaked onlookers.

I was happy in my new home. I was allowed to keep a rabbit in the back garden. For this my father made a cage. It was fronted by open wire and the rabbit had a balcony-bedroom to which he retreated up a small ramp. I loved him dearly. He was very large, snow-white, and sometimes I was allowed to bring him into the house, where he would lie like a dog before the fire. I had in turn all the pets of a small boy—white mice, a magpie, and, dearest of all, Ruff, a Skye terrier who followed me everywhere. He was my audience, and was taught to sit on a chair when I made long speeches to him. We had a lithograph of Mr. Gladstone speaking in the House of Commons. I was quite certain, at eleven, that I was going to be the Prime Minister. On another chair I placed a portmanteau, sideways, and near this my father's top hat. This was the Dispatch Box on the table before the Speaker. My mother, hearing my declamation, came upstairs and sought to rescue my father's glossy hat. I waved her back imperiously. "You are only allowed in the Ladies' Gallery" I told her, so she sat on the bed. I was moving a Bill to ensure that no Eccles cakes (great favourites of mine) should be sold with less than twelve currants in them.

My father made the rabbit box. I discovered he could make anything with his hands. I inherited this dexterity. I love tools of all kinds. Sixty years on, my friend, lovely Lady (Polly) Monckton, who lived in a Cadogan Gardens flat, used to save all her repairs for my annual return to England. I would reframe pictures, rehang mirrors, re-screw rickety tables, reverse bed-heads, renew the veneer on a chest of drawers, repair casement windows and wobbly standard lamps, sometimes re-wiring them. There would be a break, and with rolled-up sleeves and apron, I was given a delicious tea in the drawing-room. Her son Gilbert (later Lord Monckton), then a young Major-General, soon to be Chief of Staff, British Armies of the Rhine, returning home from the War Office would be greatly amused to find me, an elderly gentleman, lying on my back or up a ladder. When I was a neighbour, on the Italian Riviera, of Sir Max Beerbohm and visited him, he would ask me what I was then writing. I once startled him by saying I wasn't writing but had just finished making a small two-leaf gate-legged table out of the shelves of a decrepit walnut bookstand. I showed him a photograph of the table. He blinked his round blue eyes and exclaimed: "What fun to be you!"

I owed my skills to the early lessons given me by my father. We made a toy theatre out of the three-ply wood of the empty tea chests we could buy for sixpence, the tin edging and nails all coming into use. But three-ply wood was difficult to saw. The *Boy's Own Paper* had 'how-to-make' designs for home woodwork. I can still smell the boiling glue pot, the delicious odour of pine shavings, the fishy stink of seccotine. I can hear the scrape of a diamond-cutter along a sheet of glass, the whine of a fret-saw, the tat-tat-tat on a rebellious nail. In those days children had few and simple delights, but how intense they were! Modern boys, pampered with electric railways, radios, movie cameras, battery-driven boats, arouse in me pity rather than envy, their pleasures are so expensive and complicated. At the end of the great Market Place stood the civic Exchange, a Regency building holding the Council Chamber and the Mayor's Parlour. It stood over a bloody basement known as The Shambles, a congeries of butchers' shops lit by gas flares revealing hanging carcases split down the middle. At one corner of this Exchange there was a fabulous toyshop called Beecrofts. It was an Aladdin's Cave of delights. What hours I spent pressing my nose against the windows, envying rich little boys who could have forts with coloured lead infantry and cavalry, or roundabouts, mechanical cranes, and engines that ran on rails under bridges to a station. This toyland was wonderfully placed for me. Just across the way, on a side of the Market Place, called Long Row, much of it arcaded with wooden pillars, soon to disappear, stood the shoe-shop in which my father was employed as book-keeper. It was the superior shoe-shop of the town, elegant and expensive, supplying the needs of well-to-do citizens and the country gentry. Almost every evening I went to meet my father leaving his office, and walked home with him, a distance of about a mile. Beecrofts' toy-shop was most strategically placed on the line of march. I lost no opportunity to point out its wonders, for eventually one of them, at birthdays, Christmas and the celebrated Goose Fair, would come into my possession. There were less expensive delights that often came my way, purchaseable for threepence, which was my weekly pocket money, for by then I had progressed from a penny to twopence, and then to threepence. For this sum I could purchase a wonderful cardboard sheet of coloured designs. These might be a zoo, a circus, a castle, a railway station or a theatre complete with orchestra and scenery. You cut out the patterns along the dotted lines, gummed the sections together, and the model was excitingly complete.

With these material delights I was now discovering others. I was reading avidly. There was a marvellous series of yellow-covered paper books appropriately called *Books for the Bairns*. There were almost a hundred of these and they cost a penny each. They produced the classics in an abbreviated and simple form. Through them I encountered *Aesop's Fables, Pilgrim's Progress, The Argonauts, Heroes of the Iliad*, and Lamb's *Tales from Shakespeare*. I soon had a bright yellow line of these booklets propped up between Dr. Annandale's Dictionary, continually in use, and the Bible. I went wider afield. I read *The Jungle Book*, given me on my eleventh birthday.

53

Then at Christmas I received from a friend of my father, Sir Robert Ball's *The Story of the Heavens*, and a small telescope. He was the Astronomer Royal, and expounded the wonders of the stars. I was enraptured, and in my excitement I decided to write, in six volumes, 'The Story of the Universe'. I bought a penny exercise book and on the first page wrote, in large letters, *The History of the Stars, by Cecil Roberts. D.I. Volume I.* I noticed that Kipling prefaced his stories with a poem. I decided to follow his custom. I wrote an appropriate poem to the Moon. I worked at the poem, my first, shifting the rhymes about, and finished it in a state of mental intoxication. That evening I proudly announced to my father that I was a poet. "Good Heavens! I hope not. They die young and poor. What makes you think you are a poet?" "I've written a poem about the moon," I replied, and proceeded to recite it.

> The moon a lovely maiden is
> Who hides from me through all the day,
> Enwrapped in cloudy mysteries
> That fall away
> At even, when she kneels to pray
> The moon a lovely maiden is.

> The moon has sorrowful large eyes
> And her round face is pale with fright,
> What is the fear from which she flies
> With face so white?
> Her absence darkens the dark night,
> The moon has sorrowful large eyes.

> A maiden who has never smiled
> The shy moon is, most beautiful,
> Most virtuous and undefiled
> And dutiful—
> Yet pleasanter to kiss a skull,
> A maiden who has never smiled.

> Perhaps the moon no maiden is
> But one who goes with silent tread
> And gives a cold and solemn kiss
> To all the dead,
> And sleeps awhile upon each bed;
> Perhaps the moon no maiden is.

"Precocious and indecent," said my father. But he gave me sixpence for a copy, my first literary earnings. When he looked at *The History of the Stars* by Cecil Roberts D.I., he asked what D.I. stood for. "Doctor of Intelligence," I replied. The *History* died halfway through the first volume.

My elder brother, superciliously aloof from all my activities—he was in the high-collar courting stage and rarely visible—must have observed my obsession with pen and paper. Possibly there were visible signs on my fingers, the coming horns of the beast, as it were. He nicknamed me 'Inky'.

V

I have gone a little ahead of my story. At the age of eight I had begun to observe the world around me, sublunar rather than celestial. Momentous things were happening. I had seen the sea for the first time. I had heard a great deal about it from John and Milly. More fortunate than I, they had already seen its wonders, to be found some eighty miles distant on the East Coast. When anyone talked of the seaside, or going there, or of having come back from there, they meant one place—Skegness, or 'Skeggy', as it was affectionately called. Every year there was a great seasonal migration to 'Skeggy'. The place had a small neighbour called Mablethorpe, little more than a few houses behind a sand dune. One felt sorry for children who were taken there. It lacked a pier, pierrots and a promenade. Of course it looked on the same North Sea, and the Wash, the great watery expanse that stretched across to Hunstanton on the Norfolk coast. This shallow waste of water had sinister associations. Its tide quickly came in and out, there were quicksands. Here wicked King John of Runnymede fame, pursued by his enemies, had tried to take a short cut, and had been caught by the tide. He nearly lost his life, he did lose his baggage train. A vast treasure was said to lie somewhere in those sands.

The great fame of Skegness lay in its long broad beach. The encroaching sea was checked by a low line of grass-tufted sandhills, all artificial, designed to protect the flat Lincolnshire fenlands dyked behind. It was really a counterpart of Holland, from which it had drawn experienced engineers for dune and dyke construction. Inland there was the town of Boston, known for its Stump, a minster tower. It was an inland port by which the Dutch red bricks used in the

55

building of Tattershall Castle, now a picturesque ruin, and other buildings, were imported from Holland. Tattershall Castle had been saved by the interest and purse of that remarkable man, Lord Curzon of Kedleston, who had also saved the Taj Mahal from falling into ruin.

The fens behind the sand dunes were interlaced by dykes. Across the flat and almost treeless landscape one could see the church towers, rising from the nestling villages, and the busy windmills. It was Tennyson country. His father's rectory at Somersby lay there. When his and his brother's first book of poems was published by a Louth printer, they spent half the small profits on a carriage ride to Mablethorpe, and ran over the sands exuberantly declaiming their verses. The Lincolnshire fenland runs through *In Memoriam*, which draws its melancholy from that North Sea whose winds howled over his boyhood's home.

> The time draws near the birth of Christ;
> The moon is hid; the night is still,
> The Christmas bells from hill to hill
> Answer each other in the mist.
>
> Four voices of four hamlets round,
> From far and near, on mead and moor,
> Swell out and fade, as if a door
> Were shut between me and the sound.

In those days one week's holiday was considered sufficient for employees. Our own holiday, to be spent at Skegness, had long preparation. We were going in August, for the Bank Holiday added on an extra day, giving us, with a second Sunday and Monday, ten whole days. There was one disadvantage about this week, the prices of lodgings went up. My mother had found a place well-spoken of. This consisted of a single room with a double bed. I was to be accommodated in another room which I should share with another boy. It was an attic room that held two cots. As it was immediately under the roof, with only a skylight window raised with a ratchet, and facing south, it was insufferably hot. Also, my companion, a skinny pimply boy, had nightmares and was a bed-wetter. Against this was balanced a most romantic fact; the landlady's husband was captain of the local lifeboat crew. He wore a halo in our eyes. True, he was enormously fat and sat all day outside the front door chewing tobacco, and the lifeboat had only been called out twice in five years, yet he was a genuine captain of a genuine lifeboat crew. Once a week, to entertain the visitors and collect funds, the lifeboat had a demonstration launching. The men rolled the boat down to the sea. They were attired in large cork life-jackets, and wore black waterproof sou'wester hats and long boots. There was a gun with a rocket line and when this was fired everybody cheered.

We paid for our accommodation a shilling a night for the double-bedded room, and sixpence for mine. As it was an attic room, and shared, my mother thought it should have been threepence. The price of the lodging included the use of the cruet, and facilities for cooking. We arrived with much of our own food in a tin trunk that had *Fragile* painted on the top. The trunk contained meat and fruit pies, a leg of lamb, a tongue, a ham, all previously cooked and pots of homemade jam and marmalade. My mother could not eat any of these but there would be plenty of bread and milk available for her. In the bottom of the trunk were placed our sheets, towels and pillow-slips. The reason the trunk was labelled *Fragile* was to prevent its being put on its side, when all the juices and jams would have run over everything. We had heard stories of this kind of catastrophe. To make doubly sure there should be no mishap, my father supervised the movement of the trunk to and from the van and gave the guard sixpence to keep on eye on it. My mother made me a special white sailor suit. I had white rubber shoes, a broad-brimmed white linen sun hat and a pair of balloony paddling drawers, with the usual elastic support.

All this preparation, spread over two weeks, left my mother exhausted. I, too, was exhausted with preliminary excitement. My aloof brother was not of the party. He went with his fiancée on an Isle of Man holiday. He had a good job and could afford 'high living'.

We went to the station in a cab. This in itself was an event and John and Milly saw us off. Even the station was unusual, a sort of special station for going to Skegness. Nottingham's two other stations, the Midland and the Victoria, were below street level. You went downstairs to their platforms. You went upstairs to reach the station for the East Coast. It was therefore called the High Level station. My father, always a purist, objected. He said the name was nonsense. It should be called The Elevated Line.

When we arrived, it took two hours to go eighty miles, collecting passengers all the way, there was no cab. The luggage went off on a barrow pushed by a tough youth in a blue jersey and shorts, with very brown muscular legs with silver hair on them. I thought how wonderful it would be to have brown legs like that. It meant living a long time at the seaside. He wanted me to sit on top of the baggage. I declined. I didn't think it dignified.

There had been a shameful exhibition *en route*, provided by my father. It was not the black cotton gloves, penknife and newspaper performance. He could never resist a baby. Sooner or later he had it out of its mother's arms into his own. Then began a dangling, clucking, whisker-tickling, peek-a-boo pantomime. There was some magic in him that hypnotised infants. They crowed, they pawed his face, gurgled and squirmed in sheer delight. But when the time came to restore the infant to its mother, my father was like a man who had picked up scotch-tape. He couldn't get rid of the baby. It howled and kicked and repudiated its parents. My father, in his favourite yellow chamois gloves, was converted into an adored nursemaid. My mother and I, deeply embarrassed, tried to behave as if he did not belong to us.

On this particular Skegness journey there was an accident. A dark wet patch spread over one leg of my father's pearl-grey trousers. The alarmed parents snatched the howling child and made profuse apologies. My father, with a wave of his gloved hand, reassured them. It was as if he had welcomed the incident. "Babies must be babies," he said. He spread a pocket handkerchief over the stain, opened a newspaper and began to read. "What a gentleman!" said the infant's mother, as we parted.*

The moment we stepped out of the train I was aware of a wonderful new world. The air was buoyant, the great wide sky was full of light, and my young nose at once scented something, the ozone of the sea, unknown, invisible, as yet. The fame of the seaside town was spread throughout the kingdom by a poster of genius. Everywhere, on hoardings one saw John Hassall's coloured sketch of a merry old sea-salt, his wide trousers held up by braces over his big belly and jersey, his face beaming as he bounded joyously over the golden sands. The poster carried the legend 'Skegness is so bracing!' For once this bright jovial advertisement was no lie. The sea might not be so blue,

---

* How unlike his much-admired author, John Ruskin, who had a horror of babies. When asked to see his cousin's baby he said he could not bear 'big lumps of putty', and when he was prevailed on to see it, his wife wrote—'He likes it a little because he says it is not like a baby at all and has hair like rat's fur and a black face like a mouldy walnut.'

the sky so radiant, but there was no question of the health-giving properties of the air. It came in freshly from the North Sea over that wide flat expanse of the Wash. There were no mountains, cliffs or hills. Whichever way one looked, there was only a great clear sky in which snowy cumulus sailed slowly. And for mile on mile stretched the magnificent golden sands, with no clutter of bungalows, huts, kiosks or poster hoardings, just space and light, the beach as virgin as that on which Robinson Crusoe had been startled by a footprint.

A wide avenue led directly from the station to the sea. It was lined with shops that sold bathing attire, souvenirs, children's spades and buckets, and long coloured sticks of peppermint rock that had 'Skegness' printed throughout their length so that you never sucked the name away. There were gay balloons also, but not, as now, that ingenious variety of rubber and plastic toys. Plastics had not yet been invented, and Felix the Cat, Mickey Mouse, and all their Hollywood *confrères*, were unborn. Charlie Chaplin had not yet conquered the world, the cinema was unknown.

The great entertainment in Skegness, as at other resorts, was the pierrots. They performed on a portable stage on the sands. The *élite* sat in collapsible deck chairs, price sixpence, the children squatted in a sand pit in front of this raised stage, the crowd stood on the outer rim, their contributions canvassed by a ruffed pierrot shaking a reversed straw hat. These Thespians were, to my young eyes, gods and goddesses living an enchanted life. They made jokes, most of which I could not understand. There was a limerick song to which every member of the company contributed a verse. I heard this song so often that I knew all of the verses by heart. My mother told me that one day I came home reciting them, to their dismay. The end verse ran:

There was a young lady of Birmingham,
Who had a great habit of churning 'em.
   The hills were so steep
   And the valley so deep
Poor young men went quite wild on discerning 'em.

Puzzled by the enormous mirth this provoked, I asked my father what the young lady was churning. He replied, very solemnly, "I think she was a milkmaid, and the young men were mad about her butter." My mother reproved him.

59

Figures of romance, indeed, those laughing pierrots, mostly comely young men and women. They worked hard, sang, danced, played sketches, the stage ringed round at night with coloured lanterns, their voices rising above the murmur of the incoming tide, a melancholy background attuned to their rendering of *What are the Wild Waves Saying?* and *Speak, speak, speak to me, Thora*. This last song I knew already, my brother sang it very earnestly. I always wondered why Thora was so dumb.

I was to learn later the true nature of the lives of these summer bohemians. They were mostly unsuccessful music-hall artistes glad, in the summer season, to move out of their cheap, musty, London lodgings and get some fresh air and their keep. These were not yet the days when, their hair down over their brows, beating out a syncopated rhythm that titillated the sex glands of female adolescents, they might become 'disc' kings and millionaires overnight.

Skegness was an overgrown village during my childhood. Its full prosperity of endless rows of villas, boarding houses, hotels, hydropathic establishments, golf links, swimming pools, cinemas, and the gregarious heaven of a Butlin summer camp with everything laid on, was still to come. Later, with continental experience, there is for me nothing so depressing as an English seaside resort, mostly grey and wet, with 'shelters' on the promenade where people sit muffled up, taking the sea air, or walk the length of wind-blown piers stretching out over a sea the colour of dishwater. No wonder the English hurry over the Channel to the radiant Mediterranean, with the added excitement of strange shops and a language they cannot understand.

Even so, those were days of enchantment for a small boy. There was the first paddle in the sea, feet tender to the corrugated sand under the shallow water, the first donkey ride, a swiftly expended twopence, on a donkey that jogged slowly out and raced home at a perilous bumpy rate, the sand castles, the pierrots, the walk to the end of the pier, where a band in a blue and gold uniform played while visitors lazed in deck chairs, and some fished. At the bottom of Lumley Road, the shopping avenue that cut Skegness into two halves, a promenade ran north and south. I was forbidden to go into a park, a densely thicketed shrubbery known as The Jungle. The only thing I learned about this mysterious forbidden enclosure was that no decent girl would go into it. "Why not?" "It's full of young wolves," said my father. I was quite ready to play Little Red Riding Hood but I never got the chance to satisfy my curiosity.

There was another object of interest, the bathing machine. It was a large cabin painted in blue and white stripes, with no window but a transom and a double door. The cabin stood on a platform with four wheels. It was drawn into the sea by a horse. The sea was very shallow, so this contraption went out quite a way to reach deeper water. The horse was then detached and some steps were let down, leading from the mounted cabin to the water. The name 'bathing machine' suggested that something sinister happened to the people inside, but as the machine went so far out, I never learned the truth. Nor did I ever enter one. It was too expensive a manner of taking a bathe. We undressed in ravines on the sand dunes, where also one could lie and sunbathe out of the wind.

We were fortunate in our weather, the days were warm and sunny. The halcyon hours fled by. I had learned to swim. I came home with a souvenir. It was a pair of field-glasses made of white sugar candy. When you looked into them you saw, stereoscopically, a black and white picture of Skegness Pier and beach. When you tired of this you ate the glasses.

VI

The holiday was repeated the next year, but with a difference that cast a shadow. My mother did not come with us, the excuse being that she wanted a rest from housekeeping and also that there was the difficulty over her food. I found later that these were not the real reasons. She felt that my father should have a longer holiday by the sea. He had had a very bad nose-bleeding and heart trouble that spring. If she did not go, an extra room was not necessary, and the railway fare was less.

This time my father and I went to a boarding-house some way out, behind the sand dunes. It was the first time that I had been separated from my mother, and I fretted. My father was also unhappy. The weather was bad. The holiday was not a success. Somehow through over half a century and the vicissitudes of my life, a letter written to me on that holiday has survived. It is in my mother's beautiful clear Italian-style handwriting, descended from how many governesses, the daughters of vicars, and leading back to Italian writing- and-music masters in Elizabethan families. It seems to me typical of a letter written by a loving mother to her small son.

61

My dearest little boy,

I have just been to church, missed my little boy's company, but hope to have it for next Sunday. I am so pleased that your father and you are enjoying yourselves and that is is doing you good. Tell your father, if the funds will run to it, to stay another day as the tickets will allow nine days. Tell him he is not to buy me anything, I will be more pleased for him to stay as long as possible, and you too. I shall be very angry if he does not, it is a long time until next year. Dear Cecil, if your legs are sunburnt, get a little cold cream and rub on them. Thank Father muchly for the pears. They were beauties. I gave Ruff a kiss from you. He is waiting to go out, he lies at my feet while I am writing this letter. Tell your father I should like him to take you to a Phrenologist to see what you will be suited for. I am reckoning on soon seeing your dear faces again. I think I have emptied my budget, so will say Goodbye to little Inky, and God bless you both. Your loving mother, E.M.R.

The visit to the phrenologist on the sands! My mother was not a credulous woman, but at that time phrenologists were in vogue as much as Freudian psychoanalysts are to-day. My father would have nothing to do with this nonsense but, deferring to my mother's wishes, he asked a lady in the lodging to take me to the hoary-headed professor on the beach. Over his tent hung a sign. *Professor Sawyer, Phrenologist. Man Know Thyself.* He won my favour at once by saying, before feeling my head, "He looks a child of exceptional intelligence." I was placed on a chair before a pedestal on which stood a bald cranium in white porcelain, divided into squares and oblongs, each carrying an inscription. The professor felt my head. There was an intense silence, then the oracle spoke. The frontal sinus was very impressive. Other phenomena foretold a future of unusual brilliance. I would do well in emotional careers, such as actor, writer, musician. My two dangers were a disregard of Time, as shown below the frontal eminence, and a weak chest. Thereupon my guardian, delighted by the professor's insight, exclaimed "Yes, he has a weak chest!" She rummaged under my print blouse and the white front of my sailor collar and exposed to view my private shame, a red woollen 'chest protector' such as were then placed over the chests of delicate children. The professor was delighted, and there was an intense collaboration. "He plays the piano? Ah, he must not gallop through his scales —in everything he tends to be too fast."

The professor sat down and wrote on a sheet of paper. "Er—your name, my little man?" he asked. "Cecil," I answered. The professor beamed. "A most remarkable name borne by great statesmen and colonisers." He folded the sheet of paper and gave it to my guardian. "I have charted his future with particular attention to his gifts." She opened her purse. "Shall we say eighteen pence? The consultation was a little longer, but I was engrossed by so unusual a head." We went out of the tent. "Eighteenpence of nonsense," said my father. I felt dashed. The professor had raised my hopes after the humiliation of the chest protector.

CHAPTER THREE

The Goose Fair

I

AT HOME there was an annual event that caught up both children and elders in the whirl of excitement. It was a Nottingham event of far-flung fame, the Goose Fair. It had descended, changing its character, from a charter of Edward I that granted Nottingham in 1284 an annual fair.* It had long been a real goose fair held in the great Market Place, the largest open square in the kingdom. It had now lost its early utility and had grown into a veritable *kermesse,* celebrated with a gusto that verged on the riotous. Early in October there converged upon the city from all over England travelling shows and hucksters. Three days before the Fair was officially opened the preparations began. Steam tractors pulled great lorries and covered vans. There was a tremendous hammering and hauling, and roundabouts were erected with astonishing speed. The last to move in and take up its station in the Market Place was Bostock and Wombwell's Great Menagerie. We children used to watch for it coming into the city. Part of it could not be hidden, and we had a free view of the larger animals, the elephant, the gloomy camel, the supercilious giraffe. There were covered barred trucks in which we could hear the lions roar and the tigers snarl, and cages with monkeys, wolves and hyenas. When the show began business there was a gaudily uniformed brass band seated on a platform along the front. Over it hung a terrifying painting of lions attacking the tamer. Then out on to the platform came the lion-tamer himself, a brave figure

* In November 1290 Edward I held a Parliament at Clipstone, Nottinghamshire, in the Sherwood Forest. His wife, Eleanor of Castile, fell ill at nearby Harby and he went there to her deathbed. The route of her funeral cortège to Westminster Abbey was marked by eleven crosses, the last one being at Charing Cross.

My father in 1894, aged 36
"Your father hated being photographed and always looked fierce."

John. G. Roberts.
A Birthday Present.
from his loving wife.
April 18th 1881.

My father's handwriting in a hymnal given to him
two months after his marriage

The family ju-ju

in a frogged jacket, white riding breeches and top boots. He led, cracking his whip, a panther that he made to sit on a tub. Excited by this preliminary, the barker clanged a brass bell saying the stupendous, hair-raising performance was about to begin. We all rushed up the steps to give the entrance fee to a sequin-bosomed damsel, a circus rider, in a little pay-box framed in coloured lights.

By Thursday noon all was ready for the official opening of the Fair. It was a civic ceremony. Out of the Exchange, fronting the Square, came a solemn procession heralded by mounted policemen. There was the Beadle carrying the Mace, the Town Clerk in wig and gown, the Mayor in tricorne hat, wearing his fur-tipped gown and gold chain of office, supported by aldermen and councillors. The procession mounted a platform, the Beadle called *Oyez! Oyez! Oyez!* The Town Clerk read the official Charter and then the Mayor declared the ancient Goose Fair open. There was a great blast from the sirens of the roundabouts, the showmen clanged their brass bells, the organs of the roundabouts brayed, and under the tented canopies revolved the horses, ostriches, farm roosters, and dragons. Into the air swung the flying boats, down the switchback came the screaming passengers. The general pandemonium shook the windows of the shops surrounding the Square. The Mayor and Corporation progressed from show to show. They had a private performance in the menagerie, they were presented with bags of Grantham gingerbread and coloured candysticks of 'Nottingham Rock', then they returned to the Exchange, where they ate a goose lunch and made speeches.

The Fair opened at noon each day and went on until midnight. Children with their parents patronised it in the afternoon. I can remember my father lifting me up on his shoulder to watch a lady in flesh-coloured tights and red leather boots wind a cobra round her neck and across her shoulders. I also remember the Fattest Woman in the World, who was weighed publicly on a great scale. What happened inside her booth I never knew. But I suffered one terrible humiliation. We were in Bostock's menagerie and, open-mouthed, I pressed against the rail to watch a lioness. Suddenly it turned round and shot a great yellow stream of urine over me. I stank horribly and was hurried home. Whenever my brother wanted to mortify me he would say, "Who got peed on by a lion?"

One year there was an astonishing novelty. It was called 'The

Animated Picture Show'. You paid twopence and entered a dark tent. At the far end there was a white sheet. Suddenly the lights went out and from a hole in a box behind there came a beam of light that hit the screen. Someone began to play a lively tune on a piano. One could hear the whirring of the projector in the box. On the screen very black figures appeared and walked rapidly with jerky steps. When a pair of lovers embraced it looked like a collision. The miracle was that they all seemed vigorously alive. A fire brigade rushed down a street at a terrifying speed, though the wheels went backward, scattering firemen left and right. The piano player pounded frantically. Then, at the end of the show there was a white flash on the screen, a dazzling blank, and the lights went on. It was all over. One felt one had seen a miracle for twopence. No one had spoken a word, the titles and dialogue flashed on and off the screen. One came out stunned, blinking in the daylight. The queue outside the tent never ended. It was the event of the Fair. The lions roaring in the menagerie, the lion-tamer with his head in one of their mouths, took second place. The wonder-machine came from America, that strange land where Mr. Edison had invented the phonograph, and Red Indians slew white people with tomahawks.

It was at night that the Fair really got going, which I sampled only when I was a youth. One was hustled and jammed by good-natured crowds. But the crush could become dangerous at times. Men equipped with coloured 'ticklers', fibre tufts on wire handles, plagued the girls who shrieked and threw confetti. There were rolled-up coloured papers that had squeaky mouthpieces. When blown out they hit you with grotesque heads, but the squirts that shot flour or water were the worst.

As midnight came on the crowd got denser and denser and began mass movements in between the blaring roundabouts and the helter-skelters, down which, sitting on mats, screaming patrons were precipitated. Then human snakes began to form, consisting of lines of youngsters, hands on one another's shoulders, playing follow-my-leader. They wound up and down Beast Market Hill and Long Row, and through the fairground, indulging in horse-play that rarely became dangerous, for good-natured policemen suppressed all hooliganism. What a scene it was, with sirens, bells, the roundabouts, organs and the howling of animals in the zoo! At one end of the Market Place stood, in later years, the white marble memorial statue of Queen Victoria. She presided over an open-air pot market and two gay ice-cream stalls. There she stood, portly, with crown and sceptre, looking aloofly across the Fair towards the Exchange and its clock whose hands drew near to midnight, when sanity and quiet would return.

Once, as a special treat, I was taken to see the closing scene. The Fair lasted three days. It came to a sudden end on Saturday midnight. On this last day vast crowds pressed into Nottingham, brought by special excursion trains, and at night we had to fight a way through the packed masses. One was lifted and carried along as in a current. In sudden eddies and crushes people were bruised, clothes were torn and, good-nature running out, sometimes an ugly temper began to raise its head. The public houses were crammed, customers fighting for drinks. The scene in the Market Place became foreign in character. The sky overhead was livid, reflecting the lights and flares below. The storied shops bordering the Market Place shimmered in the night glare. As the hour of midnight approached the roundabouts and helter-skelters doubled their prices, the crowd fighting to get on them. Then, inexorably, the hands of the illuminated clock on the Exchange pointed to twelve, and its bell tolled midnight. Like a pricked balloon King Pandemonium collapsed in silence and darkness. The Goose Fair was over.

When, the following Sunday morning, the church and chapel-goers crossed the Market Place on their way to service, the great space was silent and empty. It was as if it had all been a mirage. Once more on Wednesdays and Saturdays the Square was covered with rows of tented stalls where the housewives did their shopping. But there were lasting souvenirs for a child like myself. From the fabulous Beecrofts had come a toy, a fairing. In my case it was a railway round whose circular track, placed on the floor, ran a clockwork engine and coaches.

Alas, there is no more a Goose Fair in the great Market Place, no more striking of the midnight hour by the clock on the Exchange. Time has brought 'improvements'. The Fair was banished to the outskirts of the city and thereby lost its explosive gusto. Along with the Fair went the bi-weekly tented market. In its place an ornamental Square was made. Even Queen Victoria was banished from the pot-market. She got in the way of traffic. And, saddest of all for me, cherishing a child's memories, the Exchange was torn down and replaced by a grandiose neo-classic Council House. With the old Exchange, went Beecrofts at its corner. *Sic transit gloria mundi.*

II

There were other outings besides those to Goose Fair and Sherwood Forest. A party went one day to visit Belvoir Castle. This was
another ducal mansion, the seat of the Dukes of Rutland. It stood on
a hill rising out of the flat vale of Belvoir, about sixteen miles from
Nottingham. Unlike the Portlands, the Manners family did not take
much part in the life of the city.

The second Earl of Rutland, a great favourite of Queen Elizabeth's,
in 1547 had been the Constable of Nottingham Castle and Warden
of Sherwood Forest, as well as Lord-Lieutenant of the County. He
lies now in the chancel of the church at Bottesford in Leicestershire,
near the family castle, along with seven other Earls of Rutland whose
elaborate and beautiful monuments range from 1543 to 1679.

In 1904, then a boy of twelve, I had seen the seventh duke, an old
gentleman of eighty-six, sitting in the window of the Borough Club.
As we passed my father told me to raise my cap. The old gentleman
bowed to us. "You have seen living history," said my father. And
how did he know the duke? It transpired that my father had a friend
who had a farm on the ducal estate at Redmile, the village near to
Belvoir Castle. The old gentleman often rode about his estate and
called on the tenants, sometimes taking a cup of tea with them. It
was on such an occasion that my father had enjoyed a long talk with
the duke.

How he came to be living history was thus. When a young man of
twenty-three he entered Parliament, in 1841, as member for Newark.
He shared this constituency with young Mr. Gladstone, then a Tory,
the nominee of the Duke of Newcastle who owned the pocket
borough. Thus began a lifelong friendship with Gladstone that closed
with his being a pallbearer at his funeral in Westminster Abbey fifty-
seven years later. Lord John Manners, as he was then called, was a
chivalrous and romantic young man. He was a poet also. The year in
which he entered Parliament he published a book of poems. They
were not bad poems but it contained two unfortunate lines for which
he was held up to ridicule all his life.

Let wealth and commerce, laws and learning die
But leave us still our old nobility.

Despite these lines he was an enlightened and progressive man,
always anxious to alleviate the lot of the poor, and a much loved

68

figure on his Leicestershire and Derbyshire estates. He never accepted any high political office but he was Postmaster-General for seven years and reduced the cost of telegrams from 1s. to 6d. As Lord John Manners he was in the Cabinet in 1853 when, following criticism of the events leading to the Crimean War, he had to deal with a widespread rumour that Queen Victoria and the Prince Consort had been arrested and sent to the Tower. Such was the old gentleman to whom I raised my cap. He was now the seventh duke, having succeeded his brother Cecil in 1888, and died in 1906, aged eighty-eight. He was called the Philip Sidney of his generation and Faber said of him, "He walked with a radiance round his brows like saints in pictures."

When with my father I joined a party visiting Belvoir Castle it seemed to be everything that a castle should be, immense, from its hill dominating the country round, high-towered and battlemented. Disraeli had put it into one of his novels. The present castle, however, is an architectural sham, and not really medieval. The first castle was built in the eleventh century on a former Norman stronghold. The first Earl of Rutland rebuilt it in 1528. A later duchess did not like it, pulled it down in 1800 and built a new castle at great expense but it was burned down with everything in it in 1816. Undaunted, she built another which the Prince Regent opened in 1820. She had ten children and died at forty. The bereaved duke did not remarry. The next duke, Cecil, died without a heir and the dukedom passed then to his brother, Lord John Manners, the seventh duke, destined to be Lady Diana Duff Cooper's grandfather. The old man loved tourists long before the days when annihilating taxes caused dukes to collect half-crowns from them to keep the places going. The tourists were shown everything, only one bedroom and sitting-room being reserved. The castle was open three days a week. When he met them the duke bowed. He lost his beautiful young wife bearing her second child. He married again and had eight sons and daughters. But tragedy dogged them. His daughter, Lady Kitty, drowned herself in the lake at Belvoir. Lord Cecil Manners went off to the Boer War, a journalist like Winston Churchill, quarrelled with the family, and at eighty threw himself under a train. Lord William died of fits. Lord Edward died of tuberculosis, and Lord Robert, a soldier in the Boer War, was killed, aged forty-seven, in the First World War.

Out of a hall, with men in armour, rose a great stone staircase. There were banners hanging from the high groined ceiling. The carpeted corridors seemed endless, with windows looking on great vistas of landscape. A large library had a window from which, on a clear day, Lincoln Cathedral could be seen. There were long portraits of dukes and duchesses, marquises, earls, and countless beautiful ladies, with ropes of pearls, feathers and fans. There was a long twelve-windowed Regent's Gallery named after the Prince Regent, who had often stayed there. What struck my boy's eyes most were the great Chinese vases standing in each window recess, filled with dead yellow leaves. Why should rich dukes keep dead leaves? "Rose-leaves, *pot-pourri*—to give a pleasant odour," explained my father. It was the first time I had seen such a strange thing or heard the name.

We were conducted in two parties over the castle by severe-looking elderly women who carried little wands to point at things. "Please keep on the drugget," said one of them. "Are they duchessses?" I asked. My father laughed. "Much too stiff for duchesses," he answered. But he did astonish one of them who hesitated for a name before a portrait. "By Sir Peter Lely," he said, and she gave a slight nod of assent.

Halting by a gallery we looked down into a hall where a lady and two girls passed. "The Duchess and her daughters, Lady Violet and Lady Diana," said our guide. I watched them pass. The younger, Lady Diana, was the same age as myself. I was destined to meet her and her husband, Duff Cooper, some twenty years later, at a party in a *palazzo* at Venice. She had become famous as the Nun in Reinhardt's production of *The Miracle*.

III

At the end of the nineteenth century the first rumbling was heard of the earthquake that was to shake the vast and solid British Empire. There was trouble in South Africa with the Boers, led by an obstinate old man called President Krüger, known as Oom Paul. He wore a beard and seemed to live perpetually in a frock coat and top hat. He had dared to defy Queen Victoria. To small boys he became a bogy-man. There was tremendous excitement. British soldiers left in troopships for Cape Town. The limelight was captured, through the London press, by a body of city clerks who were encouraged to enlist in the City Imperial Volunteers. They wore picturesque brown service hats with a brim turned up, carrying the initials C.I.V. They would eat the Boers.

The tobacco companies used to issue coloured pictorial cards in packets of cigarettes. These cards had portraits of British generals, with a brief biography on the back. Field-Marshal Lord Roberts, V.C., of Kandahar—affectionately called "Bobs", Field-Marshal Lord Kitchener, General French, General Redvers Buller, Field-Marshal Sir George White, Lieutenant-General R. Baden-Powell, etc. We boys did a tremendous business swapping these cards to get a complete set.

It was at this time that I experienced my first music-hall, towards which my parents had certain mixed reservations. They favoured teetotalism, witnessing the ravages of the gin parlour and beer saloons around them. They were hostile to playing cards, with their inference of gambling. There was never a pack in the house, and I remember the thinly-veiled disapproval when an exuberant neighbour, regarded by us as a well-to-do widow with an allowance of two pounds a week from a brewery that had employed her husband, produced a pack of playing cards and offered to tell our fortunes. She cut them and spread out the cards on the table and deduced from them our fates.

My parents looked with suspicion also on music-halls and rarely entered them. The theatre was in a higher category and if 'good' plays were put on they went. They took me to my first play at the local Theatre Royal. It had a columned portico, and I was overwhelmed by the plush and gilt luxury of the interior, the chandeliers, the gilt boxes, the great velvet curtain. Up in the gallery, sixpence entrance, we sat on wooden backless benches and looked down on the stage far below and into the well of the auditorium where sat the plutocrats. The play was called *The Sign of the Cross*.

The hero of the evening was the actor-manager, Wilson Barrett, who had few equals in melodrama. He had produced *The Lights of London*, which ran for two-hundred-and-fifty-nine performances in London, and toured England and the U.S.A. with great success. In *The Silver King* he had created a sensation as a melodramatic hero. Perhaps his greatest success was in *The Sign of the Cross* which he wrote himself. Dressed in a corselet and cloak, he was Marcus Superbus, a Roman patrician, one of Nero's cronies in evil living. But he met a beautiful Christian girl and she was his undoing, or salvation. Converted to Christianity, he went with her into the arena to meet death from the lions. The play made him a great fortune. It was first produced in the U.S.A., brought to England in 1895, played at The Grand, at Leeds, which he built for himself, and then at The

Lyric, London, where it created a sensation. Clergymen extolled it
in their sermons, and the strictest Nonconformists held that it
justified entering the theatre. Physically, Barrett was superbly
equipped, with a handsome face, splendid voice, powerful chest and
arms, but too short in the legs for total perfection. Max Beerbohm
did an unkind caricature of him in high-heeled boots, which he ever
after regretted.

The Empire Music Hall was another proposition. However, here
also there were exceptions that justified the lifting of the ban. There
was Arthur Chevalier, who sang Cockney coster songs. He was
famous for the well-loved *My Old Dutch—*

> We've been together now for forty years
> And it don't seem a day too much,
> There ain't a lady livin' in the land
> As I'd swop for my dear old Dutch.

It was a much applauded tribute to marital faithfulness and
felicity. There was Chirgwin, "the White-eyed Kaffir", with thick
red lips and white spats, who made negroes pathetic and lovable,
singing sentimental coon songs. There was Little Tich with yard-long
boots. He was so named after his likeness to the claimant in the
famous Tichborne case. He was a great pantomime clown.

But above all there was dapper little Vesta Tilley, the male
impersonator. She had a special allure, for she had been born
Matilda Ball in Nottingham. Now she was famous. Her number
appeared in the illuminated panels on either side of the proscenium,
the orchestra struck up a lively air, and then out of the wing marched
a young soldier in a tight-fitting scarlet uniform, a forage cap stuck
jauntily on one side of his head, a cane under his arm. A great burst of
applause greeted the figure that walked so jauntily, and sang *Jolly
Good Luck to the Girl Who Loves a Soldier*. The audience took up the
chorus. She went off and came on again, dressed as a masher, to sing
I'm Burlington Bertie, I rise at ten-thirty. Then off again, to reappear
dressed as a boy in an Eton suit and top hat and cane. He was like
the Honourable Montmorency D'Arcy, the hero of a public school
story running in the *Boy's Own Paper*. He sang a song about a dinner
he had attended with his father at which he drank a little too much.
He took out a cigar, smoked it and dizzily staggered about the stage
in his father's wake, singing

I don't know where he's going, when he gets there I'll be glad,
I'm following in father's footsteps, following the dear old dad.

Thirty years later I met Vesta Tilley at lunch at Princess Ottoboni's French Riviera villa. She had retired and was then Lady de Freece, enchanting as ever.

One evening something happened that reminded me of the seriousness of the times. The curtain rose revealing a portly woman dressed as Britannia, with shield and spear. She was appearing for a war charity fund and she sang some verses written by Rudyard Kipling that had taken the country by storm with its jingo tune.

Cook's son, duke's son—son of a belted earl—
Son of a Lambeth publican—it's all the same to-day.
Each of 'em doing his country's work
(And who's to look after the girl)?
Pass the hat for your country's sake
And pay—pay—pay!

At the close she put on a protective gilt mask and covered herself with a shield, and as she sang the final "Pay—pay—pay!" a rain of coins fell on the stage from all over the house. I was given a penny to throw. It was a long way from the gallery to the stage and probably hit someone in the stalls.

Something went wrong with the war in South Africa. The Boers, courageous, tough and familiar with the terrain, began to push the British around. Our losses mounted, the C.I.V.s got badly mauled, the campaign dragged. Some of our generals proved to be incompetent. A short little fellow, de Wet, harassed our troops and slipped through their hands. Baden-Powell, and his men were shut up in Mafeking. There were scandals over supplies and the nursing in the hospitals. A few soldiers emerged creditably. Baden-Powell, beleaguered, held on with endless ingenuity. When Mafeking was relieved London went quite mad. It was the first time the crowd had had anything to rejoice over. Another character emerged, an audacious young soldier-journalist, Winston Churchill, a scion of the Marlboroughs, who, taken prisoner, made a spectacular escape.

To pull victory out of what looked like a threat of defeat the old warrior, the Commander-in-Chief of the British Army, Field-Marshal Lord Roberts, was sent out. He had adequate troops, and a great reputation. There was a very popular oleograph of "Little Bobs". It showed the Field-Marshal sitting in his tent, before a table laden with papers, nursing on his knee a pretty child. Just outside stood an orderly, saluting, on some errand. Little Bobs looked up at him and said, "Can't you see I'm busy?" He was then sixty-eight, having achieved a great reputation in India when he made a spectacular march to Kandahar. He had just lost his only son at Colenso. The South African march was also spectacular, he went up through the country from Cape Town to Pretoria, the capital, which surrendered. It looked as if the war was over, but it dragged on, with Kitchener in command. Roberts returned just in time to receive the Order of the Garter from Queen Victoria.

Recurrent to Nottingham's Theatre Royal there was John Martin Harvey (later Sir John). He was assured of packed houses. He had found a winner, a play adapted by a clergyman from Dickens' *A Tale of Two Cities*. It was called *The Only Way*, taking its title from the last words of Sydney Carton, who, replacing one condemned to the guillotine of the French Revolution, mounted the scaffold, saying "It is a far, far better thing I do than I have ever done. It is a far, far better rest I go to than I have ever known. It is the only way." We saw the outline of the scaffold, we saw Sydney Carton mounting to his doom. The curtain fell to tumultuous applause, with not a dry eye in the House. He had other sure winners on his annual tour of the provinces, *The Breed of the Treshams*, and a dramatisation of Marion Crawford's novel, *A Cigarette-Maker's Romance*. It would be wrong to scoff at Martin Harvey for these sentimental plays. He was a very fine actor with a beautiful voice, diction and a sensitive face. He had been one of Irving's young men and was trained in the Lyceum Theatre tradition. There was none of the mumbling and back-turning of the modern school. Every syllable was clear, every movement apposite. But London resented his provincial gold-mine. It received all his productions coldly, except a fine performance in Maeterlinck's *Pelleas et Mélisande* with Mrs. Patrick Campbell. "*Il a volé mon âme, ce M. Harvey*," said Maeterlinck, seeing him in his play. He put on an epoch-making production of *Oedipus Rex* at Drury Lane in 1912. When it came on tour to Nottingham he offered a prize for the best criticism. Great was his surprise when a slim youth of nineteen stepped on the stage to receive his prize. It was the beginning of our long friendship.

CHAPTER FOUR

Into the Twentieth Century

I

THE NINETEENTH century drew to a close. 1899 was to pass into 1900. When this momentous line was crossed I was seven years and seven months old, delicate, tall for my age, fair-haired with a touch of my mother's gold in my wavy locks. There was a tremendous argument in the newspapers as to when the twentieth century began. My father produced a mathematical formula to prove that it began on January 1st, 1901, but most people had no doubt that it began on January 1st, 1900. To mark this in a proper spirit the churches and chapels announced that they would hold Watch Night services for seeing in the New Year. I was delighted with the idea. It meant one could stay up late. On this occasion we went to the Wesleyan chapel near Wilford Grove. My mother was Church of England, but she had no preferences. She was apt to wander about and sample the preaching. She admitted that the Noncomformists had the best preachers. She complained that nearly all the Anglican clergymen swallowed their words and could never get eloquently warm. They talked about "Awah Lorhd Jesas Creest" and "Awah Savyah", but she felt the Church of England had more dignity and poetry and she liked choir-boys in surplices, and regretted I had no voice. "An angel-faced corncrake," said my brother whenever I attempted to sing the hymns she liked at the piano. But she was a devoted supporter of a little neighbouring clergyman, slightly lame, saintly, and poor, who lived in a vicarage (so-called but it was one of a row of houses) that was much too large for him. He had three small children and his wife taught them and did all the housework, for though he believed that all men were equal in God's sight he wouldn't let a Board School have his children—Boarding School, yes; Board School, no. "Admirable!" said my father. His church was grim, newly consecrated in the

75

growing district. It was built of wood and had a galvanised tin roof and was adjacent to Mundella School.

It may have been Mrs. Lane, the baker's wife, who took my mother to the Watch Night service at the Wesleyan chapel, or it may have been there was no service in the Church of England one. Moreover, Mr. Lane was a sidesman there and they had a pew. My father did not go to any church, he was an Agnostic, familiar with the works of Ingersoll, Darwin and Huxley. He did not believe in the Fall of Man, nor in the Redemption. Man never 'fell'—for he never really got up. He was a mess from the beginning and would be to the end. It was preposterous to think that an All-Powerful Deity would let Himself be pushed around by the prayers of people wanting something for themselves. Also He would have to be a very conceited God to stomach all the praise everlastingly poured over Him. In the Old Testament He was a sadistic monster, as the disgusting business with Abraham and Isaac, and Job, proved. As for the churches, they all took out their own copyright on Him. The Pope, who claimed to have the keys to Heaven and Hell, declared that God did not know the Archbishop of Canterbury.

My father never expressed his views openly, I learned about them later from my mother. She was grieved by his refusal to go to church and always hoped he would "see the Light". He did not oppose my religious instruction. "It's easier for him to run with the herd," he said. He in no way tried to dissuade her or anyone else from believing what they wished, but if he was attacked he was formidable in argument.

A little before midnight on December 31st, 1899, my mother and I reached the chapel and were shown into the Lanes' pew. The place was full. My mother knelt on a hassock and prayed. I followed suit. Then she sat up and did what she always did. She pulled off her black kid gloves, blew into them, flattened them and put them on the ledge with the hymn books. The minister went up into the pulpit. He was a little man and just appeared above the Bible. He announced a hymn, reading the first line. The organ played, the choir behind him stood up, a row of black-costumed females with half a dozen men, and we all began to sing.

> As a shadow life is fleeting:
> As a vapour so it flies;
> For the old year now retreating
> Pardon grant, and make us wise.

We slowly sang the lugubrious verses. Then the minister read from the Bible a rather frightening passage about the world being devoured by flames. What if the world came to an end at midnight, and there would be no twentieth century!

After the reading there was another hymn, followed by a prayer avowing that we were all miserable sinners. Mr. Lane startled me by shouting aloud, "Praise the Lord!" as though we were to thank the Lord for being miserable sinners; then the minister took out his watch and said, "Brethren and Sisters, it is now three minutes to twelve. The Old Year is dying. We will bow in silent prayer until the New Year is born."

There followed a deep, terrible silence. No one coughed. My lively imagination began to work alarmingly. One hundred years from this night when the next century came in not one of us sitting here would be alive. No one anywhere would be alive. The men who drove the trams outside, the horses that pulled them, the passengers sitting in them, all would be dead. There would be no fathers, mothers, brothers, sisters, uncles, aunts, grandfathers, grandmothers. All the birds and animals would be dead also. No, not all. I had read that in the palace grounds at Tonga, a tortoise given to the King of the Friendly Islands in 1773 by Captain Cook was still alive and crawled about with "I knew Captain Cook" painted on its back. If I had a tortoise I could paint on it "I knew Cecil Roberts" and then over a hundred years hence people would know I had been alive.* A hundred years, two hundred years, how long was 'everlasting', and people who received 'the life everlasting' promised by the parsons, how old could they become? And what would they do all that time? My mind went round and round. The silent minutes ticked away. If only someone would cough or move, or look happy. We all seemed dead already.

There was a movement. The minister stood up. He held his watch in his hand. "Brethren! It is midnight!" A pause. "Brethren, it is now the New Year. May the Lord bless us and keep us! Let us pray." He prayed aloud, very earnestly, for everybody, for God to give us health and peace, kindness, charity, right-living, and godliness. His prayer was punctuated by "Praise the Lord!", "Hallelujah!" shouted by Mr. Lane and others. Then everybody turned round and shook hands with everybody, wishing them a Happy New Year. A hymn followed, very joyous this time, with the choir and the organ all out.

* The tortoise died in Tonga in 1966. It was believed to be 197 years old.

It felt very wonderful to be safely in a new century, despite the South African war going so badly.

The Watch Night service was over. As the organ played a voluntary we proceeded slowly to file out. "Don't put on your gloves," whispered my mother as we left the pew with the Lanes. I wondered at this, but soon saw the reason. Somehow the minister had got round to the front porch and there he stood, shaking hands and wishing the congregation a Happy New Year as it left the chapel and went into the silent midnight street.

II

The next event in my life was the death of Queen Victoria. Her death seemed incredible. She had been there so long, hieratic, frightening to her statesmen and her son Edward. I remember all the newspapers printed with heavy black borders, with pictures of the great funeral to which came the monarchs of the earth, for she was Europe's grandmother. My school closed on the day of the funeral. On a blackboard in the Assembly Hall there was a portrait of the Queen, encased in a heavy wreath. Everybody wore black.

The following event in my life was the preparation for the Coronation of King Edward. At school we all received medals and a mug with coloured portraits of King Edward and Queen Alexandra. One morning I went down to the Trent embankment to look at a ceremonial arch that was being erected. I was so fascinated that I forgot all about the time. I enjoyed myself enormously chatting to the workmen, who gave me a sandwich from their lunch. My mother, alarmed by my absence at lunch time, began to make enquiries. She learned that I had been seen walking by the River Trent. This aroused fears that I had been drowned. She went down to the river, walked about and could not find me. When she got back home, after three o'clock, I had not returned. She sent word to my father who left his office, came home, and went to the police station to inform them that I was missing. While he was there I walked into the house to find my mother, with a neighbour, almost in a state of collapse. To my surprise she was very angry, and when my father returned he took me upstairs, told me to strip, went out and returned with a cane. I knew that switchy cane, it was used when the kitchen sink became blocked. He pinned me face down over the bed and gave me half a dozen strokes across my naked buttocks. I screamed madly. I had never been thrashed before or suffered any corporal punishment either at home or at school. My yells brought my mother on the scene, who took the cane from my father saying "That's enough!" I was locked in my bedroom for the evening. At seven o'clock my mother brought me a tray with some bread and butter and a glass of milk. I burst into tears, but she was very unsympathetic and left the room without a word. When I came downstairs the next morning she said to me, "Now go and tell your father how sorry you are for being so naughty." I wasn't convinced that I had been naughty, and demurred. "There's no breakfast for you until you do as I tell you," she said firmly. When my father appeared I went to him and expressed regret for my behaviour. He lifted me up by the arms, looking into my face, and said, "You had us very frightened. Don't play the fool again!" Then he lowered me and set me down. The storm was over.

The next day we all had a shock. The King had been operated on for appendicitis. The Coronation was off.

III

The house in Wilford Grove was really too large for us. It had the advantage that my brother and myself each had a bedroom. Ten and twenty-one, we were widely apart in years and temperament. He referred to me as 'That mad kid'; I called him 'Thora' which infuriated him, for he felt he was very male, in the stag period, hotly courting and forever going out to dances.

There had suddenly appeared on the scene a piano. It was a mystery how we obtained it, since it must have been paid for. We never bought anything hire-purchase, though money was very short. My mother's friend, Mrs. Lane, had a prosperous bread shop. There were crises when my mother had to borrow a sovereign from her to tide over to the end of the week until my father brought home his wages on Friday night. Often on Saturday morning I went shopping with my mother, leading Ruff, who loved the shop smells, and the sovereign was then paid back. I loved Mrs. Lane. She had a fresh complexion, her shop smelt of new bread, and she sometimes gave me a cake out of a glass case. She always spoke to me as Master Cecil. I was very courteous to her and took off my cap when I spoke to her. She had a fat jolly husband, the Hallelujah chanter, who sometimes appeared from the bakery behind, covered in flour. He always addressed me as 'Professor'. I had once given him a discourse on how

Newton had discovered gravity. (Taken straight from *Books for the Bairns*.) "That boy's going a long way," he said to my mother one day. "Ssh! Ssh!—you mustn't make him conceited," she replied.

The piano, made by Kent and Cooper, as a legend in gilt proclaimed under the curved collapsible lid, was an upright, in polished dark mahogany with two brass candle-holders and pedals. It was in the new fashion. It did not have a fretwork front with green silk panels. It was placed in what was called locally 'the front parlour', but which was always the drawing-room to my parents. The piano occupied the wall opposite the fireplace and above it, in the place of honour, hung the Coat-of-Arms, the family ju-ju. My mother had put it in a recess over a cupboard, a *lèse majesté* corrected by my father.

I was relieved to find the tone of the piano good, for at that early age I had had an experience. Once, passing under the high walled garden of a house in the Park, the 'aristocratic' residential area (of which the Duke of Newcastle was the landlord) I heard a piano being played. The notes flowed out in the night air and, enchanted, I stood and listened to the unseen player. I did not know what the music was but until then I had not known that there was anything so beautiful in the world. I was transported to another realm. The rich tone of that cascade of notes flowed down into my young soul, a language of romance transcending words.

There was a ladder nearby and, greatly daring, I clambered up, looked over the wall and peered into a large drawing-room, well lit. There I saw a small girl sitting at a very large grand piano. The night was cold and dark, the room looked warm and rich within, but the music that came out into the still night was not of this earth. I learned later that I had heard Beethoven's *Moonlight Sonata*. Who played it I shall never know, her name, her fate. I remember the blue frock, the white stockings, the flaxen hair, the delicate hands. Perhaps now she is a grandmother, perhaps she is dead. And she never knew how a small boy hanging on a ladder by a garden wall listened in the cold night to that liquid music pouring from the grand piano.

I soon discovered that my brother was doing some of his courting with our piano. He monopolised the room and the instrument. His fiancée could play. He shut himself in with her and there he would stand, singing *When I go down the vale, love, Maid of Athens ere we part, The Last Rose of Summer*, and the inevitable *Speak, speak, speak to me, Thora*—hence my nickname for him. He was slim and hand-

Nottingham in 1830 by J. M. W. Turner, R.A.

Nottingham Castle in the sixteenth century

Lady Roberts (1600–1679), widow of Sir Richard Roberts
"Paid £5 to the poor for not being buried in woollen."

My brother, William Roberts (1881–1964), aged 24
"Speak, speak, speak to me, Thora!"

some. He was a great dancer and a taker-out of the girls, but he had a fixed passion for one girl. This had begun at the age of fifteen and it lasted until Fate separated them sixty years later. (Poor girl, if she had known what she was doomed to, for he became a lifelong invalid.) She was very pretty and vivacious. At a dance given for their wedding I took her on the floor, and, aged thirteen, told her that had my brother not got in first I would have married her. She was immensely amused. She was half-Swiss, her father coming from Zurich. He was an inventor who had been brought to Nottingham by a lace-making firm. He had died young, leaving a widow and a daughter, their only child. They derived from him the name Weiss, but instead of being called 'Vice' (White) they were called Weez, since the Nottingham folk could never achieve the correct pronunciation.

Via this 'Weez' connection and the piano, a colourful period came into our lives. Widowed Mrs. Weiss had a sister, Miss Fryer. She lived across the road and was housekeeper to the family doctor, a dark young man with whom, it was alleged, she was in love, though twenty years his senior. In this she was my rival, for, aged ten, I too, was deeply in love with him. It was some time before my mother discovered I enjoyed being ill because it meant a visit from handsome Dr. Harrison. I liked his voice and his short black moustache. and I thought it would be nice to die with him lifting me up in his arms and saying the last tender words to me. To which I would respond, just having heard Martin Harvey say them, "It is the only way."

Miss Fryer was a figure of romance. There was a glint of gold in her hair (dyed ?). She had long eyelashes sweeping over china-blue eyes. Her complexion was good, her figure creditable except, a fact noted by my father, her feet were too long. "No woman should have to wear sixes." Her elastic-sided black Sunday boots horrified him. Her bosom was roped with a number of chains, her fingers were covered with rings. Her voice was pleasant, her manner vivacious. Unhappily, she liked the whisky bottle. There was a betraying odour at times. But she dazzled a small boy's eyes. She had been on the stage, and that no ordinary stage. She had been in Grand Opera, a member of the Carl Rosa Opera Company that toured the United Kingdom. There was a heavy bound album that bore witness to her forgotten fame. It held the playbills and programmes in which her name appeared. A soprano, she had sung in Balfe's *The Bohemian*

Girl, in Gounod's *Faust,* and in the operas of Verdi, Rossini, Bizet, Bellini and Mascagni. She had a thrilling description of how she had sung in a command performance before Queen Victoria. As a comedy aside she gave a vivid account of having got locked in one of the Royal lavatories. The slip-bolt had stuck, and she was rescued by one of the royal footmen who came only just in time, for the curtain was due to rise. "Despite that, I never sang better in my life," she said. There was also a hair-raising account of an hotel that caught fire and how she was carried down a fire-escape ladder. Forgetting about the lavatory episode, she also added "And I never sang better in my life." She was always great fun, coquettish, peering in a mirror while she tucked a curl away. And generous. She often pressed sixpence into my hand and gave me a whisky-smelling kiss. She was an excellent pianist and could still sing. Why was it she had never married? She must have been very attractive in her youth. Later, at her funeral, I heard her story. She had been madly in love with a married man, a tenor in the company. His wife was in an asylum, but it was thought she would not live long. She lived ten more years before he was free, and then he married a young girl who had recently joined the company.

It was Auntie Fryer, as we all called her, who took me to see *Les Cloches de Corneville* when it came to the Theatre Royal. She had once sung in it. It was my first musical play, and I was transported to another world. Whenever to-day I hear that 'Ding Dong' chorus I am carried away to a boy's lost paradise, and Miss Fryer, gold curls, earrings and dangling chains, comes before me.

She always had to be persuaded to perform. She had a cold, or was not too well—"A little asthma, my dear"—but always did perform. Having put the music on the rack, she proceeded to take off her rings and place them on the black ledges at each end of the keyboard. She made a few runs, fluted a little, stopped, and, turning, said: "You must excuse me if I'm not in very good voice. I get no practice these days, the Surgery bell's always ringing."

Poor Auntie Fryer. It was always ringing, but that could not wholly account for lack of form. Dr. Harrison had no piano; also, she was often 'depressed' and that meant recourse to the bottle. There were certain gala evenings when my mother asked in a few friends, among them Mr. Quinn, who obliged with the flute. He was only half-theatrical. He made cricket bats by day at Arthur Gunn's, a famous Notts. cricketer's sports outfitting workshop, and played in the theatre orchestra at night. He was Irish, a devout Roman Catholic, and therefore always seemed a little foreign to us. He was a fine flautist.

In those days entertainment was a home-made restricted affair. There was no radio, no cinema to go to, no gramophone as we now know it. When its forerunner appeared, the Edison Phonograph, my brother invested in one. It had a revolving cylinder driven by a wind-up spring motor, and a large horn curled like the bell of a petunia. The records were hollow wax cylinders that were kept in cardboard containers lined with cotton wool. They were extremely fragile and must not be scratched. To remove one and place it on the machine you had to insert two fingers, slowly withdraw the record, and then slip it on to the cylinder. The sound produced was often a caricature of real music. My father detested the thing. "It has permanent adenoids," he said. I was forbidden by my brother to touch the precious phonograph.*

The end of poor Auntie Fryer was timely. My beloved Dr. Harrison was ill and might have to give up his practice. This worried her, for she would have to seek a new post. In those days housekeepers were not unobtainable jewels, they were ten-a-penny. One morning Dr. Harrison found no breakfast on his table. He rang and rang. Then he went up to her room. She had died in her sleep.

IV

The advent of the piano resulted in my having regular music lessons. The price of the lesson was sixpence for half an hour. The mistress was Miss Bewley who lived in the district. She came to the house, and my mother put sixpence on the ledge at the end of the

* The phonograph was invented by Edison in 1877. It was intended as an office dictating machine and was very expensive, $190. In 1906 appeared the popular Edison Phonograph, with a large curved horn. It held the market for a time but it was doomed. In 1887 Ernst Berliner invented the flat disk for recording. The advantages were obvious: the disks were easier to store, played longer, were less fragile than the wax cylinders, and from a single master-disk thousands of copies could be made. Edison struggled on with the wax-cylinder model until 1913 when he was converted to the principle of the flat-disk 'gramophone', with records made of asphalt. But he now had too many competitors and was forced out of business in the late twenties, despite his invention in 1926 of the 'long playing' record, revolving at 80 r.p.m. and playing twenty minutes.

keyboard. She was one of three spinster sisters. They were ardent Wesleyan chapel-goers and faithful to a chapel in the Lace Market, where their parents had worshipped. Every Sunday morning they could be seen two abreast, one behind, tall, less tall, small, marching up town to chapel. They dressed alike in black bodices with ham leg sleeves and down-to-ankle skirts and boots. Their high collars had lace frills. Julia, the eldest, wore a hat with a black curled ostrich feather. Mollie, my music teacher, had the same shaped hat with two white roses instead of a feather. Mabel, the youngest, wore a tight velvet toque. She would have been pretty but for high-powered spectacles. The eldest sister kept house and made costumes to order. Mollie gave music lessons in her pupils' homes. Mabel was a short-hand typist in an office. Poor Miss Mollie had lung trouble and took Scott's Cod-Liver Oil Emulsion, known also to me with its fishy taste. She was very punctual. She arrived and departed on the minute, timing herself with a little gold watch on a long chain, tucked in her waistband. When the lessons began she detached her watch, hanging it by a small loop on the piano candle-bracket. My eyes often looked at it to see if the ordeal was over. She was a kind but firm teacher. "Your mother is paying me to teach you and I expect you to profit by her sacrifice," she would say. Sometimes by way of reward she produced a sweet. She was enhanced in my eyes when one day she confessed to knowing a little Italian, and from her I learned what was meant by *ritardando, sostenuto, con fuoco, da capo* and *allegro non troppo*. To shorten the music lesson I tried to sidetrack her by learn-ing a few phrases from her, but she was wary. However I did learn some such lines as *Lasciate ogni speranza, voi ch'entrate* (Abandon hope all ye who enter) which she told me was what Dante saw written over the portal of Hell, and *E'n la sua volontate é nostra pace* (In His Will is our peace), found in the *Paradiso*. How very singular that thus early my ears were alert to the music of the Italian language.

There was a sad story attached to Miss Bewley's acquisition of it. As a young woman she had been courted by a handsome Italian who had come to Nottingham to learn lace-machine building. They became engaged, but she had great misgivings when he told her that they would have to be married in a Roman Catholic church and the children must be brought up in the faith, for his well-to-do father was a strict Catholic. He returned to Italy, they corresponded for a time, then he wrote to say that his parents would consent to his

84

marriage only on the condition that she was received into the Catholic Church. Miss Bewley was deeply in love, but after a terrible struggle she broke off the engagement. Her best friend told her it was God's punishment for having thought of marrying a Catholic and a foreigner.

My mother was always concerned about Miss Bewley's cough. "I don't like it," she would say, carrying sticks and coal into the drawing-room, where, in winter, she made a fire before her coming. My father enjoyed talking with her. She had read Cary's translation of Dante, and *I Promessi Sposi* in the original. My mother would invite her to stay for a cup of tea. If she did not have to leave immediately for another lesson she accepted, always protesting. "Well, really, it is too kind of you—I must go in just ten minutes," she would say, glancing at her watch and returning it to her waistband.

She started me off with Czerny's *Exercises*. From these I progressed to a little Mendelssohn and Schubert. And then came the wonderful day when I entered the world of Chopin. There was no holding me then. I was convinced I was a musical prodigy. I also read about Liszt and found a portrait of him in an album of his music—much beyond me. Ought I not to grow my hair long over my neck? "Mr. Paderewski, will you shut up!" cried my unfeeling brother, wishing to play his phonograph. I was pounding away at the *Minuet in G* of which I was soon to give a public performance. Yes, I would have hair like Paderewski's. He had a wonderful lion's mane. For my great day was coming. I had taken an examination set by the Trinity College of Music. There was to be a distribution of certificates to successful examinees. The beautiful Duchess of Portland was to present the awards. There was to be a short recital by pupils. I was to play Paderewski's *Minuet*.

I had often heard about the beautiful Duchess of Portland, but had never seen her. She lived in the fabulous Welbeck Abbey in the Dukeries, the vast mansion where a former eccentric duke had tunnelled miles underground, even building a ballroom, an art gallery and a great carriage way in the bowels of the earth. He employed one hundred workmen to do all this and gave each of them a donkey for transport, and an umbrella.

The sixth duke and his wife played such a prominent part in the public life of Nottingham that they seemed to belong to the city. Their names were always on the announcements of public events. The duke took the chair, headed an appeal. The duchess opened bazaars at charities, sat on charity committees, visited hospitals. If Royalty came to the county for some notable occasion, they always stayed at Welbeck Abbey. The duchess was a lady-in-waiting to Queen Alexandra.

A romantic story circulated concerning her. It was said that one day when the young duke was travelling to a shoot he saw standing on a station platform through which the train passed a very tall, most beautiful girl. He was so struck by her beauty that he made enquiries about her and discovered that her name was Winifred Dallas-York, the daughter of a small landowner. The story was embellished by the statement that she had been taking her father's dairy produce to market and had a basket on her arm. Whatever the truth of this, the young duke proposed to her and was accepted. They married in 1889 and had a long, very active and happy life together and when I last saw her, four years before her death at the age of eighty-four, she was still an elegant beautiful woman living quietly on the Welbeck estate.

In 1965, sixty-three years after my first sight of her, I was the guest of Signora Canonica, widow of the famous sculptor, Pietro Canonica (1869–1959) at the Fortezza in Villa Borghese, Rome, where casts of his work have been preserved for public display. Passing down the gallery, I saw two busts and to my hostess's surprise, recognised them. They were the sixth Duke of Portland and Winifred his wife, about 1896. On another shelf was the bust of a chubby baby. It was labelled 'Bambino Portland'—Baby Portland, erroneously named, for then their son was the Marquess of Titchfield, to become in 1943 the seventh duke. His father had been my chairman in 1924 when I gave the Byron death-centenary lecture in the Exchange Hall, Nottingham. What a chord of memory was plucked in that Roman studio!

Returning to the day of my debut—I had no long trousers yet, being just ten. I pleaded for them in vain. For the great occasion I was to wear black velvet shorts, black shoes, white stockings and a white silk blouse open at the neck. There was no question of a Paderewski halo. My hair was cut two days before. My father rehearsed me in making a bow to the duchess when I went on and off the platform. It was a very deep bow so that half my body became parallel to the platform. I was rehearsed and rehearsed by Miss Bewley until I was note perfect. I was not to do any pedalling.

At all times a highly-strung child, my mother regretted letting me take part in the programme. I could not sleep the night before or eat on the actual day. On returning from school she made me lie down, but it was useless. The performance was at seven o'clock. I was dressed and waiting at six o'clock when my teacher collected me. At the hall we were placed along the front row in due order for receiving our certificates. Promptly at seven o'clock the duchess, accompanied by two ladies and the Chairman, appeared. She was presented with a bouquet of flowers by a little girl amid much applause. The hall was full. Somewhere in the audience were my father and mother. The Chairman made some remarks, a lady also spoke. Then the duchess stood up and we all filed past to receive our certificates.

At last the time came for us to perform our pieces. I was fifth on the list with my *Minuet*. All went well until the fourth performer panicked. I was pushed forward to continue the programme. With clammy hands I mounted the platform. I advanced and made my bow. I heard some people laugh. Perhaps I overdid it, but the duchess gave me a warm smile. I turned and went to the piano. Two things disconcerted me. The black piano-stool was like a long bench. On this a cushion had been placed to heighten my position. It was something unusual. Also I had never played on a grand piano. A great shining lid soared above me. The whole thing looked immense. I took my seat and then the terrible thing happened. My memory went from me utterly. I sat there, frozen with fear. There was an awful silence. I felt a tear running down my cheek and in abject misery turned and looked at the duchess as I slid my feet to the floor, ready to run. She had seen what was happening. She got up from her chair, came over to the stool, sat down, put an arm round me and said very gently, "Now, dear, just play for me." It was all the confidence I wanted. The notes came, I went right through the piece without hesitation, indeed, towards the end, I played with some bravura. There was loud applause. I bowed to the hall, I gave my special bow to the duchess and left the platform warm with happiness. It was my first and last performance as a budding Liszt. When, twelve years later, I gave a recital at the Bechstein Hall, now the Wigmore Hall, in London, it was not as a pianist. I had become a poet and gave a reading of my poems.

I met the duchess several times in later years, she was one of my faithful readers, and we laughed over what she called 'Our little duet'. Oddly enough, she was the mother of a very gifted concert pianist, Lord Morven Bentinck, who died young.*

* A cousin supplies a footnote, in a letter to me, June 30th, 1965. "In the Second World War my husband and I were at the Air Training Gliding School at Netherthorpe. It was there we first had visits from the Duke of Portland from nearby Welbeck. Winifred by this time was the Dowager Duchess and several times she came with her son, the Duke. She was a most delightful old lady, like a piece of Dresden china and very charming in her Old English style. At her request she was introduced to all the officers and their wives and she took a great interest in the training of the cadets. The Officers' Mess was in the Shireoaks Station Hotel and it was here that Lord Morven played so brilliantly on the piano. He was a charming fellow and it was sad that he died so soon after the war ended, when he was only in his forties. I always remember that you were a gifted pianist, and it has stuck in my memory for some fifty years that on the only occasion I can remember meeting you the piano was your topic of conversation."—P. Woolhouse.

CHAPTER FIVE

My Native City

I

LITTLE BY little I became acquainted with my own city. Having seen Byron's home at Newstead Abbey, my father took me to see where the boy Byron had lived in Nottingham. He first came there in 1798, when he was ten, and he was last in the city in 1824 when his body, brought embalmed from Greece, lay in state in The Blackamoor's Head Inn before making the final journey to the Byron vault in the church at Hucknall Torkard near Newstead. As a child in Nottingham, Byron's experience was not a happy one. Impoverished, heir to the ruined Newstead estate, his mother having an income of only £150 a year, they lived in mean lodgings, since Newstead seemed untenable. The ten-year-old Byron was left in the charge of a drunken servant while Mrs. Byron went to London, in an attempt to get a pension for the boy peer. The servant filled the house, in St. James's Street, with her dissolute companions. The boy being lame, his mother had taken him to a brutal quack, ironically named Lavender. He twisted the boy's foot cruelly, forcing it into a braced shoe.

But there is one kind ghost in that old Nottingham house. Alas, history is almost silent concerning him. The small boy had a tutor with whom he read Virgil and Cicero. He was an American named Dummer Rogers. He loved the brilliant little boy and his love was reciprocated. Sometimes he saw the pain in his pupil's face, caused by Lavender's contrivance. "It makes me most uncomfortable, my lord, to see you sitting there in such pain as I know you must be suffering." "Never mind, Mr. Rogers, you shall not see any signs of it in *me!*" replied the boy. Who was this American, how came he to be in Nottingham, what was his history, his end? It would seem he wrote no reminiscences of his world-famous pupil. We know nothing of his end. He fades out in the mists of time, leaving a glow of kindness amid the gloom.

When my father showed me the house, No. 76 St. James's Street, it was difficult to believe the little Lord Byron had gone in and out of that door. The place was rapidly falling into decay, empty, with dirty windows and no plaque to mark its moment of history. A leaning board said: 'For Sale'.

"Shall we buy it, daddy, and live in it?" I asked. What poems I could write there!

My father laughed. "If you have six hundred pounds you can buy it—but it's too large, ten rooms, and wants a lot spending on it." Years later, a Trade Union bought it for their offices, reconditioned it, and put up a memorial tablet. It is now a well-kept suite of offices.

In 1811, the starved stockingers of Nottingham, frightened by the advent of machines that would throw them out of work, rioted and broke the frames. The military were called out. The House of Lords promoted a Bill to make frame-breaking a capital offence. On February 27, 1812, Byron made his maiden speech. It goes down in history as one of the noblest ever made in that House. He denounced the Bill. "Suppose this man, and there are a thousand such from whom you may select your victim, be dragged into court, to be tried for this new offence by this new law, still there are two things wanting to convict and condemn him—twelve butchers for a jury and a Jeffreys for a judge." He then ridiculed the efforts of the military to suppress the Nottingham riots. "The best speech by a Lord since the Lord knows when!" declared Sir Francis Burdett.

Three days later this unknown youth awoke to find himself famous. He had published two cantos of *Childe Harold's Pilgrimage*. Later he left England never to return, but from Italy he wrote of "my own county of Nottingham."

It was but a few yards from Byron's lodging near Standard Hill to the castle. As a very small boy I thought its position on the high rock dominating the town and the Trent valley was superb. I still do. What the Acropolis is to Athens, the castle is to Nottingham. Little remains of the ancient fortress, but history abides here. You see it coming into the city from Ruddington Hill, proud, dominant. William the Conqueror was aware in 1068 of its formidable site. He ordered the rebuilding of a stronghold that had been contended for by Danes and Saxons. Here Alfred the Great had clashed with the Danes of the ninth century, and negotiated a peace between them and the armies of Wessex and Mercia. William the Conqueror's wooden fort gave place to the stone building of Henry I in 1131. Where once was the keep of the fortress now stands the Castle Museum and Art Gallery. In the course of time, kings came there to hold their privy councils. For five hundred years it grew in power, knew glory and shame. Athelstan, the first crowned king of England, set up his mint here, issuing coins that bear the town's mark. The Normans held the castle, looking down upon the Normans in a French borough, the Saxons in a Saxon borough, each with its Town Hall, mint and laws. Henry II came and gave the town its first charter, in 1155. He held the castle as a royal fortress and hunted in the Sherwood Forest. Here came his son, Richard Cœur de Lion, succeeding to the throne in 1189 as Richard I. Prior to leaving on a crusade he gave his brother estates, including Nottingham. John entertained sumptuously at the castle and soon clashed and expelled Richard's regent, certain he could make himself the king. To his chagrin Richard returned from captivity in 1194, and his brother defying him, assaulted the castle. John surrendered and fled to Normandy. On Richard's death in 1199 he ascended the throne as King John. In 1212 the castle witnessed a ghastly scene. Furious at another rebellion in Wales, he ordered the hanging from the ramparts of twenty-eight Welsh boys, aged twelve to fourteen, held as hostages. Simon de Montfort, founder of our Parliament, became the governor of the castle, and after him Edward I permitted the town to elect a mayor. Edward II lived there, as also his wife, the mother of young Edward III, Queen Isabella. She cohabited there with her paramour, Roger Mortimer. In October, 1330, the young king Edward, who rebuilt Windsor Castle, and founded the Order of the Garter, decided to end the degrading spectacle of his mother and Mortimer. It is alleged that the king, with his followers, gained access through a secret subterranean passage known as Mortimer's Hole. They captured Mortimer and hanged him at Tyburn.

For a fee of threepence one could visit this passage, and, aged twelve, I expended a whole week's pocket money to do so. There was a party of six of us. The guide carried a lantern. It was a hair-raising experience, with the darkness, the dampness, the sense of drama in the bowels of the rock. I was glad to gain the daylight. Thirty years later the catacombs of Rome gave me no such sensation. When you emerged at the bottom of the twisting passage you found yourself near an inn called *The Trip to Jerusalem*. It is built into the

Rock and the title suggests the era of the medieval crusaders. It carries the legend "Ye Olde Trip to Jerusalem Inn. A.D. 1189. The oldest inn in England." The word 'trip' means a halt. As a friend observed, Edward III and Mortimer could have 'had one' there. I longed to do so, but all 'pubs' were prohibited by my parents.

It was from Nottingham Castle that King Richard III marched out to Bosworth Field where he met his doom in battle in 1485. The next tragic figure on the scene is Charles I. On the eve of the Civil War he had rested in Leicestershire before marching into Nottingham with some of the county's leading gentlemen. He took up residence, not at the castle, but at Clare House in the town. He was accompanied by his young sons, the Prince of Wales and the Duke of York, and by his nephews, Prince Rupert and Prince Maurice. A Standard in the form of a silk pennant had been made for him by a local man, Robert Large. It was flown from a red-painted pole on the evening of August 22nd, 1642. It took twenty Knights Bannerets to carry the Standard, escorted by three troops of horse and four hundred infantry called to the castle by Sir John Digby, the Sheriff. They marched to the hill behind the castle, known ever since as Standard Hill, and placed the base of the flagpole in a hole dug there. But a strong wind was blowing and the flag was kept upright with great difficulty. The herald read the Proclamation, the trumpets sounded. Hats rose in the air and voices shouted "God save the King and hang all Roundheads!" Then the Standard was taken back to the castle where it flew from the turret. But not for long. The following May Cromwell was in Nottingham and in possession of the castle. He held it until 1651 when he ordered it to be demolished with gunpowder. So the castle as a castle disappeared. "Except," said my father as we paid twopence and entered the grounds through a turnstile, "for this gateway, whose bastions are part of the old castle."

II

During a short siege of the Parliamentarians the Duke of Newcastle offered the Governor of Nottingham Castle a ten-thousand-pound bribe, which was refused. When the war was over Parliament rewarded the garrison with one-thousand pounds. At the Restoration the duke was back again. He bought the site, cleared away all the rubble and in 1674 began to build a ducal palace, which his son completed three years after his death. It was an age when dukes had a mania and the means for building. The 'castle' that now arose was a great rectangular mansion with projecting wings. Over the north door there was an equestrian statue of the first duke. What could any sane man want with these vast rooms and great staircases? It must have needed a hundred servants. It is almost unbelievable that this great block, with forty marble fireplaces, cost only some fourteen thousand pounds to build. The successive dukes soon tired of it. By the end of the eighteenth century it was almost devoid of furniture and pictures. Around 1810 it was divided into flats—thus anticipating our present age. Little by little it grew shabby and then, in 1831, the Nottingham mob set fire to it, enraged by the opposition of the House of Lords to the Reform Bill. For this destruction the Duke of Newcastle was awarded twenty-one thousand pounds in compensation. He did not rebuild his useless palace, and for nearly fifty years it remained a blackened ruin. In 1875 the Corporation of Nottingham took a five hundred years' lease. They restored the building at a cost of thirty thousand pounds, converting it into the first municipal museum of art in England. The completed Art Gallery and Museum was opened by Prince Edward accompanied by Princess Alexandra. So Edward I, Edward II, Edward III and Edward VII are associated down the centuries with Nottingham Castle.

To-day it is known all over the world for a singular reason, not because it houses examples of the work of famous Nottingham artists, Paul and Thomas Sandby, Richard Parkes Bonington,* Sir Arnesby Brown, Dame Laura and Harold Knight,† Denholm Davis, but because of its picture on packets of cigarettes. In 1877 John Player bought a small tobacco business. The made-up cigarette, instead of loose tobacco sold over the counter, was just coming into fashion. Player put his cigarettes into packets and for an identifying trade-mark he used a drawing of the castle high on its rock. For nearly a century that trade-mark on Player's has gone all over the world, being joined on the reverse side, in 1883, by a sailor's head and two ships in a lifebuoy. From that time on the Player factories in Nottingham grew and grew. To-day they employ ten thousand hands. The two sons of the founder, John D. and William G., became millionaires,

* On the back of his *Undercliff* in the Castle Gallery is written "The last drawing made by our son prior to his fatal dissolution." He died aged twenty-seven.

† Dame Laura Knight, the second woman to be elected an A.R.A., attended the local art college. Her first Academy picture hangs in the castle.

enlightened employers, and philanthropic Mæcenases of their city.

When my father first took me up to the castle and through its great galleries I did not know until then, Clumber and Welbeck still unvisited, in what grandeur dukes sought to live. Now the dukes have gone, though the first Duke of Newcastle still sits on his stone horse over the portal.

Like a young Athenian who discovers that the Acropolis and the Parthenon are part of his birthright, I revelled in this Museum and Art Gallery. It was destined to play a vital part in my writing career. One of the exhibits in the long glass cases was a Pompeian bronze copy of the famous 'Narcissus listening to Echo' in the Naples Museum, ravished from Greece by the conquering Romans. It is this statue which stood on Gladstone's desk warning him, with upraised finger, to contemplate. In reality it is not Narcissus but Dionysos with the goatskin, every line of the naked youth's figure exquisite. It was my first contact with Greek art and I returned again and again to look at it. Almost twenty years later, when I wrote my first novel, this statue, which had delighted me as a boy, supplied the theme. A young honeymoon couple see in a Naples shop a bronze copy of 'Narcissus'; the wife covets it. "I'll buy it if you'll give me a real boy," says the husband, jocularly. He buys it, and when his son is born he reminiscently adds the name Narcissus to that of John. The boy finds his fanciful name converted to 'Scissors' by his school friends. With *Scissors* I launched myself on my lifelong career as a novelist. So a bronze of the Praxitelean school started me off. I was seventy-one when in 1963 I gave a small luncheon party to celebrate the fortieth anniversary of the publication of *Scissors*, then in its twenty-first edition. As I sat at the table in my London club, a host with over forty books behind me, I saw the figure of a young boy in a sailor suit, standing in wonder before a glass case while his father explained the history of the statue. Like John Dean in my story, I, too, in Naples, bought a bronze copy of the work. It is on my desk to-day.

The rock on which the castle stands is honeycombed with chambers and passages cut out of the soft sandstone, in which Britons lived before the Romans came. These passages, it is alleged, run beneath Nottingham to the old borders of the ancient Sherwood Forest, hence the legend that Robin Hood and his Merry Men took refuge in them. One can still see a cut-out chamber, with three windows, in the castle rock.

From the retaining walls of the castle one looks down over the splendid amphitheatre known as The Park. It is a residential area, enclosed, laid out by the Duke of Newcastle about 1850. It was forest land until the middle of last century. Italian, Regency and Victorian villas are spaced out over the steep slopes. The concentric planning in terraces, drives, crescents, circuses, all wooded, shows the Nash influence. England has no lovelier residential quarter, secluded, sylvan, yet built into the heart of the city. In 1938 the Duke of Newcastle sold this estate to Lord Nuffield who presented it to the University of Oxford as part of the Nuffield Foundation.

In the days of my youth this was an exclusive area inhabited by millionaire industrial tycoons and others. If, in a shop, you gave a Park address, the bow was a little lower. In later years I had a friend, a rich and gifted eccentric, who had a lease of one of these ducal houses, fifteen rooms, hall and garden, for eighty pounds a year. Often his guest, in a dwelling crammed with art treasures, I looked down on 'St. Helier's', built by Jesse Boot, and across to a high rampart of villas known as The Ropewalk, where perched the house of 'Festus' Bailey, the poet, who died there, forgotten, in 1902.

Those late Victorian magnates, many of whom lived in the stately Park houses, were very much of a pattern. From humble beginnings they rose to wealth. They got themselves baronetcies, and established commercial dynasties. Sir Jesse Boot (chemist), Sir Thomas Birkin (lace), Sir Ernest Jardine (machinery), Sir Frank Bowden (bicycles), the Player brothers (tobacco). Their careers touched romance. A farm labourer, earning twelve shillings a week, broken in health, opened a herbalist's shop near Goose Gate. He died leaving a small boy of thirteen, Jesse Boot, to take down the shutters. Jesse studied women whose household budgets were more exacting than any known to a Chancellor of the Exchequer. He hit on the idea of retailing, at cut-rate prices. He was full of ideas. People wanted sponges ? Out of the window went the great coloured bottles of the chemists's trade-sign, and into it went sponges. The Post Office was offering the six-penny telegram. The public was shy of it. It was expensive and gener-ally carried disastrous news. Young Jesse telegraphed two hundred people in Nottingham—"Visit our special display of sponges." That advertisement, costing five pounds, created a sensation. The sponges were sold out. Jesse was on the way up. Thence a peerage, Debrett; Residence, The Park.

In 1887 Frank Bowden was compelled to leave Hong Kong, where he had been for fifteen years, through ill-health. A specialist in England told him he had only three months to live, but another advised him to take up cycling, then a new craze. He took the advice and was well within six months. This gave him an idea. He sought out the place where his crude vehicle had been made. He found a dozen men working in a shed in Raleigh Street, turning out three bicycles a week. He had found the germ of the great Raleigh Cycle Company. It caught the cycling fashion. The germ became a giant employing eight thousand people in factories covering thirty acres. Thence a baronetcy, Debrett; Residence, The Park.

In a yard in Nottingham an old man called John Jardine collected scrap iron. His son, Ernest, began to examine where the scrap iron came from, and turned machine-builder. Thence a baronetcy, Debrett; Residence, The Park.*

Mr. Thomas Birkin had ideas concerning lace manufacture. Soon a great warehouse spread over the Lace Market. Thence a baronetcy, Debrett; Residence, The Park. The age of the business tycoons had opened.

The names of the crescents, circles, avenues and drives in The Park were mostly derived from ducal families—Newcastle, Pelham, Clinton, Holles, Clumber, Cavendish. There were gates to shut in The Park, above and below the Castle, and there was no right of thoroughfare, no shops, no 'pub', no public transport. It was an enclosed arena, exclusive, umbrageous, soundless. To-day these large houses, situated some way from public transport, are a problem. Mrs. Smith, who 'obliges' for two hours in the morning, objects to the distance she has to walk. She must be fetched and taken back by car. It would be sad if this magnificent terraced amphitheatre subsided into ruin, like the Roman Palatine, full of patrician ghosts.

When as a small boy I was invited to tea at one of these houses, I felt as if I had walked into Elysium. Later, I came to know one house well. It was 'St. Helier's', the home of Jesse Boot, now become Lord Trent, named after his Jersey estate. It was here my friend Denholm Davis went to paint his portrait. Sir Jesse, as everyone called him, was completely paralysed and the most he could do, the

---

* In 1920 Sir Ernest's son, Donald, invited me to dine and meet his guest, a young man of my own age, 'very clever', working on a London newspaper. His name was H. V. Morton. We did not meet again until forty-five years later, when we dined in Rome. He had just added *A Wanderer in Rome* to his famous series.

millionaire salesman of drugs and medicines to make people well. was to insert a twisted finger in a small loop in the lapel of his coat, by which he summoned his secretary. While sitting for his portrait he was apt to become irritable and restless. Davis invited me to sittings to entertain his model with my conversation, no easy task, since the poor man was very deaf. From the terrace of his house there was a noble view across the leafy amphitheatre to the Castle high on its rock. Within a few years of these sessions Lord Trent left Nottingham forever, 'St. Helier's' was pulled down. The son who succeeded in the new peerage died without an heir. When I was a boy I had looked with awe on the great door of the house in The Park where dwelt one of the lions of Nottingham.

In those days the city's southern boundary was the Trent, an amiable river. It is navigably wide, and slides through the level Midland fields. It rarely races, and is spaced by a number of picturesque weirs and locks. It was intimate to me throughout childhood and adolescence. The school, to which I went stood in the centre of open fields, bordered on their perimeter by the river's curving embankment. Across the river were pleasant green hills. Northwards, one looked over meadows to a distant height where the Castle crowned its rock. Four bridges spanned this pleasant promenade from Trent Bridge to Wilford Bridge. On the first there was always plenty of excitement. It was the gateway by which all must approach Nottingham coming from the south. Very near it stood the far-famed cricket ground, and the Forest Football Club. Enormous crowds crossed this bridge going to or coming from the games. And for a short time, on a piece of open land just over the bridge, there was the Midlands Exhibition. What excitement it stirred in my boy's heart! It was erected mostly of plaster, almost overnight, with arcades, arabesque kiosks, minarets and Indian domed towers. Everything was snow-white. It was put up by a man with the strange name of Imré Kiralfy, who built the great White City Exhibition in London which created such a sensation. This was an offshoot. The dizzy enchantment of its exterior was more than matched by its interior. There was a great water-chute that precipitated you into a lake, there were dazzling shopping arcades where strange dark men with many rings tried to sell you oriental goods, pearl-inlaid tables, lamps, carpets, tapestries and ivory carvings. They wore turbans and sprayed scent on you. There was a Hottentot Village with real nigh-naked negroes living in kraals. They did war dances with assegais and wore leopard skins. Their women had enormous ankle rings and many of them had black curly-headed babies frankly busy at their mothers' exposed breasts. There was a maze in which you got lost, and a long hall with distorting mirrors.

The two most fascinating shows for me were 'The Enchanted Journey' and 'The Swiss Village'. The former consisted of a series of dark tunnels through which flowed a stream. You got into a flat-bottomed boat and were conveyed into scenes full of tropical wonders, through strange forests, past oriental villages, waterfalls, towering snow-clad mountains, deep jungles and over rapids; a potpourri of Asia, India, Africa and South America. The eyes of panthers glared at you, sinister snakes were looped about tropical trees, giant vultures hung in the air, and there were terrifying dark cliffs towering above you. This part had special attractions for lovers, locked together in the darkness. Finally you came to a platform in the dazzling daylight and your threepenny adventure was over.

The other attraction, the 'Swiss Village', was a stage panorama. The curtain went up on a mountain village, its chalets, with flowery balconies, dotting the green slopes. There was a road winding down from the mountains that, snow-crowned, hung over the village. A fierce stream, with a gushing waterfall, ran under rustic bridges, turning water-wheels. Presently a waggon laden with logs and pulled by oxen came down the road, and a young goatherd, playing a pipe, drove his herd over the bridge. Birds in wicker cages hung above the flowery wooden balconies and sang blithely in the bright sunny morning in that village beneath the high glistening glacier. A cobbler at the door of his chalet mended shoes. Then in the pointed belfry of the church a clock struck noon and a peal of bells rang out. Could it be that anywhere in the world there was anything so beautiful? "Oh, yes," said Mrs. Weiss, sitting with us, she had spent her honeymoon with her Swiss husband in just such a place. Then the scene changed, the sun vanished, the blue sky became overcast, there was a distant rumble of thunder. Suddenly the black heavens opened and a torrent of rain fell on the village. The thunder grew closer and now there were terrifying flashes of sheet lightning revealing the scene in a fierce glare. Up in the black mountain peaks there was forked lightning, and a tremendous cannonade of thunder. The noise of the storm lashing that poor little village was tremendous. Then it passed, the mountains became visible, a rainbow threw its many-coloured arch over the deep ravine, the sunshine returned, the birds in the cages sang again, a peasant jodelled, the ox-cart lumbered on, and the goatherd played his pipe in the happy Swiss morning. I came out of that twenty-minute panorama dazed with the wonder of that far-away scene. One day I would be rich and I would go there.

In later years when I motored back to England from my Italian villa the route took me up over the great St. Gotthard Pass, and then, descending, how often I passed through just such a Swiss village, with torrent, church, water-wheels, chalets and goatherds driving flocks exactly as I had seen them in that threepenny show by the bank of the River Trent.

One evening, a week after my visit to the Exhibition, my brother came rushing into the house. "Come on—the Exhibition's on fire— it's a terrific blaze!" he cried. We all hurried towards the Trent Bridge where we found a great crowd held back under a lurid sky. It was true, the whole place was going up in flames. The blaze was tremendous and there was a roar like a high wind. Built of timber, lath and plaster, the building and its annexes were highly inflammable. It was my first fire, and the greatest I have ever seen. The flames soaring up into the sky were quite beyond any control from the assembled fire-engines, and not all the water they drew out of the Trent had the slightest effect on them. One watched in horrified wonder, thinking of all the poor exhibitors who had lost their goods. I also wondered what had happened to the Hottentot Village, the naked warriors, the black women with babies. Their straw kraals must have been the first to go. Presently there was a new alarm. The veering wind carried the flames towards the pavilion and grandstand of the Forest Football Club. Soon it caught fire and a fresh volcano discharged its flames into the night. Built largely of wood, it was an easy prey. In a few hours there was nothing left of the Midlands Exhibition or of the Forest Football Club. For months as one passed over Trent Bridge one saw the great blackened skeleton of the vanished Exhibition. The Scenic Railway, the Swiss Village, the water-chute all lay among the black cinders of a vanished fairyland.

III

Below Trent Bridge there was an embankment by which were tethered the pleasure steamers. Downstream, beyond the rowing clubs, rose the dark thick woods of Colwick Park, some two miles distant. On a summer's day my mother would pack a two-lidded basket with sandwiches and cold tea and we would make an excursion by steamer between the green banks of the Trent. It was the very height of romance. On the deck of the *Empress* or *The Prince Consort*, two men with fiddle and harp played as we glided over the water. The beat of the boat's engines and the thrash of the paddle-wheels mingled with the jaunty music. We gladly put a penny in his straw hat when the violinist came round.

The arrival at the Park was dramatic. The water was very deep and black where the great elms threw a shadow. It was said that boys who ventured to swim there had been drowned. How carefully we went down the gangway to the bobbing landing-stage! The swans glided away, very white on the black water. We advanced into a dim grove of trees. It was all very Wagnerian, or like a scene in *Swan Lake*. There I was, dressed in a striped print blouse with white sailor collar, shorts, white socks and strap-over shoes. I wore a round sailor hat with a red ribbon streamer. My slim pretty mother had a flowered print dress, a green leather belt round her waist and, as always, a little inset of crocheted lace just peering over her neckband. Sometimes my father went with us, and sitting on the deck of the steamer he would smoke a cigar and fold his yellow-gloved hands over the ivory handle of his ebony walking stick. He wore a 'boater' straw hat a little rakishly and sat, one leg over the other, displaying an elegant foot.

After a short walk down the elm avenue we came to an open space with a long lake full of water lilies and spanned by a rustic bridge. Above this, on a terrace of green turf, was the long façade of Colwick Hall. No one lived there now. There was a café and the long salon was let out for dances. The grounds had a sad, deserted look. Outside the park there was the Colwick Park Racecourse. Clearly the place had been forgotten by Time. Yet once it had known fashion and gaiety, the seat of fox-hunting Squire Musters. He had brought to this Georgian mansion in 1805 his young bride, Mary Chaworth. She had been Lord Byron's boyhood's love and for her he had written his first poems. He had often ridden over from his semi-ruinous seat at Newstead Abbey to proclaim an adolescent passion for the pretty daughter of Squire Chaworth at Annesley Park. Four years his senior, she had treated his declarations with disdain. Then she married hard-drinking Squire Musters, who brought her to Colwick Park. He was coarse and rollicking and her married life was unhappy. Still attracted by her, Byron paid a visit to the Hall to see her again.

She was now a young mother. They were both fated to tragic ends. During the Reform Law Riots the Hall was invaded by the rioters on the same night that they fired Nottingham Castle. She fled with her children to a shed by the lake until help came. Her mind affected, separated from her husband, she died from shock. After Byron's death Thomas Moore found among his papers "Lines written shortly after the marriage of Miss Chaworth", which the poet had never published.

> Hills of Annesley, bleak and barren,
>   Where my thoughtless childhood strayed,
> How the northern tempests, warring,
>   Howl about thy tufted shade!
>
> Now no more the hours beguiling,
>   Former favourite haunts I see,
> Now no more my Mary smiling
>   Makes ye seem a heaven to me.

So once again the lugubrious Byron legend hovered about us, but on a summer's day, with the ducks quacking, the swans gliding on the lake, with the lunch basket opened on the grass and a half-penny ice in my hand, old sorrows did not touch my happiness, and at evening there was the steamer ride back to Trent Bridge, with the musicians playing and the sunset gilding the river.

In Nottingham itself there were other attractions. I loved to go with my mother to the open market held in the Market Place on Wednesdays and Saturdays. It had a festive air with its rows of awning-covered stalls. There was an avenue where hung the white bodies of plucked fowls, and cocks with red combs dangling. There were vegetable stalls with an earthy tang, shoe stalls with their leathery odours. Once my mother bought me a pair of shoes for five shillings. She thought them a great bargain, but my father was so incensed that I should wear anything made of cheap leather that he insisted on them being given away. There were cheese stalls, linen stalls and across the way the open pot-market with plates, cups and saucers displayed on the ground. The hawkers picked them up and flicked them with a finger to show they were not cracked. Later, above this display of crockery, stood Queen Victoria, high on her pedestal, with crown and sceptre. Just a short distance away were two spots of vivid colour. They were the striped blue and white awnings of Mrs. Capocci's and Mrs. Solari's ice-cream stalls. They shone with polished brass, on wheeled carts that could be trundled away. Behind one of these ice-cream stalls stood Mrs. Capocci. She had a darkish skin, black hair, large glittering earrings and wore a vivid bodice over which she threw a many-coloured shawl. She also wore a triangular piece of linen on her head. It was my first contact with anything Italian. For a halfpenny one could have a cornet or a small boat of ice-cream. I always patronised Mrs. Capocci and avoided her rival. She was more generous. She raised the lid of her ice-cream bucket, plunged in a wooden spade and slapped the ice-cream into the cornet. Mrs. Solari always levelled off the top.

Just off the Market Place was Cheapside, along which on Wednesdays and Saturdays were displayed the farmers' baskets offering chickens, butter, eggs and livestock, so that one side was dubbed The Poultry. I used to see parked there, a luxurious (for those days) automobile. In it sat two boys, brothers of about fifteen and sixteen. They were the sons of a Councillor Halford. He was a handsome well-built man, partner in a prosperous estate agency. I looked with deep envy on those two public schoolboys waiting for him in the car. To me they seemed to have everything. They had a handsome father, were well-dressed, good-looking, and reflected the family prosperity. They had a sister Kathleen, who had a trained 'concert voice', and with whom I danced later. The younger god in the car was destined for fame. He became Major Frank Halford, with a genius for designing aero-engines. Sir Geoffrey de Havilland discovered him, and the famous Moth pioneer plane emerged in the First World War. He served with distinction in the R.A.F. and from his fertile brain came the Napier, Sabre and Gipsy engines which made aeronautical history. Singular indeed that two local boys of about the same age, one Captain Ball, V.C., one Major Halford, should seal their fame in the field of aviation.

In streets leading out of the Market Place were some lovely eighteenth-century houses. Very justly did Daniel Defoe declare that Nottingham, spread over its hills above the Trent, was a pretty town—"One of the pleasantest in England." One day I trespassed into Bromley House. It had been built in 1752 for Sir George Smith, the banker. Through an elegant doorway I daringly went up a fine staircase, peered on the first landing down into a leafy garden, and then went through a swing door, to find, under a rococo plaster ceiling, a long room that was a library! I saw *soignée* ladies come in and change books. It was a private subscription library evidently catering for 'the County set'. I went out, dazed, making a vow that one day, in the affluent future I planned, I would belong to it. I never have, though happily it survives in all its neo-Palladian beauty. Then there was Newdigate House, with elegant iron gates and railings. It had housed the French Marshal Tallard and his officers, taken prisoners in the battle of Blenheim. It was rare for a Commander-in-Chief to be taken prisoner with a group of high officers. Camille d'Hostun, duc de Tallard, was a Marshal of France. With him were the Marquis de Montperroux, General of the Horse, the Marquis de Hauntefeuille, General of Dragoons, the Marquis de Silly (a name that drew mirth), and among a number of aristocrats a Comte de Horn whose ancestor was the famous Governor of Gelderland under Charles V, who was decapitated by the Duke of Alva. There were twelve noblemen in all, a rich bag. The prisoners arrived with their own valets and cooks. The Marshal was soon famous for the garden he made at Newdigate House. He was the first person in England to cultivate celery. The officers became very popular and brought a touch of the French Court to a provincial town. When Marshal Tallard returned to France in 1711, Nottingham lamented its elegant prisoner with his good manners, his fine garden, his excellent cuisine and wines.

Naturally there was the legacy of a little scandal. Daniel Defoe, visiting the garden, was impressed, but could not resist reporting on another aspect of the distinguished hostage—" 'Tis said that this gallant gentleman left behind him some *living* memorandums of his great affection and esteem for the English ladies."

Near Newdigate House is an inn called *The Royal Children* which recalls other distinguished visitors. The name was derived from the children of Princess Anne, the daughter of James II, who, when in residence at the Castle, were the playmates of the innkeeper's children, about 1688. The inn sign is the shoulder-blade of a whale used to indicate that whale oil was sold there. The inn was one of the first places to use lamps instead of candles and torches.

IV

When the Market Place was cleared of everything on Sundays, on the site of the pot-market there was the 'orators' corner. Here they had their little rostrums. It was a field-day for religious and political cranks. They offered their various recipes for salvation to a rabble of unemployed or odd listeners. The 'hot' revivalist thumped, shouted, denounced, sang hymns and glorified the Lord. Side by side, the Atheists, Agnostics and Socialists held forth. One preacher of local fame was an old ex-pugilist, William Bendigo, who had been 'saved'. Once upon a time he had had a colleague, William Booth, a Revivalist open-air preacher, who had gone ahead, founded the Salvation Army, and gained world fame. This rankled with Bendigo. He held him up as an example of sinful pride. "You all knew Bill Booth, who used to preach here, a God-loving 'umble man. Alas, my brethren, how success can destroy a man! Since Bill Booth put on a bloody weskit, banged a drum and shouted about Blood and Fire, he ain't known any of us 'umble servants of God. He eats with princes, and consorts with publicans and sinners."

In 1905 I was fated to see General William Booth, founder of the Salvation Army. He was Nottingham born, and in that year the city sought to honour him by conferring on him its Freedom. He was then seventy-six years of age. Born half-Jewish on his mother's side, in a small house in what was then considered the slummy part of the city, he had known considerable poverty, and at thirteen worked in a pawnbroker's shop in a squalid district. Since then he had made the blood-red banner of his Army known throughout the world, and among all the Christian agencies devoted to the welfare of the sick and poor his stood highest in the esteem of the people for its coura-geous campaign in the darkest corners of the land. Those brass bands, those sisters with the tambourines, those 'Captains' with their peaked caps, praying, preaching, singing, beating the drum at street corners, were the shock troops of Christian evangelism. A dynamic personality, inspired by a passion to alleviate poverty, candid, and respected by kings and statesmen, Booth had made even Cecil Rhodes kneel down with him in prayer, in a railway carriage. Now General William Booth had been called back as a 'distinguished native son' to receive the accolade of his city. He was to live seven more years and die, blind and mourned by millions, at eighty-three.

On the appointed day of the Freedom ceremony he drove into the Market Place in an open carriage. Waiting in the crowd with my mother, a boy of thirteen, I remember the striking figure he made as he slowly drove by, standing up in the carriage, hatless, his great white mane streaming in the air, his beard flowing down over his scarlet waistcoat and blue tunic with its red collar, as he acknow-ledged the salute of the crowd. Erect, tall, he was the very image of an

Old Testament Prophet. How little did I know then that exactly sixty years later, I, too, would make a journey to the Council House in that Market Place to have conferred upon me the same Freedom of my native city, or that, in 1917 and 1920, two notable figures, both personally known to me, were to be my predecessors. One of these was Captain Albert Ball, a lad of twenty. His astonishing bravery and skill in the air over the battlefields of the Western Front during the First World War, had made him the nation's hero. He was credited with having brought down forty-three of the enemy's planes. In 1917, on leave from the Front, he was received and decorated by the King, entertained by the Prime Minister, and by the leaders of the nation. He made a visit to his parents. This occasion was used by his native city to pay him its highest tribute. What a small smiling boy he seemed as he drove to the old Exchange, and what a lovable gallant lad he was! I had known him, four years my junior, since he was a boy of fourteen, at the house of his father, a former Mayor. He had a shy, withdrawn nature. "I hate this killing business," he said, but, dedicated, he fought with a fierce chivalry. Honours fell fast upon him—V.C., M.C., D.S.O., with four bars, Croix de Guerre, Legion d'Honneur, the Russian Order of St. George. They wanted to keep him home, a fine recruiting asset but he would have none of it. He was the spearhead of the Royal Flying Corps which, before the Battle of the Somme, had achieved ascendancy over the Germans. He returned to the Front, brought down another three planes, and then was reported killed, the special target of the enemy, only a few weeks after he had received the Freedom of his native city.

The other recipient of the city's Freedom, in 1920, was a very different character, Sir Jesse Boot, founder of the great drug business, a model employer of labour, and a tireless benefactor of his native city. He was now seventy years of age and had long been tied to a paralytic's chair. As a small boy I knew of Sir Jesse, one of the gods of the city's industries, powerful, rich and benevolent. Daily as I walked with my father to his business I would see the magnate's car going to Boots' office by the Midland Station. The car had been constructed to take an invalid's chair, and there, high up and visible, he rode down the street from his house in The Park.

Sir Jesse was a Primitive Methodist Nonconformist, a staunch Liberal, a great figure in party politics, and when the leaders, Asquith, Lloyd George and others came to address local audiences, he entertained them and took the chair at the mass meetings. In the days following the great Tory landslide of 1906, when the Liberals achieved power with a large majority, H. H. Asquith was the rock and Lloyd George was the volcano. Another eruptive force was the youthful Winston Churchill. I heard all of them in my cult of public speaking, and my boy's enthusiasm was all for the fiery little Welshman. I was in the opposite camp to my father. In those days what passions were aroused by politics! The Albert Hall was crammed to the ceiling. Until the big guns appeared the crowd sang political hymns. The great organ thundered, the massed voices chanted "The Land! The Land! God gave the Land to the People." It was the era of Lloyd George's attack on the House of Lords, the 'backwoodsmen' who came up like tottering hermits to throw out the Welsh fiend's diabolical 'People's Budget'. Yet within six years he was to become 'the saviour of his Country' in the Great War. Thirty-five years later, discredited and deserted, he was to take refuge, three months before his death, in the very House of Lords he had threatened to abolish.

As the multitude, near hysteria, waited in the hall, an invalid chair was seen being slowly hauled up the steps to the platform. In the chair sat crippled Sir Jesse, his hands cruelly twisted by arthritis. The hall went mad. The acclaim was more for him than for Asquith, Lloyd George or any Cabinet Minister for whom he took the chair. I had my first personal contact with him when, a youth, I sold some poems which Boots used for calendars. After he had published two I was told Sir Jesse would like half a dozen and I was taken in to see the great man. I trembled inwardly. "So you're the poet!" he said, accusingly, then added with a chuckle—"You don't know that I've been one too! When I was a youth I won ten shillings in a competition for rhymed verses celebrating Day and Martin's Blacking." He proceeded to recite the verses with gusto. "Now," he said, "We like your poems and we'll take half a dozen. I suppose you'll give us a cut-rate?" "Oh no, Sir Jesse," I replied, "you're dealing with genius not merchandise!" He stared at me. "I like that! Perhaps you've got something there. Very well—three pounds a time," he said. That was our first encounter. I went dizzily out of his office. I was destined to conduct other business with him later, and to be a guest at his house and at his villa in Cannes. I was present in the Exchange Hall when he received the Freedom of the city. He was lavish with benefactions and was the virtual founder of the University of

Nottingham, on a site given by him. I was his guest at the laying of the foundation stone.

In my desire to hear all manner of speakers I went to Tory as well as Liberal and Labour meetings. I heard smooth A. J. Balfour, insolent baby-faced F. E. Smith, *l'enfant terrible* of the Conservatives, and self-possessed, bland Bonar Law, but neither their eloquence nor their arguments caught me up like the Liberal leaders. One day I was destined to speak, in a junior rôle, from that same platform, as the young Liberal candidate for East Nottingham. But that was a long way off. Perhaps the most memorable performer of all was that Irish *condottiere*, T. P. O'Connor. He was an infallible tear-jerker with his carefully preserved Irish accent and his harrowing story of the potato famine in Ireland, which he had witnessed as a 'bhoy'. The wrongs of 'ould Oireland' enabled him to pluck every chord on his harp. Churchill, young and pugnacious, I heard and first saw in a fog-filled skating rink in 1909. He was then the pink-faced thirty-five-year-old President of the Board of Trade. I was astonished to find he had trouble with his aitches; he said 'at 'ome', and 'the 'orrible situation', and had an impediment when any esses came up. In later life I noticed how he turned this defect into an asset—the pause, the expectancy, and then the magnificent volley of the perfect sentence. There was also a touch of the imp in him that delighted the crowd. "Give it 'em, Winnie!" they cried. And Winnie gave it 'em.

CHAPTER SIX

Mundella

I

I HAVE RUN ahead in the years to come. In 1905, aged thirteen, when I stood in the street and cheered old General Booth, the cap I waved was my Mundella School cap, maroon with a gold circle on it. Through all the extraordinary vicissitudes of my long life there seems to have been a directing finger of Fate steering my craft through many rapids and shoals. How extraordinary that, destined to love Italy with a passion next to that for my homeland, to visit and live there through a great part of my life, to write about it in my many books, to never cease being engrossed by the miracle of its beauty and history, I should be fated to go to a school with, of all names, an Italian one!

Mundella: where did the name come from? When I went there I never thought to ask. It was a commonplace to me, being a school located in a district where I lived. No one ever told me it was an Italian name. Unusual, yes, like 'terracotta' and 'demerara', but anglicised, its native origin forgotten. Only in manhood was my curiosity aroused, and rewarded. I learned with some pleasure that the school had been named to honour a great and good man, now undeservedly forgotten.

Early in the nineteenth century an Italian named Antonio Mundella came to England as a political refugee from his home at Monte Olimpino, a tiny village close to the Swiss-Italian frontier station at Chiasso, known later to all Italy-bound tourists taking the St. Gotthard line into Italy. It was a pretty little place within easy reach of Lake Como. The Italian refugee settled in Leicester, where he found work in a hosiery factory and married a Leicester girl. In this city his son, Anthony John Mundella, was born in 1825. He went to the National School until he was nine. The family being poor, he then started work in a factory. He soon proved to be an exceptional boy. He moved later to Nottingham, and at the age of twenty-four was made a partner in a well established hosiery firm. With this firm he built for himself a considerable fortune, owing much success to his shrewd and capable mother. He became a captain in the Robin Hood Volunteers and began to take an interest in politics. At the age of forty-three, an ardent reformer, he became Liberal M.P. for Sheffield which he represented in the House of Commons until his death nearly thirty years later. He was a prime mover in the Education Act of 1870, and was one of Gladstone's most esteemed supporters. In 1875 he introduced the revolutionary Factories Act. Probably inspired by his own child labour, this act reduced labour from sixty to fifty-four hours a week. It increased the age of full-time workers from thirteen to fourteen, and half-time workers from eight to ten. For this he received as a token of gratitude a bust by Sir Edgar Boehm, subscribed for by eighty-thousand factory workers, chiefly women and children.

In 1881 he succeeded in making compulsory education universal. In 1886 he entered Gladstone's Cabinet as President of the Board of Trade, and became a Privy Councillor the following year. As the President of the Board of Trade he developed what grew to be the South Kensington Museum. He was a quiet-spoken man, extremely conscientious, shunning publicity. When he died in his London house in 1897, a memorial service was held for him in St. Margaret's, Westminster, attended by all the heads of State, and he was buried in Nottingham with civic honours. What a success story, the Italian refugee's son, sent to work at nine, building himself a fortune by the age of forty, a model employer, abolishing the cruelty of child labour, establishing a great national museum, and in the British Cabinet at sixty-one.

To this record, let me add a personal note. In 1916 I reviewed *The Life of Abraham Lincoln*, written by Lord Charnwood. It remains to this day the best-written concise history of that President, buried under innumerable pedestrian tomes. Its author was a man of varied gifts, sometime Lecturer at Balliol College. We entered into correspondence and later I was his guest at his house in Eaton Square. He was then a man of fifty-six, grave, courteous, and a rewarding conversationalist. He was the brother of Sir Frank Benson, the actor, and had been for many years an M.P. before receiving a peerage. His daughter, Theodora, had won some fame as a novelist.

It was in his drawing-room that John Drinkwater read the manuscript of his play *Abraham Lincoln*. One day when leaving his house
I noticed a bust standing on a table. "It's of A. J. Mundella by Sir
Edgar Boehm, given to him by some grateful factory workers," he
said. Very surprised, I told him that I had been at Mundella School,
and asked him how he came to possess it. "Mundella had a daughter,
Mrs. Ruby Thorpe of Nottingham, and I married her daughter,"
he replied. Such was the man who had given his name to the school to
which I now went, twelve years of age, shy and apprehensive, with a
three-year scholarship.

I am always amazed at the ferocity with which, in after life, some
men attack their old school. According to them it was a period of acute
misery during which they learned little, were bullied by sadistic
masters and savaged by their fellows. The more privileged and
distinguished the school, the more bitter their recriminations. Sir
Osbert Sitwell, for instance, in *Who's Who*, recorded his contempt—
"Educated during the holidays from Eton," he wrote. Of my period
at Mundella I can only record that it spanned three of the happiest
years of my life. I was taught by able and sympathetic masters under
a headmaster, a strict disciplinarian, who set a high tone for the whole
school. Newly built, surmounted by a bell tower, Mundella was bright
and airy, terracotta in hue, set in the centre of playing fields bordered
by the River Trent. The classes were small, rarely more than fifteen,
and we received individual attention suited to our mental capacity.
At no time can I have been an easy boy to deal with. I was precocious,
highly strung, of a sensitive disposition. I could be audacious and
nigh irrepressible. But I was ridden with a light snaffle, otherwise
there might have been mental disaster. I was not a good all-round
scholar, my usual position being in mid-form, but in certain subjects
I was ahead of my contemporaries. The school became a stage for me,
and it was not long before I established a certain leadership and acted
a rôle with much bravura. In constant collision with my tormented
masters, I was damped down, but never extinguished. I was, they
said later, 'an exasperating entertainment' but I was always handled
with good humour. One day, after a particular passage between us,
my form master said, a little irritated, "Roberts, I can foretell what
will be the end of you. You'll either sit on the Woolsack or hang on
the gallows." "In either case it will be an elevated position, sir," I
retorted. "That will cost you twenty lines. You will write out
'Cromwell, I charge thee, fling away ambition; by that sin fell the

angels'." "Oh, sir," I protested, "Isn't that unfair? Won't it give me a distaste for Shakespeare and spoil my handwriting?" He looked at me, burst out laughing and said: "Preposterous child, I'll settle for ten lines!" We lived happily on such terms.

II

The school was co-educational, consisting of one hundred and fifty boys, from twelve to fifteen or sixteen, and the same number of girls. We were strictly segregated. We occupied the right wing classrooms, they the left. We only met when assembled in hall for morning prayers or on official occasions. We were not allowed to speak to each other, and it was a strict rule that if by chance we met in a corridor the boy must stand aside until the girl had passed. In effect it was two separate schools in one building. On an occasion when three boys were caught in the gymnasium giggling with some girls, they were caned before the whole school, perpetrators of a heinous offence.

Nervous, aloof at first, I began to find my feet at the end of my first year. My form master was reticent and painstakingly slow. I did not know then that he was tortured by rheumatism. Alas, poor man, his name being Wardle, my rapier tongue dubbed him Dawdle, and it stuck. When he found out he reproached me very gently and told me why he dawdled. I apologised, filled with contrition, and after that we were on the best of terms. At home I had grown some hyacinths, and I took them, one January day and placed the bowl on his desk. He was very pleased and asked who had brought them. When I put up my hand he said, "Thank you. 'If winter comes can spring be far behind?'" I asked him what it meant. He explained that it was a line from a poem by Shelley. None of us had ever heard of him. He left the classroom and came back with a book from which he read us the *Ode to the West Wind*. The words and music lifted me to near-delirium. I went home shouting through the streets "If winter comes can spring be far behind?" I shouted it to my mother in the kitchen, and to my father when he came in.

In the second year I lost dear Dawdle, and fell into the hands of a young man just down from Oxford who was regarded as a god, but not by me, because he had a Blue for cricket. He had dark brown hair heavily greased and plastered over his sleek head. He was once rude to me and in class one day pointed at me and said, "Perhaps our

Omniscient One will kindly tell us?" I called him Herr Cokernut, and it stuck. Then he left, and I fell into the hands of Mr. Broadburn. He became my life. He had pointed wax mustachios, a red face and shiny trousers. He was a born teacher. He handled me at my most critical chrysalis stage. I had got my first long trousers, moreover it was a tailor-made suit. I felt a Beau Brummell. I believe it was the only tailor-made suit in the school. It was brown and beautifully cut, even my father admired it. I was thirteen, and the way in which I came by it was this. Next door to us they had a lodger, a young man I now know was a Jew, but at that age I had never met one. The poor young man was consumptive, lived in one room and ate out. My tender-hearted mother, hearing he was sick in bed, went in to see him. She took him some food and nursed him for a week. He was a tailor's cutter employed at a very good shop. My mother invited him to supper occasionally. Then at Christmas he took my breath away. He bought me a moated fort, complete with drawbridge and soldiers. Later, when I went to Mundella, he told my mother that if she would buy the cloth he would make me a suit. I was measured. I could hardly sleep, waiting for the finished product. He was a fine cutter. I had a battle over that suit. My mother said it must be saved for Sundays. I pointed out that since there were only fifty-two Sundays in a year I should be grown out of the suit before it was worn out. My father agreed with me. So I appeared at school in trousers, conscious of enormous prestige.

I now had other ideas about a Sunday suit. I had transferred my allegiance from the *Boy's Own Paper* to *The Captain*. It was a glossy monthly that catered for public school boys. It put ideas into my head. Its school stories were illustrated by H. M. Brock, who drew handsome boys dressed in Eton suits. They lived in beautiful Tudor buildings, had fun in dormitories, and the masters wore gowns and and mortar-boards. I asked my father why he did not send me to Eton, even if I had to fag and would be birched on a block. "There is only one reason why you cannot go to Eton, my child. It costs three hundred pounds a year, and I haven't got it."

Very sad. Well, the next best thing was to have an Eton suit. I was already wearing an Eton collar. When the subject of my Sunday suit came up I asked for an Eton suit. My request met with opposition from my mother, and ridicule from my brother. "You'll look nice going about in a 'bum-freezer' and a top hat, little Lord Fauntleroy!" he said. I pointed out that, with his usual ignorance, he was wrong. Little Lord Fauntleroy wore a velvet jacket, knickerbockers, and a lace collar. Happily my father was on my side. He had once worn an Eton suit. There was one difficulty. My kind friend the tailor was no longer there. He had been carried away after a fearful hemorrhage to a sanatorium and passed out of our lives.

A problem arose over this suit. Was there any tailor in Nottingham who knew how to cut an Eton suit? Well, perhaps there were ready-made ones. I was immensely relieved when it transpired that no one in Nottingham stocked ready-made Eton suits. So a tailor must be found. It was my father who, after some enquiries, discovered the tailor. Alas, he was the most expensive tailor in town, he cut Eton suits for the sons of the county gentry. My rôle of D'Arcy Mont-morency of St. Simeon's College seemed in jeopardy and I was not to be an H. M. Brock figure of elegance. Luckily my father knew the tailor, one of the customers of his shop, and a price was agreed on. He measured me. I had two fittings. The price had been fixed at thirty shillings as a special favour. How that thirty shillings was raised I never learned. "I hope you will realise you are a very fortunate boy," said my mother. I agreed. Within two weeks the suit was delivered in a long cardboard box with white tissue paper. When I tried it on it was a flawless fit. I could hardly wait for Sunday morning, to accompany my mother to church. There was to be another occasion for wearing the suit, then unknown to me.

III

The defeat of China by Japan in 1894 enabled the Russians to obtain a lease of Port Arthur. They completed the Trans-Siberian railway and occupied Manchuria. This alarmed Japan, nervous of Russian penetration of Pacific waters. On February 8th, 1904, the Japanese Fleet under Admiral Togo treacherously attacked the Russian Fleet and sealed it up in Port Arthur. The Russo-Japanese war had opened. In subsequent fighting Russia suffered defeats on land, and their fleet was ordered to take refuge in Vladivostock but this, too, was blocked by Togo. In October, as a rescue operation, Russia despatched its Baltic Fleet. It steamed into the North Sea, jittery with rumours of Japanese submarines, a new weapon. Off the Dogger Bank it mistook some British trawlers for submarines, opened fire and damaged some of them. England, already pro-Japanese by virtue of the Anglo-Japanese Alliance and of her old suspicion of Russia, blazed with indignation. There was a diplomatic crisis and a mood of tense belligerency. The British Fleet shadowed the Russian Fleet, under Admiral Rozhestvenski, until well into the Atlantic. The Russian admiral sailed on for Port Arthur and his doom. On May 27th, 1905, in the Straits of Korea, Admiral Togo sank or captured the whole fleet. Russia sued for peace. Britain was swept by pro-Japanese fervour. The little Japanese sailors were the heroes of the hour. They had made mincemeat of the great Russian Bear. A song, launched at the music-halls, was taken up by the public. It was a tearful little song set to a catchy tune about a Japanese sailor saying goodbye to his sweetheart.

> Farewell, my little Yo-San,
> When I am o'er the ocean
> I'll think of you.

It was in the wake of this pro-Japanese fervour that a visit to Mundella was paid later by Baron Kikuchi, the Japanese Minister of Education, a frock-coated smiling little man He walked through the hall between a Guard of Honour to the platform decorated with the British and Japanese flags, while we all sang the Japanese National Anthem, set to a jerky piece of music that mercifully drowned our bad Japanese, painfully rehearsed. Before giving his address the Baron was presented, in the name of the Mundella girls, with a large doll, a present for his daughter and a souvenir of his visit. The Chairman of the Governors introduced the Baron who then proceeded to address us. He told us that both the Eastern and the Western nations owed their present greatness to the self-sacrifice and devotion of their people, and reminded us that in fifty years Japan had been raised from obscurity to a place of power by the perseverance and heroism of her people alone. He urged us to be true patriots and support the Anglo-Japanese Alliance, for the good of both countries and the world. He could not foresee, and we could not foresee that in less than forty years some of the sons of the boys he was addressing would perish miserably from forced labour, or in Japanese war-prisoners' camps; or that Hiroshima would be obliterated by the first atomic bomb to be used in warfare. He smiled, we cheered.

It had been arranged for one of the boys to make a speech of thanks to the Minister for his visit. The School Captain was too tongue-tied.

My form master suggested me. It was my first and last official appearance. I was leaving the school in two weeks. The master wrote out a speech that I was made to learn. He rehearsed me and rehearsed me, until I was word perfect. I was to take three minutes. He even rehearsed my gestures. "Why do you tuck your left hand in the top of your waistcoat?" he protested. I could not tell him I had seen an engraving of Disraeli addressing the House of Commons in that manner.

The eventful day came and with it my great moment. The Headmaster looked my way. I advanced to the platform. I was now almost the tallest boy in the school. My fair hair was plastered down. I had put a yellow and red-tinged chrysanthemum in my left lapel. These were the Japanese national colours, and I had a battle to be allowed to retain this gesture. I wore a spotless Eton collar, a black tie, and my cuffs just emerged from the sleeves of my Eton jacket, a detail watched by my father.

There was an expectant silence after I had advanced. Nothing came from my mouth. Those rehearsed words had completely slipped from me. There were a few desperate seconds of near panic, everyone looking at me. Suddenly I launched myself extemporaneously. After a dozen sentences, oblivious of my surroundings, I went on with growing confidence, buoyed up by some kind of magnetism. I felt *en rapport* with my audience. And then I came to the end and bowed. There was loud applause. So I had not muffed it. Later, filing out, my special friend thumped me on the back. My form master spoke to me, looking severe. "Well, you made a mess of it, didn't you? Not one word of what you learned. And you took five minutes instead of three." "Sorry sir," I replied, not feeling at all sorry. He put a hand on my neck and pressed it. "I've an awful feeling that you're going to grow into a public menace," he said, but his eyes smiled, and I knew he was pleased.

Out of that experience, I was conscious of a discovery. It was as if I had found a wonderful instrument I could play. I was no good at so many things. In the athletic field I was abject, no one wanted me on his side. Other boys easily surpassed me in examinations. I had curious blanks. Euclid, Algebra, Physics, utterly defeated me. And now I had discovered something innate in me. I had, to use a later expression, the 'wave-length' of an audience. But where I could use it and what use it would be to me I had no idea.

IV

It was in my second year that I found a new friend, Donald Richardson. He was a year my junior and not in my form. Two boys more dissimilar could not be imagined, but from first sight I loved him intensely. It was not a *schwärmerei*, it was a warm mutual affection. He was short, sturdy, black-haired, with a broken nose, and dark-eyed. He could do all the things I could not do. So opposite in many ways, the positive and negative poles of our characters had a magnetic pull in all we undertook. He had also in his background a certain glamour. His father was the Liberal-Labour member of Parliament for South Nottingham, a constituency in which I lived. This fact brought with it a disturbing division of loyalties.

In the great landslide of the General Election of 1906, when the Conservatives went down to ignominious defeat, the sitting candidate, Lord Henry Cavendish-Bentinck, was thrown out. He was one of my gods, although I counted myself a follower of Asquith and Lloyd George, my sympathies being with the under-dog, and the under-dog meant for me the wretched coal miners living in the prohibited territory around Clifton Colliery. Even so, Lord Henry, as he was called, occupied a particular niche in my boy's heart. He was tall, aristocratic, the half-brother of the Duke of Portland and the brother of Lady Ottoline Morrell. He was so liberal-minded and advanced in his views that he often infuriated his party, which at times was on the verge of repudiating him. He did not hesitate to walk into the Liberal Lobby if he believed in the particular reform they supported. With his pretty wife, he was very popular in his constituency. I knew him because as a small boy I often accompanied my father to the party meetings. On one occasion my father took the Chair for him. They could neither of them speak. They er-er-d, but Lord Henry looked so kind and handsome and had such a beautiful accent that he fascinated me. Once he patted me on the head; it was like a papal benediction. He was at this time about forty-three. He was an Etonian. I wrote a poem about Eton College Chapel, which I had never seen, and gave it to him.

> O place of sacred memory
> Where youth so careless came,
> I knew not then that I should be
> So zealous of thy name;

> What joys we often lightly prize
> When in our hands they lie,
> What visions of the dead days rise,
>   What pain lives in a sigh! . . .

He said he had read the poem to Lady Henry and they both liked it very much.

Despite the popularity he enjoyed after representing the constituency for eleven years, the great landslide of 1906, demolishing Mr. Balfour, almost all his Cabinet, and two-thirds of his supporters, also unseated Lord Henry. The man who unseated him was the father of my school-friend, Donald. Poor Lord Henry, but also dear Donald.

This friendship brought me an enriching experience. I found myself in the midst of the Richardson family. I was a very lonely boy, and was not a good mixer, possibly other boys found me too egocentric. Then again I was socially aloof. The atmosphere of my home was not that of theirs. My father and mother, engrossed in each other, kept themselves apart. My only brother, in temperament a complete opposite to me was virtually a stranger. Grown-up, courting, he was always out of the house. Such odd moments of contact that we had left him puzzled and antagonistic to my intense enthusiasms. He had called me 'Inky', an allusion to my early writing activities, and 'that crazy kid'. We were destined to remain strangers to each other for the next sixty years until death separated us. He had some admirable qualities. He was balanced, calm, a good husband and father, but he never achieved the slightest comprehension of his ebullient brother. We lived in totally different worlds, mentally and socially. He bore with great fortitude, from his thirtieth year until his eighty-second, an affliction that made his life a perilous hazard.

A highly sensitive boy, alone in the house, left to my own resources, I had no experience of the gaiety and variety of life in a large family. When Donald took me to his home and I met his vivacious brother and sisters, his forthright rugged father and his gentle mother, it was another world into which I stepped, vivid, argumentative, robust, a nest lined with comparative affluence. There were two sisters, the elder, Dorothy, reticent, the younger, Muriel, a quick-tongued tomboy with whom I had vivid duels, for she loved mocking me. There was a tall elder brother, alert and affable, and always in the background gentle Mrs. Richardson, quietly amused by our dog fights. Donald introduced me into this circle like a *rara avis*, and I was always ready to astonish them. I stood in awe of the father only, abrupt but genial. He was a Member of Parliament, in touch with the great world unknown to me. Strong in character, a doughty political champion, he had built up a sound wholesale grocery business. Owing to his parliamentary duties he was often absent and left much of the business management to his able elder son, Arthur.

Their home had an aura of historical legend. Just off the Market Place, up a thoroughfare called Friar Lane, lay a row of fine Tudor houses in a quiet cul-de-sac named Friary Yard. These houses were part of an ancient Carmelite friary housing the White Friars. Now sub-divided, the Richardsons lived in the end house which opened into the second house which they kept empty, the other three houses in the row being used as offices. They stood strangely quiet and remote from the bustle of the Market Place. The empty second house had a wide oak-banistered staircase. The place was reputed to be haunted by a friar. When I was taken up the stairs to see the great rafters, I experienced 'the shivers'. The whole place was spooky. The house the family inhabited was dark, low ceilinged, with massive oak beams and wide, open fireplaces. There was a heavy oak Gothic front door opening on to a small hall. But the most surprising asset of this ancient place was the enormous square garden at the back of the house. There were two lawns divided by a path that went down to the bottom of the garden, where a great chestnut tree nobly flowered. Under this there was a heavy stone table of great antiquity. I felt that Robin Hood might have had his lunch on it; perhaps Friar Tuck had once been an inmate. This large garden was entirely enclosed on three sides by buildings belonging to various offices. It was an oasis of quiet green beauty in the very heart of the city. It was not the ghost, or the long dead friars that gave an aura of legend to the place. Here a pair of lovers had come after their elope-ment. Every visitor to Haddon Hall is told the story of John Manners who eloped with Dorothy Vernon around 1565. This most thoroughly preserved of medieval houses, above the sparkling Derbyshire Wye, is a perfect setting for a romantic story. From it Dorothy Vernon, daughter of the house, whose infatuation with John Manners of Belvoir Castle is said to have been opposed by the family, eloped with her gallant lover. They came to Nottingham and lived in The Friary. John Manners bought the house from a descendant of James Strelley to whom, on the dissolution of the monasteries, the property had been given. A Borough Record states that on November 28th, 1573, the Mayor and some of his brethren "dined with Mr. Manners at the Frears". The house continued to be owned by the Manners family (the Dukes of Rutland) until 1802. My friends the Richardsons lived in it until it was demolished in 1928, as part of a street-widening development.

It was not these lovers, John and Dorothy, but the ghost of one of the friars that stirred my imagination. He was said to have murdered a brother friar and his guilty spirit haunted the place. One winter's evening Donald took me home to supper. A log fire blazed in the great fireplace, the lights were dim, the whole setting was just right for our purpose. All the family were there in the living-room. "He's written a poem about our ghost!" announced Donald. I was called upon to read it, which was just what I was eager to do. It was a long poem and ran to eight pages of quatrains. I read it with great fervour and was rewarded by a burst of applause. It was Muriel who was at once downright. "Now, you don't believe the story about that silly ghost, do you?" she demanded. I affirmed that I did, not willing to have my poem shattered. Donald, ever loyal, stood up for the ghost.

In the Richardson drawing-room there was an enlarged photograph of Donald's father standing by a seated thickset man. This was none other than the famous Right Honourable John Burns, the first artisan to reach the rank of Cabinet Minister in the 1905 Government. One day I saw him going out with his host. I looked at him with awe, my first Cabinet Minister. Twenty years earlier, a Socialist candidate at Nottingham, he had received only five-hundred-and-ninety-eight votes. He was one of eighteen children, his mother could not write and had signed his birth certificate with an X. He left school at the age of ten. In 1881 he drove the first electric tram in England. At thirty he had become a leader of the unemployed who, in 1886, demonstrated in Trafalgar Square. He carried a Red Flag. The police sought to break up the meetings and a year later, forcing his way into Trafalgar Square, he was arrested along with aristocratic R. B. Cunninghame Graham, the Scottish laird who had joined the cause. It was called Bloody Sunday. They were sentenced to six weeks' imprisonment.

He was now a national figure and never out of the limelight. He had been the leader of the London Dock Strike and won for them a rate of 6d. an hour. In 1892 he was elected M.P. for Battersea, one of the first three Independent Labour Party members, a new party, appearing in the House. In 1905, he was in the new Cabinet. Nine years later, now a Liberal, a Privy Councillor, he was again in the Cabinet. Opposed to the declaration of war with Germany in 1914, he resigned and passed out of public life. Andrew Carnegie left him $5,000. With this and his Cabinet's Minister's pension, he devoted the rest of his life to collecting books on the history of London, on which he was an authority. He died at eighty-seven, quite forgotten. He should be remembered for one sentence he invented. He wrote "The Thames is liquid history." Such was the singular man who glanced at an awe-struck schoolboy of fourteen as he passed me in the hall of the Richardson home.

It was at The Friary that I met my first live actress. One afternoon I found there a beautiful young woman, with blonde hair, lovely eyes, and an enchanting smile. Donald whispered that she was an actress. She was playing the lead at the Theatre Royal in *The Waltz Dream*, a musical comedy by Oscar Straus, on tour after its London success. Her name was Effie Mann. How came such a glamorous creature to be shedding radiance in the Elizabethan gloom of The Friary ? Donald enlightened me. She was the daughter of the famous, or notorious, agitator, Tom Mann. He had been sentenced to gaol for leading a dock strike in Sydney, Australia. He was a friend of John Burns. So when his daughter arrived in Nottingham, with all the glamour of a successful musical comedy actress, she was invited to the Richardson home. Donald and I fell in love with her. Of course we went to see *The Waltz Dream* and found her still more entrancing. I had a copy of the waltz and played it on the piano *ad nauseam*. Ever since that encounter that waltz, anywhere, evokes the lovely Effie Mann, my first actress, so responsive to the adoration of two school-boys.

At the Salzburg Festival in 1950 I found myself taken to a theatre to see a musical comedy, a respite from the incessant Mozartian menu. To my delight it proved to be *The Waltz Dream*. Like its composer it had enjoyed a long life, and this occasion was made memorable by the fact that Oscar Straus, on his eightieth birthday, was present to conduct his overture to the second act and received an ovation. The next morning on the bridge at Salzburg I met a friend who introduced me to Oscar Straus. The reminiscence of my first hearing of *The Waltz Dream* gave him great delight.

At the General Election of 1910 my hero, Lord Henry, was re-elected. He retained the seat for nineteen years. But I was sorry for my friend's father. However, Arthur Richardson soon found a safe seat as member for Rotherham which he represented for some years.

The Richardson home with its family vivacity, its prosperity, and close touch with stirring events, opened a new window in my restricted world, and always there was solid Donald, a little puzzled by but firmly loyal towards his flamboyant friend. After schooldays our ways parted and then across some fifty years we met again. He had remained faithful to Nottingham and become chairman of the flourishing family business. He was my guest at the Council House when I received the Freedom of the city.

This political background to my friendship was not without effect on my ambitious spirit. I began to think of politics. By 1910, being then eighteen, I was an ardent Liberal and made my first political speech before the local Cosmopolitan Debating Society which had invited me to speak. It was a socialist hotbed with a vigorous following. On the day of my address the hall was crammed. All I remember of that occasion is the near riot I created by my provocative line and of a fat red-faced woman sitting in the front row who exclaimed in a loud voice, stirred by my attack on the socialists, "Listen to 'im, the saucy young pup! I wouldn't be 'is mother for anything!" To specially annoy them I carried a monocle on a cord. It was a stage monocle, a piece of plain glass. I wore a black stock tie like Lord Henry's. My elegance was an affront to proletarian equality.

V

At fourteen I possessed only two assets that prevented me from being classed as a hopeless sap and an odd kid. I was very light on my feet and, perhaps because of this, I was a good boxer, early tuition having come from Milly's brother. I won a school paperchase, to everyone's amazement, including my own. And in the school gymnasium I became a successful flyweight. I was so light that it was like hitting a balloon, I bounced away. Our gymnastics master was a grim, thick-set Swiss, with a broken accent and no sense of humour. There was an unfortunate occasion when, under instruction, I leapt up and caught him such a whack on the nose that he was more outraged than hurt. He stared at me and said, "You are wild boy with 'orrible temper." This was very unjustified, but he would not let me put on the gloves again, and chased me over the beastly vaulting-horse and parallel bars. I was not to be frustrated. I found some cronies who liked boxing. We none of us had any gloves, but we discovered that the instructor hid the gymnasium key behind the door of the lavatory. When the school closed, in we went and had a lot of fun.

Possibly I got rather conceited about my prowess. One day a chunky boy came up with two others and said, "You fancy yourself, don't you? Well, I'll take you on." I saw it was a plot and I didn't like the look of him, but I could not retreat. We agreed for six rounds of two minutes the next day. As we parted a loyal friend of mine said to him, "He'll eat you up."

The next day when we started there were about a dozen boys. I lent the time-keeper my five-shilling Waterbury watch. We took off our shirts and began. We were the same height. He was much heavier. It was a baffling encounter. He couldn't get near me, but no matter how often I hit him it had no effect, he just smiled. At the end of the second round we were both breathless and I had had some nasty jabs. I decided in the third round it was now or never. In a wild mêlée I tapped his nose and he began to bleed freely. The blood got all over our gloves, our faces and our bodies. The referee wanted to stop the match, we ignored him. The fourth round was a frightful mix-up. Towards the end we were both so breathless we could only stand and look at each other. With a good-natured grin on his bloody face he said "Shall we stop?" "Yes," I said. We shook hands, he put an arm round my shoulder and, to my surprise, gave me a bloody kiss on the cheek. Later my second said "All professionals do that in the ring." We took off our gloves and put on our shirts and coats. Unfortunately there was no washing place in the gym.

On the way home something was happening to me. My left eye closed up, my lower lip was numb, and swelled and swelled. I entered the house timidly. My mother stared, horrified. I explained we had had a boxing match. "Have you seen yourself?" she asked, and took me to the mirror. I was certainly a terrible sight, my eye closed, my lip like a Hottentot's, my face plastered with dried blood. Otherwise I felt all right. "This nonsense has got to stop, I won't have you coming home looking like a hooligan," said my mother. Then there was my father to face when he came home. He looked at me, heard my account, and said quietly, "You weren't born a beauty, and you certainly haven't improved yourself." That was my last fight.

VI

My other enthusiasm was very different. When I was twelve I wanted to become an artist. It all started with a box of paints that Miss Fryer had given me for Christmas. It was a beautiful flat mahogany box. When I raised the lid there were two rows of colours pots under a glass top, a porcelain sub-divided mixing-trough, and four camel-hair brushes. The very names were lovely and exciting —Sienna Brown, Ultramarine Blue, Vandyck Brown, Chrome Yellow, Vermilion Red, Burnt Umber. There were two tubes of black and white paint, and a small book with pictures for colouring. A girl friend told me of a painting class. You paid sixpence and had an hour's tuition. I worried my mother into joining this. The lessons were given by two elderly sisters who lived in a large house in Arboretum Street. What had been the long drawing-room had been converted into a painting room. Some twenty children sat at a long table and the two sisters moved up and down, leaning over us and showing us how to mix the colours and spread them. One of them had a ring with three stones that flashed. They fascinated me. My mother said they must be diamonds. She called on them. She described them as "ladies in very reduced circumstances". For a long time I thought this was a description of their costumes. What struck me most was a thick pile carpet on the stairs fastened with very shiny brass rods, and at the top of the stairs a lavatory with a chain-pull that had a porcelain handle with flowers on it, and a seat cover that lifted like the lid of a mahogany box. It was all very rich in my young eyes. I was also sorry when the class came to an end. I sat next to a pretty little girl who told me that her elder brother at the end of the table was leaving his preparatory school soon and was going to Eton. I looked at him with wonder. He did not seem a bit elated. Then one evening, as I was leaving, I was bowled over. A brougham drew up, a coachman got down from the box and opened the carriage door for my companion and her brother. It was like seeing Cinderella set off for the ball.

I became very friendly with Katherine and Robert. We exchanged paintings. One evening Katherine gave me an envelope addressed "Master Cecil Roberts." It had a delicate scent. When I opened the tough envelope, there was a sheet of glossy paper with *Clumber Crescent, The Park,* embossed in black letters. I read "If your mother is willing, will you come and have tea with us next Saturday at four o'clock." I could not contain my excitement, and said eagerly to Katherine, "Oh, yes, thank you, of course I'll come."

The great day arrived. I was twenty minutes too early and walked up and down the Crescent before I pressed the bell by the heavy Gothic door of the large house with a high-walled garden. My mother had very carefully superintended my dress. I shone from head to foot, but I was a little doubtful about my white stockings, it was their first outing. It seemed a very long time before the door opened, revealing a stoutish gentleman in a black tailcoat. For a moment I thought it was Katherine's father and then something told me he was the butler. He closed the door behind me and said gravely, "Please come this way, sir." Sir! I crossed a large square hall, pillared, with a very slippery floor, and turned into what seemed a drawing-room with a grand piano, large chintz-covered chairs, china ornaments, and then on through a French window that opened on to a terrace. Before me was a large lawn with elm trees at the end. There were croquet hoops on the lawn. There was a swing awning and some basket chairs and an oak table beyond these. The butler had only got half-way when Katherine and Robert ran towards me. Their mother followed. She was a short, dark, thin-faced woman with smiling eyes. She held my hand as she said "How nice of you to come, Kathy and Robert have told me so much about you. You have quite a lot of fun at the class, don't you?" There were other elderly people at the table, and an old gentleman with a shawl although it was a warm July day. There was a thin elegant lady dressed in a heliotrope costume. She had a long neck covered by a high collar and sat in a cane chair holding a white silk parasol. She had an 'air' and I learned she was my hostess's French cousin, called Madame Somebody. To my utter astonishment Katherine and Robert talked to her in fluent French. Later I learned they had had a French governess, and, more surprising still, that their mother was French. Presently there was a procession across the lawn. A maid in a snow-white cap and apron with wide bows laid a cloth on the table, and behind her was the butler with a very large silver tray holding a silver tea service which he placed on the table. Then the maid reappeared with a four-tiered stand holding bread and butter and cakes. We were all served.

I was standing with a cup in my hand when I felt myself poked in the back by a parasol. I turned and the French lady spoke to me. "Boy, what is your name?" she demanded. I told her. "Cecile—but that is a girl's name!" "No, madame," I protested, "In England it is a boy's name. There is a famous man called Cecil Rhodes, a pioneer in South Africa." "He writes poems!" said Katherine, coming to my defence. "Yes? Will you recite one?" asked Madame Somebody. She had very bright eyes and very red lips, and a high pitched voice. She was like a strange bird. "I know one in French, by La Fontaine," I said.

"Please—recite it," she said with an alluring smile.

Very steadily I recited *La Cigale et la Fourmi*.

> La Cigale ayant chantée
> Tout l'été,
> Se trouva fort dépourvue
> Quand la bise fut venue.
> Pas un seul petit morceau
> De mouche ou de vermisseau.
> Elle alla crier famine
> Chez la fourmi sa voisine,
> La priant de lui prêter
> Quelque grain pour subsister
> Jusqu'à la saison nouvelle.

She clapped her hands when I finished and said something I did not understand. Encouraged, I said I knew a poem about painting. She asked me to recite it. I complied. My father had taught me it.

> La peinture à l'huile
> Est très difficile
> Mais c'est beaucoup plus beau
> Que la peinture à l'eau.

"*Charmant!*" cried the lady, shaking her parasol.

After tea we played croquet, a new game to me. It was a wonderful day. When I got home I breathlessly described the tea-party. My mother asked me what the ladies wore. I was not very good at remembering, but I described the huge silver tray, the cakes and the white parasol of the French lady.

"You must now write thanking your hostess," said my mother.

Alas, soon after that the family left Nottingham and I never saw any of them again. By a singular coincidence a friend of mine took a lease of that house some thirty years later, and on return visits to my native town I often stayed there. The ghost of my first French-woman, holding a white parasol, was in that garden. What was her history, what was her fate? I shall never know.

When I went to Mundella we had a French mistress, but she had no allure. She was a wizened spinster with a wart on her face. My first French reading book was called *Sous Terre*, all about coalminers. My next book was Alphonse Daudet's *Le Petit Chose*, about a poor young man who was an usher in a French boarding school. We were to have much in common, for in due course I, too, became *Le Petit Chose* in an English boarding school.

VII

It was in my second year at Mundella that the splendour of a new world opened for me. I was already since ten an omnivorous reader, eating my way through the glorious inheritance of English literature. I was now introduced to Macaulay's *Lays of Ancient Rome*. They went to my head. I stood on the bridge with brave Horatius, I looked on the temples of his gods. As I walked along the Trent embankment with my Skye terrier Ruff, I turned that quiet river into the turbulent Tiber. "O Tiber, Father Tiber, to whom the Romans pray!" I shouted.

One weekend we were told to learn twenty lines of Tennyson's *Ballad of the 'Revenge'*. On Monday morning we had a *viva voce*. When my turn came, full-throated, I declaimed my twenty lines, and, these said, I went on.

"Stop!" cried my form master. But I couldn't stop, I was in full course. "Sit down, Roberts!" he shouted. "Sir, I know the whole poem!" I cried, and went on. He banged the lid of his desk. "Will you sit down. I have to hear other boys!" he protested. I sat down, aggrieved.

What do boys recite these days? I cannot see them carried away with the verses of Auden, Eliot, Graves. They lack the sounding line, the mounting rhetoric, the grand sweep of sound and passion. With Byron one could stand and address the ocean in lines worthy of its majesty: "Roll on, thou deep and dark blue ocean—roll!" Eliot and Auden have nothing to say to it.

Break, break, break at the foot of thy crags, O Sea
But the tender grace of a day that is dead will never come back to
me,

sang Tennyson. They have no knowledge of any heartbreak. No one
could find himself stirred by Mr. Prufrock's "patient, etherised upon
a table", or

> I grow old . . . I grow old.
> I shall wear the bottoms of my trousers rolled.

An anaemic muse shuffles along after the giants, and there is nothing
into which a lad can put his teeth as in my boyhood.

One day at the beginning of a new term two boys entered the form
room wheeling a hamper of books. They proceeded to dole these out,
six on each desk, all new, smelling fresh, brightly bound. They were
a geography reading book full of pictures, Stevenson's *The Black
Arrow*, Carlyle's *Heroes and Hero Worship*, Ruskin's *Sesame and
Lilies*, Shakespeare's *Julius Caesar*, and a small red-bound book,
Palgrave's *Golden Treasury of Songs and Lyrics*. They were our
reading books for the new term. We were permitted to take them
home for weekend reading. I started with *The Golden Treasury*, first
reading Gray's *Elegy in a Country Churchyard*. That weekend I lived
in a state of delirium. I went through the *Elegy*, then discovered
Keats' *Ode to a Nightingale* and Shelley's *Ode to the West Wind*. I
stayed up in my bedroom, spread over the bed, book in hand, until
called down for supper.

"Thou wast not born for death, immortal bird!" I declaimed,
addressing my mother, who looked very surprised. When my father
arrived home I greeted him with

> O Wild West Wind, thou breath of Autumn's being,
> Thou, from whose unseen presence the leaves dead
> Are driven, like ghosts from an enchanter fleeing.

"Shelley," he said. "Where did you find that?"

I produced the thin volume from my pocket. He glanced at it, and
said, "I had it for a school prize. Keats, Shelley, Wordsworth,
Swinburne. They've been pygmies since then," he said.

In those exciting days I read and I read. "Your eyes will fall out if you don't stop," said my mother, ordering me up to bed. "Blow out that candle!" she would shout from the foot of the stairs, detecting a ray of light under my bedroom door.

The school had no library. Just down the road in a row of small villas there was a little crippled hunchback man, Mr. Erasmus Horsley, with a wonderful library. There were books in all rooms from floor to ceiling. I had the run of these shelves. He guided my selection. I was in and out of the house, a *rat de bibliothèque*. I began to acquire a few books with my saved pennies. There was Nelson's blue-bound sevenpenny series, then the fabulous *Everyman Library*, a shilling a bound volume. For sixty years that little red *Golden Treasury* has stood on my bookshelf. On the fly leaf is inscribed 'C. Roberts. Form 3c, 1906'. Because it is of the same size it stands next to an Aldine Press edition of Catullus, published in Venice in 1502, bound in Paris by Tout. I am told it is worth £100, but if one of the two had to be sacrificed, the Aldine would go, for the other holds the essence of entranced boyhood. It bears the school stamp. Did I fail to return it? I do not know. It does not trouble my conscience.

With this new discovery of the wonders of literature the piano lapsed in favour. My mother, glad to economise as my school demanded various sums for caps and subscriptions, stopped the lessons. Also, I had become rebellious. How cruel children can be! She had bought me a Church of England Hymnal with music, and liked me to play her favourite hymns, which I detested. I caricatured them. There were also two religious songs she loved. I thought them frightfully saccharine. One was called *The Heavenly Gardener*. It had a cover picture of Jesus walking in a garden carrying in His arms a small child. The closing line of this song about a defunct child was "Then came the Heavenly Gardener and took my bud away." The other was a lachrymose dirge about the death of a small boy. The opening line was "Close the shutters, Willie's dead." I guyed these songs mercilessly, to my poor mother's chagrin. Perhaps she was thinking of her two lost children. I lament my conduct now.

CHAPTER SEVEN

The Author Emerges

I

MY THRIFTY mother was the Chancellor of our domestic exchequer. I know that she worried over income and expenditure, whereas my father lived in the clouds. He never complained, he never longed for anything beyond his reach. A teetotaller, he indulged in smoking very moderately. He was always well-dressed, and since he carried his six-feet-one-inch well, walking very erect, fussy over shoes, linen and gloves, he had an air of elegance. He walked slowly. I had never seen him hurry. I therefore had no trouble keeping up with him when I went with him from his business in the Market Place down to Wilford Grove. "We could set our clock by him," said a neighbour. There was another immaculate walker who came into my ken twice a year. He was not as tall, but he was as particular in his dress, as punctilious in his manner. He seemed to be an incurable optimist. He was Mr. Samuel Ellis, the Prudential Insurance Company's agent. He called twice a year to collect the premiums of the Life Policy my mother had taken out on my father. Whereas the latter believed this was an unpredictable world to which you must show a stoic front, Mr. Ellis oozed optimism. He walked through life bestowing bland benedictions. "Soapy Sam" was my father's verdict on cheerful Mr. Ellis.

One day there would be a knock at the front door. There was Mr. Ellis, in a bowler hat in winter, in a straw hat in summer. Summer or winter, he wore grey spats with pearl buttons, and carried a small black bag exactly like that of the doctor's. A noticeable thing about his spick and span attire was a white slip carefully adjusted to show along the edge of his vest. He wore a stiff white choker and a stock tie with a gold horseshoe pin. His white cuffs just emerged from his sleeves. He was florid, with sandy grey hair, wavy and parted down the middle.

If I answered his knock on the door the greeting was always the same. "Ah, my little man, is your dear mother at home?" Inside, shaking hands with my mother, he sat down at the table and opened his black bag, taking out some papers. He wore a gold ring and had well-manicured hands. He picked out of his vest pocket a pair of gold-rimmed *pince-nez* glasses attached to a thin black cord and perched these on his nose. Smoothing out his papers, there would be some talk about the company's policy bonus. Obviously all was going well with the Prudential and its clients. My mother opened her cashbox and counted out some money. He wrote a receipt, and gathered up the money into a little linen bag, closed with a tape. "I think that is quite correct?" he would say, handing my mother the receipt. All this was strictly solemn business, but sometimes there was a welcome deviation. He would push towards me across the table-cloth a silver sixpence, saying "My boy—I've no doubt you have expenses to meet." "Oh, thank you, Mr. Ellis," I cried, beaming and pocketing the sixpence. The business completed, he would now become social. Replacing the *pince-nez*, snapping close the bag, he would say, "I trust Mr. Roberts is in his usual good health?" In return to this question my mother, bringing forward a cup of tea, would enquire about his. "My dear Mrs. Roberts, I am most happy to say that Mrs. Ellis and I are in excellent health for which we are very grateful to the Almighty. Ageing, of course, the years run on, but mellowing gently." Then, looking at me—"What a bright boy! What pleasure he must give you! Alas, alas, Mrs. Ellis and I have not been rewarded in this manner, although the Lord's mercies towards us are many. Excellent health, a happy home, few worries —and this reminds me of something I heard the other day." And then he would produce the funny story with which he always came equipped. It was a very proper story at which we could all laugh. This delivered, he stood up. "Well, I must be getting on my rounds. This had been a most agreeable interlude." He would put his hand on my shoulder, looking fondly at me. Then my mother conducted him to the door. "Goodbye. Goodbye—till I come again!" I heard him call. The semi-annual visit was over. My mother put the receipt with other papers in the cashbox, and I had had a windfall of six-pence. "Such a nice man, always pleasant," said my mother. I wholly agreed.

On one of these calls, business transacted, the funny story told, he took from his wallet a newspaper cutting. It was from the local newspaper. "I saw this letter—an excellent letter. What surprised me was the name of the writer—Cecil Roberts. Is it a coincidence, or is he a relation?" he asked. "No, I wrote that letter," I said. He stared at me. "You, my boy, you wrote that letter! Is it possible!" he exclaimed. "Yes," said my mother, "he wrote it—he's always busy writing something." Mr. Ellis replaced the cutting in his wallet. "I shall treasure this. I always felt he was a most unusual boy—most unusual! I shall read it to Mrs. Ellis and tell her who wrote it. Our political sympathies endorse every word!"

My mother, alarmed at the effect on me of this open praise, immediately demurred. "We are very surprised they printed it, but I suppose they have to fill up the paper," she said. "Ah yes, ah yes—still—" commented Mr. Ellis, giving me a warm smile. He had not wasted his sixpences. What Mr. Ellis did not know, and what I could not tell him for fear of my mother's reproof, was that I had been an author for over a year.

There had been a number of exciting excursions arranged for us at school. One was a memorable visit, at schoolboy prices, to see Sir Frank Benson and his Shakespearean company acting in *Julius Caesar*, which my form was then reading. Sir Frank toured the provinces with a repertory company that was the training ground for young men from the universities who wished to become actors. A number of famous actors had passed through his hands. We sat in the dark auditorium while Antony harangued the crowd, Casca sneered and lean Cassius led Brutus on his way to doom. For many of us it was our first experience of the theatre and of the immortal bard given human shape. We were thrilled to the marrow, incapable of knowing whether the acting was good or bad. Then someone at Mundella arranged for a party to visit Clifton Colliery and descend the mine. We were reading *Sous Terre* in the French class, so this was an appropriate visit. I contributed to the school magazine a description of that visit. "Thousands of tons of coal are consumed every day, yet hardly a second thought is given to the toilers who are working in the bowels of the earth for their daily bread," I wrote sympathetically, and I assured my readers that pit ponies were not blind when brought to the surface, only dazzled. Thus at fourteen I had become a journalist. In the July number, 1906, the index said: "Down a Coal Mine" by C. Roberts, Form 2c. It was my first time in print. I slept that night with a copy of the magazine under my pillow, and at daybreak assured myself I really was an author.

Three months later I was again in the magazine, this time with an illustrated article. "Henry Kirke White" by C. Roberts, Form 3c, said the November number. 1906 was the centenary year of Henry Kirke White's death. He had died at twenty-one. Nottingham had a claim to three poets, Byron, Kirke White and 'Festus' Bailey, the last two of spurious fame. Byron, though not Nottingham born was closely associated with the city, having resided there and at his nearby seat, Newstead Abbey. Bailey won fame at twenty-three with *Festus*. "Order it," wrote Tennyson to FitzGerald, "you will most likely find it a great bore, but there are really very grand things in it."

Bailey was one of those one-poem men who went up like a rocket, spluttered brightly and was then engulfed in darkness. Some of his verse went into all the anthologies, it had the right note of noble uplift in the era of Samuel Smiles' *Self-Help*, another transient splutter.

> We live in deeds, not years; in thoughts, not breaths;
> In feelings, not in figures on a dial.
> We should count time by heart throbs. He most lives
> Who thinks most—feels the noblest—acts the best.

Bailey, with a Civil List pension of £100 at forty, lived to be eighty-six, a long-extinct volcano. During fifty years he added and added to *Festus* and buried it beyond resurrection. When a boy he had seen Byron lying in state at The Blackamoor's Head, High Street, Nottingham. Henry Kirke White was another rocket of brief flight. He was a butcher's son born in 1785 in the meat market, The Shambles, where, almost under the old Exchange, his father had a shop, the place marked later with a plaque. As a boy he worked at one of Arkwright's stocking looms. A solicitor then took him up, and encouraged the boy to study Latin. Precocious, he learned Greek, Spanish and Portuguese. He wrote a book of poems called *Clifton Grove and other poems* of which the Duchess of Devonshire accepted the dedication. Southey praised his book, Wilberforce became interested, and, desiring to become a clergyman, patrons sent him with a Sizarship to St. John's College, Cambridge, in 1805. The twenty-year-old boy distinguished himself in classics and in 1806 came out first of his year. But he overworked, was consumptive and died in his rooms on

October 19th, 1806, aged twenty-one. His early death gave his name a touch of sorrowful drama. Southey compiled *The Remains of Henry Kirke White* and added an account of his life. It passed through ten editions by 1823 and was also published in the U.S.A. Possibly because of his Nottingham origin Byron became interested and enshrined him in some verses:

> Unhappy White! while life was at its spring
> And thy young muse first shook her joyous wing
> The spoiler came, and all thy promise fair
> Has sought the grave, to sleep forever there.

This was more than Byron did for Keats and Shelley, doomed to follow White within less than two decades. Byron went farther. He wrote, "Setting aside his bigotry, he surely ranks next to Chatterton. It is asonishing how little he was known, and at Cambridge no one thought or heard of such a man till his death rendered all notice useless. For my own part I should have been proud of such an acquaintance; his very prejudices were respectable."

The Byronic aside about White's bigotry arose from the fact that the boy was pious and wrote some hymns that got into the hymn-books. His "Onward, Christian Soldiers", somewhat changed by an editor, still goes marching on.

On the centenary of his death Nottingham noted the date, and the *Nottingham Guardian* had an article, with a block portrait. I made my second contribution to the school magazine with a notice of the poet. I coveted that portrait for my article. It happened that my father knew the Advertisement Manager of the newspaper. Together we went with my request and, elated, got the loan of the block. I had now staked out my claim at school, I was an author. But I had a grievance that rankled. In my three years there I never gained a prize. This seemed very unfair. In one subject I was easily ahead for four consecutive terms, in the General Intelligence Paper, and for that subject there was no prize. Fifty years later I had my revenge. A 'Distinguished Old Boy', I was invited, for the second time, to distribute the prizes at the annual Prize Day. It took place before a thousand assembled parents and scholars in that very hall where Sir Jesse Boot had presided over those delirious political demonstrations. On this occasion I gave the Headmaster a cheque for two thousand pounds to establish two annual travel prizes, to be awarded to the two top competitors in a General Intelligence Paper. When the Headmaster sent me the set paper of one hundred questions, answered by the winners with 94 and 91 marks respectively, I learned how far a younger generation had progressed since my boyhood. I could not have answered more than sixty per cent of the questions.

II

In my second year at Mundella there was a theatrical production, put on by one of our masters. What excitement those rehearsals provoked! I do not recall the name of the pageant-play in which I found myself cast. It presented a collection of famous characters from English history, Chaucer, Shakespeare, Queen Elizabeth, Marlborough, Dr. Johnson, Nelson. We somehow came to be gathered in an English manor house, but on the stroke of midnight we all resumed the figures of puppets, a kind of *Boutique Fantasque*. Inevitably, my muse having been demonstrated, I was cast for Shakespeare. My mother and Miss Fryer went to work on my costume. Blue hose were made from a pair of shrunken cotton long drawers, dyed. I had a noble white doublet, made out of an old silk blouse, a splendid red cloak lined with blue satin, buckled shoes, and, a tremendous labour for my poor mother, a really splendid ruff. To this was added a brown velvet cap with a large ostrich feather supplied by Miss Fryer. It was part of my rôle to carry an enormous portfolio and to read out of it a long poem in couplets, making play on the titles of Shakespeare's works.

The Merchant of Venice and Hamlet met
On a rainy Twelfth Night so they both got wet.

The hall was packed, our parents were present, the Headmaster held a reception afterwards, the evening was a great success. In succeeding years I have been at many first nights in most of the capitals of Europe, at royal, gala and charity performances, with a riot of tiaras, diamonds, decorations and uniforms, but there was never such a first night as this, when the heart was young and one stood tip-toe on the verge of life. We did not know then we were a doomed generation, that within a decade half of us would be lying under crosses in foreign soil or at the bottom of the seas.

III

It was about this time that my father had embarked on a personal adventure. He had turned inventor. Every Sunday night, with my assistance, there came up from the cellar of our house a series of washing tubs, dolly pegs and scrubbing board. It was after the Sunday night cold supper. These articles were laid out in the scullery ready for eight o'clock on Monday morning, laundry day. Next morning there arrived a middle-aged woman, Carrie, who, for half a crown, did the day's washing. She was sturdy and deaf, a good-natured worker but a disreputable character. For Carrie, unmarried, lived with a coal miner in the Forbidden Land. She represented Sin. Her life was stormy. She arrived on various occasions with blue bruises on her arms and face. Sometimes she had a black eye. The explanation was always the same, she had slipped somehow, or fallen down stairs. But rumour informed us that she was often very violent outside The Cremorne at closing time on Saturday night. "She's a good worker and her life's her own affair," said my mother.

She came with a string bag and in it was an apron, a mob cap, and a bottle. She took off a battered straw hat with a drooping black feather, a rabbit-skin boa, turned up her sleeves, put on the apron and began to ladle boiling water out of the copper. At eleven o'clock there was a break. She was provided with a glass of stout and some bread and cheese. At lunch she sat with us, the kitchen being hung with wet things if the day was rainy. She sat at one end of the table very demure and quiet, not hearing a word. My father, on entering the dining-room, gave her a slight bow before seating himself at the opposite end of the table. She responded with a sad smile. My mother could have banished her to the kitchen, but she thought it "unkind to the poor soul". So there sat Carrie, in our world yet not of it. Towards five o'clock the things hanging on the lines in the backyard were taken in and folded, ready for mangling. This took place the next day with my reluctant assistance. The following day there was a stretching and sprinkling of sheets preparatory to ironing. My mother was a good ironer. She also starched and ironed my father's stiff collars and cuffs, and my Eton collars. I was made to wear a clean collar each day. I became adept at pulling the corners of the damp sheets with my mother, and at folding.

But rainy Mondays created a problem. The sheets were still wet when Carrie departed at six o'clock and they had to be hung on lines in the kitchen, obstructing passage from the dining-room to the scullery. To deal with this situation my father turned inventor. He devised an apparatus like a small capstan that was attached to the central joist of the ceiling. Into this capstan were thrust a dozen long wooden rods. On these hung the laundry, high overhead, and concentrated in one place. It was very ingenious and a great success, so much so that neighbours began to ask for a similar contraption. My father sighted a fortune. To secure the profit of his own invention, he decided to take out a patent. When he embarked on this he had no idea what a long and costly process it was. There were people called patent-agents who had to be commissioned to see the thing through. Also a model had to be submitted to the patent-agent. This involved the employment of a pattern-maker who made, in hard smooth wood, a facsimile of the invention. And as the capstan had to support the lateral strain of the rods, this had to be a special hard wood and the holes had to be reinforced with metal. This involved a metal-worker.

The patent process took six months, with journeys to various people in London. There were then five shilling return excursion trips from Nottingham to London. The train left at noon, and returned at 2.30 a.m. My father came back exhausted on his half-holidays and was at his office at nine the next morning. For this patented production he had to register a trade name. He hit on an ingenious one. His name being John Godber Roberts, he took the first two letters of each name and called his invention *Jogoro*. It was to restore our family fortunes. Alas, having patented it, he could find no firm to take it up. For almost a year he interviewed one company after another, his hopes raised and dashed. Finally, he decided to have two hundred manufactured at his own expense. They were brought home and filled the attic bed-room. With individual effort he sold about fifty, then tired, disillusioned, he gave up. There, cramming the attic, lay the unsold *Jogoros*.

All this happened during my fourteenth year. We none of us spoke of this failure. But Carrie remained enthusiastic in its praise. She even succeeded in selling half a dozen to her various employers and received a commission.

I had now entered on my last year at school. I was to leave two months after my fifteenth birthday, which fell in May, 1907. All hopes of an extra year, which would have been a most rewarding time for my opening mind, vanished with the *Jogoro* disaster. This last year at school was the best of all. I was deliriously happy. Every day a new wonder sailed into my ken. There were now Macaulay's *Essays* and Milton's *Lycidas* in the English Literature class. My father knew his Milton and started me on *Paradise Lost*.

"Of Man's first disobedience, and the fruit" he taught me to declaim, and I followed with:

> High on a throne of royal state, which far
> Outshone the wealth of Ormuz and of Ind,
> Or where the gorgeous East with richest hand
> Showers on her kings barbaric pearl and gold,
> Satan exalted sat.

"There's the glory of the English language for you!" he said. How he would have denounced the impertinence of T. S. Eliot's belittlement of Milton!

He was aggrieved we were not taught Latin. He found, secondhand, a primer and started me off, again, but I had homework and he was often tired, so it came to nothing. But he never weakened on my diction, my deportment, my manners, and my clean shoes. He gave me that birthday two pocket-sized volumes, excitingly illustrated, of Pope's rhymed translation of the *Iliad* and the *Odyssey*. The marvellous Greek world burst on my vision. I sailed to Troy, I stood on its ramparts with Helen, I wept with Achilles over the body of Patroclus and, as Hector, said farewell to Andromache.

I was now busy in the correspondence columns of the *Nottingham Guardian* attacking an old Tory who wrote under a pseudonym. There were my contributions to the Mundella Magazine, and some twenty poems written out in an exercise book, entitled *The Collected Poems of Cecil Roberts*. Gone was my enthusiasm for the piano, boxing, painting, but I was still faithful to my Muse. I now began to question accepted customs. Every morning in school we assembled for prayers. This was followed by a hymn. I was in revolt against some of the verses we sang. "God moves in a mysterious way His wonders to perform" was grand to sing, but already I had begun to think some of His ways were very mysterious, such as snatching away Milly at ten years of age and letting kind young Mrs. Gee die of agonising cancer, leaving four small children. "Rock of Ages cleft for me" sang splendily, but I didn't want to hide in any rock or have it cleft for me, a troglodyte.

I soon found I must not ask awkward questions or think for myself. There were 'mysteries' not to be explained. One just believed, as everyone else did. I was already puzzled why a bishop should live in a palace, wear gaiters and ride in a limousine whereas Jesus had nowhere to lay His head and had to walk everywhere, no lace frills on His gown, or a jewelled staff. And how was it bishops so often seemed to have been to Eton and Oxford whereas Jesus had never attended even a National School? Could He write, I asked my form master one day. He looked very astonished, and told me not to ask foolish questions. But was it a foolish question? It seemed to me that among the twelve disciples only four of them could sign their names.

Then there was sex. We were forbidden to speak to a girl in school, but not a thing was taught us to explain an increasing manifestation. I had already experimented with myself, and exchanged information with my schoolfellows. One evening, reading *Paradise Lost*, I came upon

> There they their fill of love and love's disport
> Took largely, of their mutual guilt the seal,
> The solace of their sin, till dewy sleep
> Oppressed them, wearied with their amorous play.

I read it out to my father and asked him just what it meant. Quite calmly he said "They were enjoying each other physically, having sex. Milton was in the Puritan camp and professed he didn't like it. Actually Milton did. It comes out in *Paradise Lost*." My father opened the book and read

> Adam from his fair Spouse, nor Eve, the rites
> Mysterious of connubial Love refused
> Whatever Hypocrites austerely talk
> Of purity and place and innocence,
> Defaming as impure what God declares
> Pure, and commands to some, leaves free to all.

"'Free to all!' That must have shaken the Puritans!" said my father. He answered my questions in detail.

"Can I get a baby?" I asked.

138

"Possibly in a year or so, but if you're sensible you'll wait another ten. Sex can be not only a great pleasure but uncontrolled it can also become a disastrous obsession."

He gave me the key to a great deal that had puzzled me in the books I was reading. He did it with no subterfuge or hesitation. So that was the clue to the Helen-Paris business and all the commotion around Troy!

Then there was Death and the Hereafter. I was surrounded by people who seemed to know exactly what was going to happen to them after they had died. It was as if they had booked a seat for a celestial performance and knew every item on the programme. But what different programmes they had! As a child I recall that the Mormons had descended upon us and struck fear through the neighbourhood. Mild young men with beards and a strange accent tapped at doors and left pamphlets describing a wonderful Heaven promised by the Prophet Dowie. We were all kept indoors, for it was said these Mormon missionaries, seeking to populate Salt Lake City, were kidnapping children, and young girls were put into harems. Then there was an Evangelist called Gipsy Smith who once a year visited the Wesleyan chapel and held revival meetings. I was so eager to have a good look at a gipsy that I begged my mother to take me to one of his meetings. It was crowded. He sang hymns with a beautiful voice and then addressed us all as sinners, giving us details of the wonderful Hereafter we were going to miss if we were not 'saved'. Then he told us to close our eyes and sing. Presently he shouted, "Yes, sister, I see you! Come to Jesus! He is waiting for you!" I took a peep and saw a sobbing young woman assisted to the altar rail by a sidesman. Other 'sisters' followed, and a few men. "Praise the Lord! What a harvest for Jesus!" exclaimed Gipsy Smith. "Ten—eleven—twelve—Come to Jesus, brothers, come to Jesus, sisters!" he exclaimed ecstatically. Then he said "Let us sing for joy—for sinners saved!" and the organ played fortissimo and the congregation sang lustily while a silver collection (minimum sixpence) was taken. When we filed out the 'saved' were led off to the vestry. I asked what was going to happen to them there. My mother said she did not know. When I asked my father he replied: "They get signed up—it's a way of swelling the congregation." Sixty years later I went to a Billy Graham revival meeting. It was the same technique on a colossal scale, hymns, denunciation of sin, a glowing heaven for penitents, worked up emotion, and mass hysteria. The

Church of England did not have revival meetings. "Don't sinners get saved in the Anglican church?" I asked. "Yes," answered my mother, "but it's done in a dignified way. They don't shout about it."

Death. I had first been aware of it when I looked on Milly in her coffin. In my twelfth year I came very near to it. I had rheumatic fever and was in bed a month. It had compensations, I became quite important. I had frequent visits from my adored Dr. Harrison, I had lots of books, my father and mother read to me, and, most exciting and lovely, a fire in my bedroom. Sometimes in the gloaming, before a lamp had been brought up by my mother, I would lie there and watch the firelight playing on the ceiling, hearing the evening sounds outside. The jumping shadows took shapes, the fire would settle and sigh, and, the room darker, panic would seize me and I would shout, bringing my mother upstairs to comfort me. How vivid those firelit sick-bed memories remain! Some fifty-four years later, staying in a lovely Italian villa in Alassio, I was ill with influenza. It was a late winter afternoon. Suddenly a storm in the mountains cut off the electric light. We were without heating also from the oil-electric generator. My hostess had a log fire made in the French grate of the bedroom. While the maid sought for candles the firelight leapt over the walls and ceiling. Once again I was a small sick boy with a fire in his bedroom. Some lines, laden with memories, took form in my head. I had a pencil but no paper, so I wrote my verses round the blank margin of *The Times* newspaper. I was no longer in Italy in 1958, I was in a back bedroom in England in 1904, before those 'loved long since and lost awhile' had gone with the years.

> When I was a small boy it was nice to be ill
> In bed, with a fire flickering in a room warm and still,
> With long shadows walking on ceiling and wall
> And my mother's soft hands smoothing pillow and shawl.
> And now I'm an old man I remember, with tears,
> That room with the firelight far off down the years,
> And while the light's fading on a life flickering out
> I lie alone wondering what it's all been about.
> The room is so still and a shadow waits there—
> Oh, hands that once nursed me, oh face once so dear,
> Come closer, come closer in the firelight's warm glow,
> Ere, one journey ended, on another I go.

IV

The morning hymn-singing in the school assembly was presided over by the Headmaster. At no time did I have any personal contact with him, except if I must count a smile he gave me the morning after the visit of the Japanese Minister, in aloof acknowledgement of my performance, and when, on leaving school, I went to say goodbye to him. He was an austere figure. Facially, he had a singular resemblance to my father, but he was querulous and lacked his height. Fresh-complexioned, he parted his hair in the middle and had slightly slanting eyelids that gave severity to his expression. (In later years I noticed that Joseph Conrad had the same kind of eyes.) He had a resonant voice and was always well dressed. Woe to the boy who was dirty or slovenly. There was an awful moment one morning as he passed our ranks going to his desk on the dais when he stopped before me. My heart gave a thud, but the offender stood next to me with a crumpled collar, ill-tied tie and not too clean shoes. I am afraid I heightened the contrast. He slowly surveyed the wretched boy. "Tomorrow I hope you will not dare to appear in this disgraceful manner," he said, and then passed on. There was an awful silence. When he read announcements he wore *pince-nez* and at the end of each paragraph peered over them, looking to see if we were listening. He read the morning Lesson very well. The grandeur of the Authorised Version lost nothing in his delivery. Neither the Church of England clergymen nor the Wesleyan ministers could match him in the majesty of his oratorical tones. When censuring us he was Jove thundering, and we, his minions, cowered. As a Headmaster he created for the school a high reputation. About that time I was reading *Tom Brown's Schooldays*, and here was Dr. Arnold.

Tender and beautiful are my memories of those morning gatherings, the Lesson, the prayers, the hymn, with the light streaming in through the long windows, the masters assembled in a line at the end of our ranks, the assistant chemistry master at the piano, our young faces shining, our treble voices piping. It is an unfading legacy from the dawn of my life. I cannot to-day hear "Lord, behold us with thy blessing once again assembled here" (for beginning of term), and "All things bright and beautiful, all creatures great and small", without a catch in the throat, and a sense of the debilitating years heavy upon those of us who have survived. The morning light and the evening light are so sadly different. I was always too sensitive a boy never to be unaware of the menace of Time; my ecstasy in a bright unfolding world was always touched by a warning of mutability.

CHAPTER EIGHT

Goodbye, Boyhood

I

"Shades of the prison-house begin to close upon the growing boy."
As my fourteenth year opened I was made aware of our mortality.
Miss Fryer, found dead in bed, was a great loss. No more would
she take off her rings at the piano, and give us extracts from *The
Bohemian Girl* or *Faust*, calling up the spring-time of her years with
the Carl Rosa Opera Company. The next shock was the news that
Dr. Harrison had sold his practice and was retiring to Devon. I did
not know then that a consumptive's doom awaited him, or that
consumption was to play such havoc among those I loved. In those
days it was a great killer, my music teacher, my doctor, one of my
form masters, a devoted secretary, were all foredoomed.

I went across the road to say goodbye to the doctor, holding back
the tears in my eyes. He was young, handsome and kind. I recall the
chill touch of his stethoscope on my bare chest, and the coldness of
his hand on winter days when I lay stripped before him. He told my
mother, taking off the ear-plugs of the stethoscope, that I had a
'murmur' but he was sure I would grow out of it. He was the first of
a long succession of doctors on two continents who were to fuss over
my heart. "I think you should have a cardiogram," the latest doctor
would always say. "But I've already got a dozen," I would protest,
and knew quite well he would insist on another. Every doctor has
his own little ring of specialists that he starts you running to. Up
and down Harley Street you go, ringing one of a tier of bells,
pausing in those stately communal waiting rooms, glancing at old
copies of *Country Life*, often feeling you are to be 'tried for life'
and called up for a death sentence. My cardiograms looked like the
peaks of the Dolomites. Young Dr. Harrison was the first to be
puzzled.

143

He received me in his sitting-room on my farewell call. I was shown in, school cap in hand. I explained why I had called, saying how sorry I was that he was leaving, how . . . And then I choked. He was smoking a pipe, got up from his chair, and came to me. Putting an arm round my shoulders, he took the pipe out of his mouth and led me to the window looking on the garden. He told me where he was going, to Devon, to a house overlooking the sea. He would be married soon. He ran his hand through my hair and smiled at me with his dark eyes. "I believe you're going to be a six-footer like your father," he said. "You're having a lot of fun at school, I hear. Someone showed me an article you wrote about going down a coal mine. Are you going to be an author?" "A poet!" I replied, to be explicit. "Ah—be careful. They've a habit of dying young!" he said, laughing.

The new housekeeper looked in. They were lining up in the surgery, she warned. "Coming," he said. He held me for a moment, then he stooped and kissed me. "Goodbye, young man," he said. We went out into the hall, his arm about me. He opened the door. Somehow I went down the steps. He died within three years. He was only thirty-five. Was it that schoolboy infatuation which has always made me happy in the company of doctors? So many have been my friends.

II

At the end of my fourteenth year my brother got married. He had played so small a part in my life that I scarcely missed him. He was tall, goodlooking, a lively dancer, and devoted to his boyhood sweetheart. On the night of his marriage, when he left the house for the last time with his bride, going to a new home they had furnished, my father came back from the hall door into the sitting-room. I was surprised to see tears running down his face. "I don't like turning the key on the boy," he said to my mother, and pulled out his handkerchief as they held each other in their arms.

I moved into my brother's back bedroom and took over his wardrobe and dressing-table. The piano was now wholly mine. He would not want it for singing *Speak, speak, speak to me, Thora*. I had now progressed as far as Chopin's Black Key study and the Drum Polonaise (Op. 53). I had been bewitched by Vladimir de Pachmann and was to remain bewitched for another twenty years. He had

Sir William Skipwith of Cotes and Prestwold (1549–1610), and his wife, Dame Jane, daughter of John Roberts (1555–1630)

Sir John Bale of Carlton Curlieu (1551–1621), and his wife, Dame Francesca (1549–1629)

On the back panel five sons are shown in armour, a daughter, and a son who died in infancy. The first son on the panel, George, married Elizabeth Hartopp, who re-married Sir William Roberts. The fifth son on the panel, Edmund, married Joyce, daughter of Sir Richard Roberts

Sir Richard Roberts of Sutton Cheynell and Thorpe Langton (1564–1644)

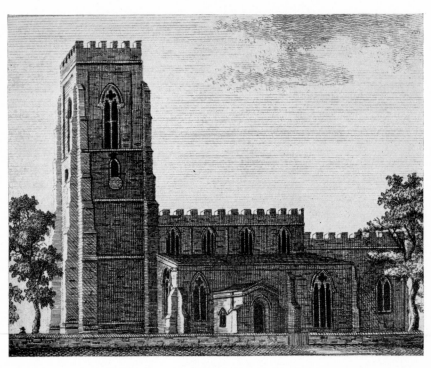

St. Peter's, Church Langton, 1780

spoken to me once. I was standing at the entrance to the Mechanic's Hall where he had come to give a concert, for which I expended a shilling. He dropped some papers at the back entrance and I was quick to pick them up. "Tank you. You are a goot boy!" he said. "Give heem a teeket," he said to his attendant. He gave me a 7s. 6d. ticket. I did not say I had a ticket, which I gave to someone, and proudly sat in the fifth row. In 1965 I met an old musician in whose house in Rome the pianist had passed his slightly mad last years. He told me that Pachmann used to put on a dressing gown once worn by Chopin (stroked by George Sand?) and sit down to play, lost in a dream. I found the cemetery in which he was buried in Rome in 1933, aged eighty-five, and put some flowers on his grave in memory of my boyhood's enchantment.

In 1906 there was another musician who delighted me, a young man named Harold Bauer. I learned many years afterwards that he was English, not German, born in London in 1873. He began as a child prodigy playing the violin. When he was twenty Paderewski heard him and was so impressed by his keyboard ability that he said he must become a pianist—"And besides, you have such beautiful hair!" said Paderewski, who was himself famous on that score. Bauer had already decided that he could not become a great violinist, so he switched instruments. He had no teachers. By 1900 he was established as a concert artist. He often appeared in a trio with Kreisler and Casals, or in sonata recitals with Thibaud. He made his debut in the U.S.A. in 1900 and went on tour. When he came to Nottingham I scraped up a shilling to hear him play. There was a comic episode. While he was playing a black cat walked on to the platform and solemnly approached the piano and sat down. The audience broke into laughter and with great sang-froid Bauer turned, as if he were playing to the cat. When he came to the end he picked it up gently and left the platform to immense applause. In 1946 I met him in a friend's house in New York. I told him that I had heard him in Nottingham forty years earlier. I reminded him of the cat. His face lit up. "That cat! I never had such luck again. It made my concert!" He was now grey and old but when he sat down and played for us a Weber waltz it was clear that he had lost none of his magical soft touch. He told me that as a very young man he saw Isadora Duncan, then quite unknown to him, dance. It affected him so much that it gave him the idea that if into the rhythm of his hands on the keyboard he could get the rhythm of her body in motion, he would achieve finer gradations of tone. Twenty years later in San Francisco Eugène Ysaye brought to his studio Isadora Duncan, now famous. They arranged to give a dance and piano recital together, the whole programme being Chopin. One of the pieces was the *Étude in A flat*. He played it as the music indicated, with a great crescendo followed by a diminuendo at the end of the phrase. Isadora Duncan said he was playing it wrongly. He insisted that he wasn't, that he was playing the music as it was written. "No, it can't be like that," she said, "because if it is I have nothing to do with my arms at the end!" So he yielded and played it as she wished. A long time after he discovered that in the original manuscript edition Chopin had written it to be played exactly as Isadora Duncan had wished.

Now, sole possessor of the piano as I pounded away at the Polonaise, the Black Key study, my mother would look in and say "Not so loud, you'll annoy the neighbours!" In little more than a year, by a stroke of Fate, I was to lose my piano, but already I knew I was not a born pianist. The ambition was there but the innate gift was missing. The pen, not the piano, was now predominant. Shelley, not Chopin, was beckoning me.

Poor Miss Fryer's visits from across the road, bringing with her the score of *Aïda* or *La Traviata*, Novello editions with Italian text running between the music, had awakened another interest. I learned a few lines of Italian. These were not the first. Before this, a plumber had visited our house to renew some piping. My mother had threatened the landlord, saying she would leave if the repairs were not made. He was a skinflint and came in a pony and trap to collect the rent of twelve shillings each week. The plumber was an engaging young man and I talked to him. He grew into a fabulous creature. He had visited Naples, Genoa and Venice!—a stoker in a British cruiser sailing the Mediterranean. He had even seen the Coliseum and the leaning tower of Pisa, and had ridden in a gondola. His ship was laid up for two months at Naples for repairs. During that time he had learned some Italian. Could he talk to Mrs. Capocci, who kept the ice-cream barrow in the Market Place and went home once a year to her native village near Monte Cassino? He had not tried that. He taught me some Italian verses. I learned them avidly.

> Stare a letto e non dormire,
> Sempre servire e mai piacere,
> Sono sufficienti per morire.

To stay in bed and never sleep,
Always to serve and never please,
Are enough to make you die.

I thought this wonderful and marched about the house reciting it.
I asked who had taught him Italian. He winked and said—"A nice
little teacher in my bed." I wondered then why he had learned
Italian in bed, it seemed an odd way to study. I had no idea whether
my Italian was intelligible, I learned it parrot-wise. Almost twenty
years later I recited it to an Italian friend. He laughed and said it
was perfectly good Italian. From the Verdi scores and Miss Bewley I
picked up a few lines, and there for many years my Italian stopped.
I was thirty-five when, in Venice, I began to read Dante's *Divina
Commedia* with a young university student in my pension, glad to
earn a few lire. *Nel mezzo del cammin di nostra vita . . .*

III

On my fourteenth birthday my pocket money was raised from
threepence to sixpence.* This enabled me to enlarge my library. I had
found a second-hand shop that sometimes sold books for as little as
threepence. For sixpence the range was much larger. My pocket
money also, one July day, enabled me to take a young lady out for
tea, and thereby provoke a commotion, the first 'trouble with a
woman' in my life. The manner of it was this. I often played in the
back garden with a racket and tennis ball. A stone wall provided the
rebound of the ball. Sometimes it happened that the ball went over
the wall into the neighbours' garden. Greatly daring, if the coast
was clear, I would go over the wall and retrieve the tennis ball. The
neighbours were disagreeable people; not the wife, who was a fluffy,
timid little woman, who seemed in terror of her husband. He was an
older man, very arrogant in manner, who never spoke to anyone and

* In 1961, fifty-five years later, a secondary school master asked me to
conduct over the Forum a party of twenty boys, aged fifteen to sixteen, with
whom he had flown over to Rome at Easter. I learned that the week's trip
cost them £30 a head, that their pocket money was upwards of £1 a week,
and that most of them were also taking summer holidays abroad with their
parents. Some had cine-cameras, and hailed taxis. I was stunned, but hid it
from their sophisticated young eyes. But they spent less than a group of
American schoolboys for whom I performed the same office, who flew the
Atlantic for two weeks in Italy at a cost of £150 per head.

carried himself like a lord of creation. The wife wanted to be friendly, but dared not. We called him the Old Nabob.

One day I was about to go over the wall to retrieve my ball, a trespass I preferred to going to the front door and asking for it, when, to my surprise, there was a small girl in the garden. She picked up the ball to give it to me. I thanked her and we talked. She had a slightly freckled face, a snub nose and red hair. It was a rather comical face and she had merry blue eyes, and very nice teeth. I asked her what her name was, "Serena," she answered. "Serena—What a pretty name!" I said. She asked for mine. "Cecil!—What a funny name!" she replied, with a giggle. I refused to be rebuffed. I learned she was thirteen and staying with her aunt because her mother was in hospital. She lived in Birkenhead. Our talk was checked by the Nabob's wife, calling her in. Whenever I went into the garden with my racket she appeared, and I made sure my ball went over the wall. She was lonely, poor Serena, cooped up in that house.

We became great friends. One day I asked her if she had ever been to Clifton Grove. I offered to take her there and give her tea. You could get tea, bread and butter and jam for sixpence. That meant a shilling's outlay, but with last week's pocket money in hand, and this week's coming, it was possible. I should still be twopence short, the cost of the double passage over the half-penny toll bridge. but I could tap my mother for this. I suggested next Saturday afternoon. She would ask her aunt. The next day she said it would be all right. We agreed to start at half-past two. It would take more than an hour to climb Clifton Grove and reach the village at the top. Our excursion must have been about the time of that of a Nottinghamshire coal-miner's son, D. H. Lawrence, aged twenty-one, who took a girl there and gave her tea in one of the cottages, an incident to be used later in his novel *Sons and Lovers*.

On Saturday, in possession of one shilling and twopence, we set off. I did not know she had 'told a fib'. It transpired that she had not asked her aunt. We set off on a lovely July afternoon. She was full of life, quick on her legs, and her funny little face was always in ripples of laughter. She told me a lot about her home, her younger brother and sister, also sent away. Her mother was in hospital and her father was an officer on a merchant ship. She had just had a post-card from him in Australia.

Clifton Grove was a lovers' haunt. It was sylvan and romantic.

You walked through meadows at the side of the Trent, and came to a steep ascent with a wide grassy avenue arched over with massive elms. Far below, at the bottom of the steep bosky hillside, flashed the silver river. "Let's go down," she said. I warned her it was very slippery, but she wanted to go, so down we went, hand in hand, bouncing from tree to tree. At the bottom, breathless, we lay down in the grass, and threw pebbles in the river. Suddenly there was a cloud in my heart. I thought of how I had stood in the ferns in Sherwood Forest with Milly, and how she had died soon after. How awful if Serena died too.

We clambered back up to the top of the Grove, went over a stile and on to one of the tea cottages in the village of Clifton. An elderly man, clad in a rough tweed jacket, knickerbockers and woollen stockings, looking like a gamekeeper, accompanied by a lady and two dogs, passed us. "That's the Squire" said the old woman at the cottage gate. We looked on him with awe. He was Sir Hervey Juckes Bruce, related to the extinct Cliftons through his mother, and lived at Clifton Hall. I did not know then that he was also related to the eccentric Lord Bristol, Bishop of Derry in the eighteenth century. Nor could I know that one day Sir Hervey's second son would marry in Russia, where he was at the British Embassy, the great ballerina, Tamara Karsavina, or that their son was destined to begin a stage career in a play of mine, to be produced thirty-three years after I had seen his grandfather clomp by the cottage.*

We had our tea out in the garden, under an apple tree. The old woman brought us a large brown earthenware teapot. We gobbled up everything. After tea we went to look at Clifton Hall, with its porticoed entrance façade and fountain. The peacocks called from the balustraded terrace garden. I thought of Sir Gervase Clifton, who had fought at the Battle of Bosworth Field, and of great Queen Elizabeth's tribute to his descendant, when speaking of her four Nottingham knights:

---

* Frederick Hervey, fourth Lord Bristol and Bishop of Derry (1730–1803) an eccentric Mæcenas with £80,000 a year. He built a vast mansion at Downhill, Co. Londonderry, and a Palladian villa at Ickworth. He travelled in such state on the Continent that he gave his name to a number of hotels. He spent much time in Italy, dressed as a prelate wearing a white hat edged with purple, a coat of crimson silk, a black sash spangled with silver, and purple stockings. He died at Albano, Italy. "God has created men, women and Herveys," it was said.

Gervase the Gentle
Stanhope the Stout,
Marcham the Lion
And Sutton the Lout.

It was all very romantic, looking at the ancestral home of the Cliftons. We went into the old church and examined the tombs of the Cliftons ranging from the fourteenth century, and shivered before a charnel chamber which showed skulls and bones, erected in 1631 by a Sir Gervase Clifton to the memory of three of his seven wives. Was he a Bluebeard? Awed, we stole out, hand in hand. Somewhere a clock struck the hour and warned us we must be going. It was seven o'clock when we reached home, tired but happy. We had had a lovely excursion. Serena said she would go in by the back door as her shoes were very muddy.

About nine o'clock that evening my mother went to the front door. Presently she returned, rather flushed, and said to my father, who was reading, "Will you go and speak to that awful man!" It was the Nabob, raving about my abducting Serena. Presently my father returned. The calmest of men, he had a glitter in his eye and an air of triumph. He cross-questioned me very closely. When I told him I had spent a shilling on two teas, he laughed. "Taking ladies out is an expensive pastime," he said. My mother asked what he had said to the Nabob, which seemed so effective. "I told him that instead of making such a fuss over two innocent children he should marry the woman he's living with. I heard about that a year ago," he continued, seeing my mother's surprise, "and it appears to be true. He hadn't a word to say."

Poor Serena! I never saw her again. She was not allowed out in the garden. I suppose she went back home. I am sure some boy fell in love with her merry snub-nosed face. But what a fuss over an innocent adventure!

IV

When a boy I often made the excursion to Clifton. It had a fabulous rector, Dr. Rosslyn Bruce, a man of about forty, related to the Squire. He lived in a large Georgian house behind a high brick wall. Inside the grounds he had a menagerie. His hobby was the care and breeding of animals. Horses, monkeys, mice, birds, rats, iguanas, snakes, ferrets, fox terriers, of which he was a champion breeder, a bear, and, once, an elephant, all lived behind that high brick wall. One day I met him carrying a ringtail monkey. Boldly I spoke to him and he took me through the magic door to see the menagerie. He hunted twice a week, knew everybody, was loved by everybody, was cheery and robust, and when one winter he gave a course of lectures on Dante I attended, now a boy of eighteen. He was a racy fluent lecturer and he introduced me to the wonders of Dante's world.

The rector was the grandson of Sir James Bruce, Bart., who had fought at Waterloo. At Oxford he became Secretary of the Union, having contested the presidency with Hilaire Belloc. He rowed for Worcester College and was a fine all-round athlete. Endowed with enormous personal charm and a bohemian sense of adventure, he started work as a bank clerk in Edinburgh but gave it up to take Holy Orders. As a curate in Soho he shared rooms with (Sir) Nigel Playfair, the actor-manager, and with his sister Kathleen Bruce, who was studying sculpture. She became the wife of Captain Scott, the Antarctic explorer, and the mother of Peter Scott, the ornithologist. Bruce was also an early friend of James Barrie, who may have found in him, always full of fun and mischief, 'the boy who never grew up'.

In 1912, after eight years as rector of Clifton, Bruce went to Birmingham and then to Hurstmonceaux, Sussex, the beautiful rectory made famous by the books of Augustus Hare. He lived there until his death thirty-three years later, aged eighty-four.

When I published in 1951 my novel *A Terrace in the Sun* I was astonished to receive a letter from him. He was then eighty and I thought he had long forgotten the small boy to whom he had shown his animals at Clifton. After some complimentary words on my 'Nottingham novel', he reproached me for a liberty I had taken. I had described his nephew, the Squire, driving to church in his carriage with a liveried, cockaded footman on the box seat. "What on earth do you mean by giving Sir Hervey gout, in order to have him drive to church so pompously—nonsense! The Hall was only five hundred yards from the church and he walked through his private gate into the churchyard." He was quite right but in order to give a picture of squirearchal state, having seen Colonel Sir Hervey Bruce (of Clifton descent) drive forth into Nottingham, I had transposed the scene. "I must congratulate you on your career—it doesn't surprise me. You were a most inquisitive, intelligent boy."

The writing was firm. For over eighty years he had brightened the world with his rich personality, whether taming pets, running a campaign for better conditions for stage children, for poor young widows with babies, acting as chaplain to the troops in France, going on missions with Noel Buxton to the Balkans and America, organising a Maypole dance on the village green at Clifton, or lecturing on Dante—"An unpleasant man to live with, I am sure". He had always a contagious zest.

V

I was now in the last year of my school days. I would be fifteen next May and leaving in July. It was a grief to me that I could not have an extra year, as my form master had suggested. It would have been a year of expansion in fields of growing interest, but the *Jogoro* fiasco had shattered any hope of remaining at school. Scholastically, I had not been a success. An examination paper paralysed me. My algebra, mathematics, chemistry, physics, were lamentable. In English Literature, the Essay, General Intelligence, I was easily ahead. "You could do anything if you gave your mind to it," said my form master reprovingly. Nevertheless, in the life of the school I played a vivid rôle. I enjoyed every moment. And I was fortunate in falling into the hands of a sympathetic and tolerant master. I must have tried him severely. Called up to his desk to have a paper corrected, I said, "Sir, your tie is on one side. May I put it right?" "Beau Brummell, that is an impertinence!" "No, sir," I answered, "it is a proof of affection." The form bellowed. He threw up his hands. I put his tie straight, to general applause. We ran together on easy terms of give and take. He never ceased to feed my enquiring mind on quite irrelevant subjects. I never appealed to him in vain. When I went back to address the school, as a 'distinguished old boy', there he was, lined up with the masters, ageing. The smile was the same. I shook his hand and I was warmed to see the pride he had in me. Later, revisiting Nottingham, on a second-hand bookstall I found some of his library, with his notes in the margin, and I learned he was dead. I bought half a dozen books as a souvenir of my boyhood under him.

But those years were far off. I was concerned about my immediate future. What was I going to do? You could not earn a living by being a poet. My father spoke to Lord Henry Bentinck. One of his supporters was a solicitor. I was taken to see him. The result was highly satisfactory. I would go as office boy at five shillings a week, and if I showed promise he would give me my articles and I would become a solicitor. It seemed a wonderful opportunity, but not to me. Perversely, I wanted to write. I had tried to get on two local newspapers, *The Guardian* and *The Journal*. They would have nothing to do with me. So it was to be the Law.

My last day at school dawned. I was in a highly emotional state and felt none of the jubilation of my schoolfellows, who behaved as if they were getting out of prison. The Headmaster sent for me, I went with trepidation. He was an austere figure. I was shown into his study. "Ah," he said, getting up from his desk, peering at me with his keen eyes. "You are leaving us. What are you going to do?" I told him. "Very good, very suitable. You should be a great success," he said genially. "You have been a bright note in the school, your appearance, your manners—" he paused, and added with a smile— "your eloquence. But not exactly a scholar, eh? Well, goodbye, my boy. Good luck!" He shook my hand and walked me to the door. I found myself outside. I had never thought he had been aware of me, and was dumbfounded.

Alas, the unpredictable course of Fate! That man, so disciplined, so admirable a figure, a few years later, in retirement, one morning cut his throat with a razor.

There were no classes on this last morning of school. I had, since the age of eight, contracted a habit of saying goodbye to familiar things when going away. Now I went through the school, the gym, the laboratories, the corridors, classrooms, touching something in all of them, saying quietly "Goodbye". And there were farewells with school friends. The faithful Donald was remaining another year and I was fearful our contacts would be less frequent. He was dependable, and had poise whereas I, imaginative, emotional, faced a hundred deaths, unnecessarily. At last, around noon, when the school was almost empty, there was the parting I dreaded most. I waited until the classroom, in which our desks had been cleared, was empty. Over the frosted half-panel of the door I peered in. My form master sat at his desk busy with some papers. I went in and he looked up. "Ah, Roberts—I wondered what had happened to you," he said, turning in his chair. Surely he could not have believed I could leave without saying goodbye! I walked up to him. "Well, it's a bit sad, isn't it? We shall miss you—torment that you are!" "Have I been a torment, sir? I'm sorry," I answered. He laughed, got up and put an arm over my shoulder. "No, no—I should say—an entertainment. It's been a pleasure teaching you," he said.

We stood there. I wanted to say something. I just couldn't, I, who always had so much to say. The lump in my throat blocked the words. I could hardly see him for swimming eyes. He said nothing for a few moments, and gave me a hug as we crossed to the door. "Thank you for everything, sir. Thank you, thank you," I stammered out. He shook my hand, and, desperate, I escaped through the door. On the half-landing as I went down there was a lavatory. I hurried in, bolted the door and let the tears come.

CHAPTER NINE

The Visitation: 1. Church Langton

I

THERE WERE two volumes on my father's bookshelf of which I took little notice. One was entitled *The History of Market Harborough*, the other *The History of Langton*, by the Reverend Harwood Hill, an antiquarian, published in 1867. On top of these heavy volumes lay a small book entitled *The Visitation of the County of Leicestershire in the Year 1619*. The only interest these volumes had for me was for pressing papers I had gummed together. My father often consulted them, and my mother, watching him turning over the pages, said to me with a twinkle in her eyes, "Don't disturb your father. He's visiting the ancestors."

For me the dead were dead and I could not imagine what interest they might have for him. Later, I received some instruction in these volumes though at the time, a boy of twelve, I was not interested in Thomas Roberts who died in 1460, or Sir William who died in 1633, or Sir Richard in 1644. But from these pages I learned what a pedigree was. There they were, Robertses on Robertses, line on line, from William Roberts *de Stanton Lacy in Comitatu Salop*, around the thirteenth century, descending through several generations until one, Thomas, married an heiress, *Hickson de Sutton Cheynell in Com' Leicest*, and settled at Sutton Cheynell. Marriage of a great-grandson to another heiress brought into the family the estate of Thorpe Langton near Market Harborough.

"You can't trust any pedigree," said my father, showing me the pages. "A lot of Debrett and other such works are flattering fiction. What the genealogist can't find he often guesses at. The murderers, suicides, gaolbirds and blackguards are dropped in the well of Time. Sometimes the compilers miss the main line and get side-tracked with a collateral, like a railway truck wrongly shunted. Since everyone has ancestors everyone has a pedigree, if he can trace it. The Old

Testament is full of 'Isaac, son of Abraham, begat . . .' Wealth was measured by flocks in Abraham's time, and by land since Norman times in England. There were no companies with shares, no stock exchanges, no directors of big businesses. If you owned five thousand acres you were somebody, and when you married an heiress you married more acres. Being 'landed', the families stayed in one place, the deeds they possessed were kept in their houses, in a 'muniment' room. From these it was easy to compile a pedigree. That's how the 'landed gentry' became an institution in our social history. Most of the marriage deeds and wills up to the eighteenth century register the transfer of land and property. If you had none of these you were nobody and no record of you existed."

A 'Visitation' was a check made by the College of Heralds, a corporate body originally established by Richard III. The check made in 1619 had been conducted among the Leicestershire families by William Camden, Clarenceux King of Arms, with two assistants. It was an office with perquisites. "It still is," said my father, and read to me a page from the 'Visitation'—

> Prince Charles for his first entering into the Tiltyard gave to the Kings of Arms, Heralds, the Pursuivants of Arms, twelve scarves of his colours, being those colours, nine yards a piece, of rich taffeta, fringed with deep gold fringe, and to every man a white beaver hat with silver bands and feathers of his colours, and twenty pounds in monie, the 24th of May, 1619.

"They must have looked gayer than those doddering gold-laced and plumed Heralds who go out on to the terrace at St. James's Palace to announce the reign of a new sovereign," he commented.

The front page of *The History of Langton* had a border in bright colours, of the arms of the lords of the manors whose pedigrees were set forth, and there, in the middle of the top row, was the Roberts family coat-of-arms—our 'Ju-Ju' as we called it out of my father's hearing. It was described in the 1619 'Visitation' as *Arms. Per pale argent and gules, a lion rampant sable. Crest. An heraldic antelope's head erased per fess argent and gules.* My father patiently explained what all these heraldic terms meant. It was exciting to learn that I was a young lion rampant.

He knew his way through a labyrinth of names spreading over two pages, "Full of inaccuracies, of course". He taught me the meaning of *filia & haer, uxor*, of *filius ob. sine prole* (no heir), of *renupta* and *relicta*. I wondered about Sir Richard Roberts's sister Lucia, born 1584, first Mrs. Thomas Acres who, widowed, then married Thomas de Chaney, 'alias Giles de Bosworth'. What had he done, causing him to assume another name ? There is no answer out of Time. And how came James Roberts, much farther down the line, to be slain at Maastricht on June 21st, 1747, fighting on the French side, in the Dillon Regiment ? His grandfather had been a captain in King Charles I's Army. "Probably the bad boy of the family, in debt. The Dillon Regiment was the equivalent of the Foreign Legion in those days," said my father. It had been raised in 1690 by Viscount Dillon in support of the exiled James II.

One could go on asking questions. The girls of the family often had delightful names. Susan was recurrent, and there was Jocosa, and Eleanora and Francesca and one, Sence, who seems to have derived her name from a local river. Like my father, I shall always wonder about Katherine who married '. . . Ciampanti, Italiano, de *Com* South Italian.' Where was Signora (or Contessa) Katherine Ciampanti buried ? Did he take her back to Italy ? What kind of a life did she have in Campania, Puglia or Calabria in the seventeenth century ? How different must have been the sun-scorched mountains of her new home from that of Sutton Cheynell's green level fields! And how did Signor Ciampanti come to meet and woo Katherine ? We shall never know.

In my tender years the family history was without interest to me, it was only later that I began to understand my father's obsession. Like my mother and brother I was apt to be amused by his veneration of the family coat-of-arms, crudely painted on a board and framed. Perhaps it was to correct my indifference that he decided, soon after my fifteenth birthday, to make a 'Visitation' of the ancestral places in Leicestershire. He had forgiven me the *lèse majesté* of having been born in Nottingham. I was now approaching an age at which he found me receptive and companionable. Instead of the annual holiday at Skegness he decided to spend part of it in Leicestershire, taking me with him.

Just before my birthday I had been given and taught to ride a cycle. It was second-hand, of the local Raleigh manufacture, a bargain at twenty shillings. I think now that he had the Visitation in view when he bought me the cycle. He occasionally rode one himself, borrowed from a friend. He rode it with singular dignity, very upright and austere. "Don't lean over the handlebars like a lout," he said, admonishingly. It was on cycles that we set forth on August 27th, 1907, a day carefully selected, as it transpired, our baggage restricted to two valises on the carriers. My mother was apprehensive. "You must walk up the hills, and you must not get wet," she said.

We started off at eight o'clock. Our first destination was Market Harborough, some forty miles distant, which bordered the 'Langton terrain' as my father called it, as though we were still landed proprietors. The River Trent sparkled as we went over the bridge. The excursion steamers to Colwick Park had not yet got up steam, the cricket fans were not yet pouring over Trent Bridge. Our first incline was Ruddington Hill, up which we walked and from the summit looked across the vale of the Trent to Nottingham, the Castle on its rock proudly dominating the skyline. There was not a house around us. Two miles out of the city we were in the heart of the country. We passed Clifton with its green, its eighteenth-century brick dovecote with 2,300 nesting places, and came to Bunny, which I thought a delightful name. It had had a famous squire, an eccentric wrestling baronet, Sir Thomas Parkyns. He was as gifted as he was eccentric. He wrote a Latin grammar, built a crazy hall with a castellated tower, and a picturesque school with mullioned windows, in which he had the village children taught the three Rs and some Latin and science. He was an able lawyer, collected stone coffins, but above all was an enthusiastic amateur wrestler. He supported a professional team and had all the village youths taught the art. When he died in 1741 he had planned a standing wall-monument in the church, life-size, showing him in a wrestling stance, with hands extended for grappling.

After Bunny came a famous hill. It was considered so steep that the automobiles then coming into use were taken there for a test by their proud owners. They 'crowed' if their wonder-cars got to the top. I knew its testing quality already, having encountered it in a school paperchase. Needless to say we walked up the hill, with three pauses *en route*. The descent eventually brought us to the village of Rempstone. I had no idea how soon this tiny place was to play a memorable part in my personal history. The village lay back from the main road and was scarcely visible. We had not progressed very far beyond it when my father stopped and got off his cycle. I soon knew why. He took off his cap, breathed deeply, looked around and said with dramatic emphasis—"My boy, we are now on the border of Leicestershire. What air!"

There seemed no difference in the air whatever but certainly there was in him. He drew it in through his nostrils and the happiness suffusing him became visible. Indeed, on that unmarked borderline of the two counties there began a transformation of temperament that endured through the next five days of our excursion.

My father opened the valise on the carrier. To my surprise he had brought two books and a notebook. The books were *The Visitation, 1619* and Hutton's *Battle of Bosworth Field*. The notebook was an oblong manuscript in which he kept notes about the family. My brother called it 'The Ju-Ju Book'. Its entries were most beautifully written. It was indexed. He now opened this. I did not know until that moment with what forethought our excursion was planned. I was now to learn. He looked up and down the road with its leafy hedges on either side. We were on a little bridge over a stream.

"This is the King's Bridge," he said. "It's over King's Brook. It has taken its name from King Richard III. Today is August 27th, but in the Old Style calendar it is now August 16th. If we had been here exactly four hundred and twenty-two years ago we should have seen a most remarkable sight. The Tudor claimant to the throne, Henry of Richmond, had come out of Wales and King Richard was going to meet him. It was the last great battle of the Wars of the Roses, the white rose of the House of Plantagenet and the red rose of the House of Lancaster. For thirty years England had been torn by a conflict in which over 100,000 men had died, a very high percentage of the population in those times. It left the land desolate, the people starving. One bad king is a misfortune. two bad kings in conflict are a great curse. There was little to choose between them. This morning, that is, August 16th, 1485, Richard marshalled his troops in the Market Place at Nottingham. He was fond of Nottingham Castle. It was in the centre of his kingdom and he often kept court there, attended by the local gentry. One of his most faithful supporters was Sir Gervase Clifton. Richard made him a Knight of the Order of the Bath at his Coronation. As you know, his descendants are still at Clifton Hall.* Do you know how the Plantagenets got their name ?"

---

* Clifton was granted as a fief to Alveredus de Clifton by an illegitimate son of William the Conqueror. The manor of Clifton was presented by King John. In 1632 Charles I wrote to Sir Gervase Clifton after a visit, "The greatest pleasure the King took in his entertainment was in your barge and the watermen." Sir Gervase fought with the Royal Army. A descendant, Sir Arthur, was Colonel of the Royals at Waterloo.

I confessed my ignorance. "The founder of the family was named Folk," continued my father. "He lived a century before the Norman Conquest. For his sins a priest ordered him to lash himself with a branch of broom—prickly stuff—in Latin the *genista* plant, hence Plantagenet. Richard was a strange young man. They called him Richard Crookback. He wasn't anything of the sort but he was small, only five-feet-four, sturdy, with his head sunk on his shoulders. He had a lion's courage in battle. But he was a murderer, the two young Princes in the Tower, and all that, though some swear that he didn't do it. Well, who else should? Like most scallywags he had a deep streak of religion. He had intended marshalling his troops in Nottingham Market Place early on the morning of the 15th, but that happened to be the anniversary of Our Lady of the Assumption, and he was a devout Catholic. So he reviewed his troops early on the morning of the 16th, this very day, four hundred and twenty-two years ago. He set off into Leicestershire where, he had learned, Henry Richmond had come out of Wales. Richard came over this very bridge. He liked playing the rôle of king and he rode on a white horse richly caparisoned, coated in mail, wearing his crown like a knight's crest over his helmet. He was attended by a bodyguard. Two divisions of foot soldiers marched in advance, five abreast. Then came the baggage, and after that another two divisions of foot soldiers, their flanks lined by the cavalry, all told, about seven thousand. It must have taken them an hour to pass over the bridge, a procession almost a mile long. They reached Leicester about sunset and there, wisely, Richard rested the night. Well, let's follow him." My father looked at his watch. "It's ten o'clock, we're Richard's vanguard this morning. I suppose this brook took its name from the fact that Richard and his soldiers drank here. Bunny Hill must have made them thirsty."

The notebook went into my father's pocket. "You must remember," he said, "that King Richard was a very young man and young men are apt to be flamboyant. He was brave, a good soldier, and he enjoyed being king. A lot had happened to him in a short time. He married at twenty, he was crowned king at thirty-one. In the same year, 1484, his only son died. He received the stunning news while at Nottingham Castle, his principal residence, in the heart of his kingdom. The next year his wife died and he was killed, aged thirty-two. He had many enemies, he had had a great number of heads cut off and was charged with doing away with his two young

Title page of the manuscript of Polydore Vergil's *History of England*

Polydori Vergilij Vrbinatis Anglice Historie
Liber Primus:

BRITANNIA omnis que hodie Anglia est
insula est in oceano contra gallicum littus
... divisa in quatuor partes ...
quarum unam incolunt Angli: altera Scoti:
Walli: quarta Cornubienses. si omnes aut lin-
gua vel moribus seu institutis inter se differunt. Anglia ... incolam ita nuncupata ...
... est ... quippe que in
duos et triginta dividitur conventus: quos vocant comi-
tatus: in quibus rectores eorum iudicia faciunt incolis: iusque
reddunt. Novem ex his complectuntur ... illud terre ... totum
tum: quod ... in meridiem vergens inter Thamesim flu-
men et mare iacet. Reliqui conventus ea parte Anglie
continentur: que a Thamesi amne usque ad agrum Scoticum
extenditur. Hec autem prima Britannie pars ab ortu et austro:
terminatur mare oceano: ab occidente Wallis et Corn-
bis finibus, a Septemtrione Tueda fluvio: qui Anglos
a Scotis ... dividit ... et si longa prosspi-
gentibus admodum plena ...
... tamen frequentes habet colles: et illos quidem ma-
gra ex parte arboribus vestitos amoenissimos que Vallos
in quibus homines ... sertim montes qui ex parte ...
non ... sed ...
domicilia habent: vicatim habitant: ad evitandos (ut mea
fert opinio) vehementes ventorum flatus: quoniam insula
suapte natura, maxime ventosa est. Vnde fit: ut aque
stes ex nobilitatis per rura incolarum bonos passim ibibant
in mortes:

Anglia

Hic ad tardin
annos ... sunt
omnis una ... qui
altiore ...
contra meridie
est: incipit: et
huc usque producti
... spatio ...
tri trecentum
et viginti miliu
passuum. At pars
hec totius insu-
le optima

nephews lodged in the Tower of London, one the heir to the throne he had coveted. No wonder he was uneasy as he marched to encounter Richmond."

We remounted out cycles. It was a bright, lovely morning. I was excited to know that King Richard, his crown on his head and seven thousand soldiers in line, was following behind.

We had not gone far, coming to the first Leicestershire village of Hoton, when my father suddenly turned left, up a side road. "We're going to Prestwold Hall," he cried over his shoulder. We followed a long park wall on our left until we came to an open drive that led through a wood. After we had gone along this for some way my father got off his cycle by a path leading to a small church that seemed deserted, deep in the wood. "We're going to see the first of the Leicestershire Robertses," he said. "She's Jane Roberts, actually born in Northamptonshire just over the border where her father had married an heiress and settled. Wait here, I'll have to ask for the key at the Hall."

He set off on foot down the drive. I went into the quiet church-yard, walked round the church and suddenly had a view of Prestwold Hall. Before the long façade of the Hall there was an enormous lawn with flower beds. The far side of the lawn had a low balustrade shutting it off from the sweeping meadowland. One could not conceive a setting more noble. Presently my father returned with the key of the church. "It's almost twenty years since I was here," he said. We entered. It was dim, silent, more like a private chapel. My father took out his notebook and sat down. "I'll tell you something about the Skipwiths who once lived here. This church is a jewel and it owes the preservation of its monuments to one of those freak tricks of history, for a Cromwellian got hold of it, and that saved it during the Civil War, and after, from the barbarian Roundheads."

It transpired that the Skipwiths of Prestwold, and Cotes, another nearby property, had been here from the time of Queen Elizabeth. William Skipwith, buried here, had been knighted by James I when coming down from Scotland to succeed Queen Elizabeth on the throne. Sir William's son, Sir Henry, had backed the Royal cause during the Civil War, with disastrous results. He had had to sell the Prestwold estate, owing to heavy fines. The purchaser, Sir Christopher Packe, was a Roundhead and a great supporter of Cromwell. He was a Lord Mayor of London, a Governor of the Merchant Adventurers and one of the petitioners who wanted Cromwell to assume the crown. At the Restoration he lost his honours and retreated to the obscurity and safety of Prestwold. "He was lucky not to lose his head," said my father, "but let's be grateful to him— he saved the Skipwith monument we've come to see." He rose and went to an alcove on the right of the chancel. "Here's Sir William Skipwith. He died in 1610 and his wife put up this monument to him, and to herself! For sheer beauty it ranks with any in the county."

It was certainly a masterpiece of funerary art. The old knight was in armour, with red knickerbockers, his sword at his side. Just below him, projected on a ledge, lay his wife in a mantle and wimple. Sir William, gorgeously attired, had fifteen angels guarding his coat-of-arms. There was an epitaph above. The whole monument was in perfect preservation, a joy to behold. (Plate p. 144.)

> Here lieth the body of Sir William Skipwith of Cotes, Knight, and Dame Skipwith, his last wife being the daughter of John Roberts of Woolstone in the County of Northamptonshire, Esquier. He departed this life in the year of our Lord 1610 and she lived twenty years after him, at whose cost and charges this monument was erected A.D. 1631.
>
> His first wife was Margaret Cave relict of Sir Thomas Cave of Stanford in Leicestershire, Esquier, by whom he had four sons and four daughters, whereof is Sir Henry Skipwith, Knight and Baronnett.

"You see," said my father, "that his second wife, Jane Roberts who paid for the monument, wasn't going to give the first wife a place, although she produced four sons and four daughters. No monument of her, only a mention. Second wives are apt to be like that—so here's Jane as large as life. She certainly got her money's worth."

On an inset tablet above the effigies there were some verses which my father read out. They were written by Sir John Beaumont, a Leicestershire neighbour. The art of writing ran in the family for he was a brother of Francis Beaumont, the dramatist.

> To fame a man who in these gifts excels,
> Which makes the country happy where he dwells,
> We first conceive what names his line adorn,
> It kindles virtue to be nobly born.

This picture of true gentry must be graced
With flattering jewels round about him placed.
A comely body and a beauteous mind,
A heart to love, a hand to give inclined,
A house as free and open as the ayre,
A tongue which joyes in language meet and fayre,
Yet can when need requires with courage bold
To public ears his neighbour's grief unfold,
And these we never more shall find in one,
And yet all these are closed within this stone.

"Sir William's son was made a baronet by James I in 1622 but he was soon out of luck," said my father as we left the chancel. "He was a Royalist and in 1643 entertained Charles I sumptuously, a bold gesture during the Civil War. Cromwell's Parliament fined him £1,114 'for his delinquency', that's about £25,000 to-day and he was compelled to sell Prestwold and Cotes, when in came the Packes."

In the church there was a monument to Sir Christopher Packe, resplendent in the robes of a Lord Mayor of London. There were other Packe monuments; Hussey, kneeling in front of a *prie-dieu*, with his portrait engraved on it, offering to an angel the model of the church which he had restored; a mural of Major Packe leading the charge of his regiment at Waterloo, where he fell. We stopped in front of a monument covered with a loose sheet which my father carefully removed. "I've never forgotten this," he said. "It's to young Charles Hussey Packe. He died at Eton in 1842 when he was about fourteen. The statue's by Westmacott, one of his finest works."

The sheet removed, the recumbent figure of a beautiful boy was revealed. It seemed as if he had just fallen asleep, the young head resting on a pillow, the delicate throat exposed by the open shirt. It mingled pathos and delicacy and caught at the heart. "Poor boy," said my father, replacing the sheet.

Through the open door we saw the sunlight on the vivid green turf as we turned to go out into the living day. "We should be grateful to a family that keeps all these monuments in such fine preservation," said my father, locking the church door.

II

We soon reached Loughborough, cycled through it and took the road to Leicester. We came to Mount Sorrel, a depressing-looking village but it had a charming domed rotunda crowned by an urn, on eight Tuscan columns, an eighteenth-century conceit. Behind it there was a steep hill. We parked our cycles and taking our lunch packets decided to eat on the hill, the straggling village below us. I said something disparaging about the place but my father said it had known its hours of importance. There had been a Norman castle here, King John had slept here, King Richard had been here. It had seen Wolsey, Charles I driven back from Leicester, and Cromwell marching from Nottingham Castle, now in his possession. It was here, having lunched, high above the village and the Quorn country, I began my diary. My mother had given it to me on starting out. "You can make notes of our trip in it," said my father, "and in later years, if you keep it, you will find how much interest and pleasure it will store up for you." I have a lifetime gratitude for the habit then inculcated.

We spent no time in Leicester and struck the southbound road for Market Harborough, but we did not take the main road. We left the city by a small road, Gartree, once the straight Via Devena built by the Romans. It was an almost deserted country road devoid of villages and houses, with green undulating fields, typical of the open Midlands, *sans* wire, a green grass country loved by the Quorn and the Fernie packs.

"Houghton, Billesdon—young George Villiers, Duke of Buckingham, went to school in that village, a son of a Brooksby squire,* Skeffington, Rolleston, Noseley, Carlton Curlieu, the Langtons, this landscape's full of ghosts of dead Robertses," said my father. "When I was twenty I was lent a hard-mouthed nag by a friend at Skeffington and we followed the Fernie. I came home with a broken collarbone, plastered with mud. I was courting your mother and I couldn't put my arm around her for a month!" My father laughed. "We're now crossing the Sence, a Roberts girl took her name from it, though the family preferred Susan and Katherine. I once had an idea of calling you Trent Roberts but your mother vetoed it." We dismounted. The road had almost vanished, the track went over the gated fields. "It picks up again to Carlton Curlieu where we're going," he said.

We were in the Hundred of Gartree. The Roman road had once cut at right-angles a Bronze Age trackway. He began to tell me about

* The Villiers of Brooksby died out after five hundred years and the great house became the home of Admiral Lord Beatty.

the Hundred Courts that met to govern subdivisions of the county. I was bewildered by the terms he used. Pipe Roll, Fiscal Hundred, Bailiwick, Court Leet, Frankpledge, Wapenstake, Soke. Charles Roberts had owned a soke of Thorpe Langton around 1660. All these words were new to me. I had never encountered them in Dr. Annandale. It transpired that Eleanor of Castile, had sublet a farm to William de Boyville until the year of her death in 1290. How did my father know that? A great-great aunt at Skeffington had been Mary Boville and claimed descent from him. Suddenly we were back into Nottinghamshire history for Queen Isabella, whose lover, Mortimer, had been caught and executed by her son Edward III, once owned the Hundred which had belonged to Eleanor of Castile.

I learned all this sitting upon a fence, plagued by August flies. It went down in my diary that night with some additional facts given me from my father's notebook. Queen Isabella's Hundred of Gartree was owned eventually by King James I. He leased it to a William Ireland, whose son, in turn, held a lease for thirty-one years from Charles II. The King gave the rentals to his queen, Catherine of Braganza. In 1677 the High Sheriff of Leicestershire contested the legality of Ireland's lease and was upheld in the Court of Common Pleas. "You can squeeze history out of every Hundred," said my father. "That High Sheriff was your grandfather at eight removes."*

After a rest in the warm afternoon we cycled on to Carlton Curlieu, only half a mile off the Roman road, a pretty little village on the high ridge that looked across the vale to the blue line of the Charnwood Forest. It was a nest of Bales, Robertses and Palmers. "The Palmers are still here," said my father. "There's their house, some say its the finest Elizabethan mansion in the county." We came to a few cottages and red-brick houses near the church and rectory. There was not a soul in sight. The place looked dead. "I'm afraid it's dying out," he said, as we stacked our cycles by the churchyard wall. "This village was flourishing as early as 1066, and even in 1575 when the Bales held the manor."

The church had a fine Norman arch and a tower much restored. Inside there was a splendid alabaster tomb with the effigies of Sir John Bale and his wife Francesca. They died in 1621 and 1629. The old knight lay in armour, his feet resting on a gauntlet. His wife lay just a little behind and above her husband, in ruff, wimple and pleated

* *The Victoria County History of Leicestershire*, Vol. IV.

robe. On a wall panel above the tomb were Sir John's five sons in armour, with one daughter, and a babe in swaddling clothes denoting death in infancy. "Have a look at the youngest son, Edmund. He married Sir Richard Roberts' daughter, Jocosa. His sister, Francesca Bale, married Sir Richard's son, Sir William Roberts of Barwell. His brother George's widow, Elizabeth, married, secondly, Sir William Roberts of Sutton Cheynell, his wife's uncle. If you can work out that you're a clever boy!" said my father, laughing "When you follow the intermarrying among these local families you wonder we were not all born idiots." My father read again from his notebook. "There's another family connection here. Sir Richard's grandson, the Reverend Dr. Roberts, was the rector. He married Ann Palmer, daughter of the Lord of the Manor after the Bales. The poor man had a bad time of it. His wife died in childbirth at twenty-three. Their only son Benjamin, a student at Cambridge, died aged eighteen. The Doctor had trouble during the Civil War. The Cromwellians turned him out of his living but he came back in 1660 and read The Thirty-Nine Articles. One wonders how he existed all those years until the Restoration. Well, that's enough family history for to-day," said my father, closing his notebook. As we left the church he showed me a memorial stone to Ann Roberts, with the Roberts arms impaling those of Palmer. (Plate p. 144.)

Years later, reading Burton's *Description of Leicestershire* (1623) I found something more about Carlton Curlieu:

"I cannot here let pass one observation that has been made of the residents of this town—that all who have been here born have a harsh rattling kind of speech, uttering their words with much difficulty, and whirring in the throat, and cannot well pronounce the letter R; which whether it be by some peculiar property of the water, soil, air or by some secret effect or operation of nature, I cannot well discover. Mr. Fuller seems so certain of the fact, that he places it among the wonders of the county, and thinks it comes from some occult faculty in the elements of the place, as lisping was to the tribe of Ephraim. (Judges XII. 6.)"

That they could not pronounce their Rs is very singular considering there must have been many Robertses around, at the manor and the rectory in the seventeenth century!

III

It was nearly six o'clock when we came into Market Harborough, having passed a sign on the main road that said "To the Langtons", an excursion to be reserved for the morrow. We came to an inn called The Three Swans. It was very old, dating back to the latter part of the fourteenth century. In 1517 it was called Ye Sygne of Swanne and remained known by that name for over two hundred years. The inn sign had been first forged in the seventeenth century. In 1780 two other swans were added to the sign and the inn then became The Three Swans. An outstanding example of fancy iron craftsmanship, it is reputed to be the finest sign in England. The inn actually issued its own tokens known as 'Swannes' for use as change by its customers. It was patronised by royalty and the nobility throughout the centuries, particularly as a venue during the hunting season.

It was the first hotel I had ever stayed at and was an exciting experience. The charges were—Breakfast, 1s., Lunch, 1s. 6d., Dinner, 2s. The room we occupied, with a double bed, was 3s. a night.* We economised by lunching out, buying bread, cheese and fruit from the shops around the market. The hotel fascinated me. There was a Boots with a green baize apron. I knew he was going to be deprived of his prey, our boots! In our valises on the carriers there were shoe-cleaning outfits. The hotel had a coach entrance, a wide archway leading into a long stable yard with sixteen horse boxes. There were bandy-legged little grooms with light grey cloth leggings and long coats with large pockets. They all seemed red in the face. "A doomed breed," commented my father, and pointing to two automobiles by a hand pump, added—"Their executioners!"

After we had washed in our room, and before dinner, we went out. My father seemed to know every inch of the long straggling town. I learned that in the time of Queen Elizabeth it was famous for the making of shoes. "They probably caught the trade from nearby Northampton, the town of footwear," observed my father. "Shoes, horses, and horse-shoes, of course."

We came to the fourteenth-century church, with one of the finest

---

* The Three Swans still flourishes. The lofts over the stables have been converted into an attractive Elizabethan dining-room and there, fifty-eight years later, May 2nd, 1965, I had an excellent lunch which cost 18s.

steeples in England. It was beautiful inside. It had known turbulent scenes during the Civil War. The Royalists under Prince Rupert had plundered the town and camped in the church in 1642. Three years later, after the fatal battle of Naseby, rashly fought at Prince Rupert's prompting, the Royalist cause was lost. Charles I fled to Leicester. The Parliamentarians chased the King's army through Market Harborough, which they occupied, filling the church with their prisoners. The well, where the fleeing Charles watered his horse, at Tur Langton, is still called after him.

We returned in time for supper which we ate in candlelight. The romance of this setting was heightened by a waiter who wore a brilliant red waistcoat and side-whiskers. "A transformed groom," declared my father. After supper I entered up my new diary, plaguing him with questions. While I was writing and he was reading, a slightly intoxicated gentleman came up, bowed to my father and said —"Excuse me, sir, but aren't you severe?" My father rose, bowed in return. "I don't know, sir, for what reason you consider me severe. I don't think my son here would agree. I've always regarded myself as an amiable man!" he replied genially. The merry gentleman exploded into laughter. "Sir, you miscomprehend me! I was asking if you were Sir Vere Isham."

"Alas, no," replied my father. The gentleman apologised, bowed and withdrew. I asked my father who was Sir Vere Isham, and if he looked like him. "I don't know, I've never seen him, but the Ishams are a famous Northamptonshire family at Lamport Hall near here," he answered.

"Sir Vere Isham—it's a wonderful name," I said.

"It is, my boy. With a name like that you want £20,000 a year to support it, and I expect he has!"

I thought of my father's comment fifty-five years later, at a large luncheon party given by my friend A. L. Rowse, in the great dining-hall of All Souls' College, Oxford. My neighbour was Lady Lenanton, Carola Oman, the biographer, daughter of the historian from whose books I had been taught English history. I saw, from a place-card, that her other neighbour was Sir Gyles Isham, who had on his right Agatha Christie. I asked him if he was from Lamport and had his father been Sir Vere. Yes, he was. He seemed to expect me to say something more but I did not wish to hold up the general conversation. He could not know that I was no longer in that noble dining-hall but in a low candle-lit room at The Three Swans, where a waiter in a red waistcoat served us and a bibulous gentleman had asked my father if he was severe.*

IV

When I awoke the next morning my father was shaving and the sun was streaming into the room.

"Now my boy, up you get! We're going ancestor-hunting with the Quorn and the Fernie!" he cried.

He was in a very gay mood, humming some lines of *The Leicester-shire Lass*. Quite a change had come over him in the past year and my mother had been worried by a depression that hung about him. He was by nature a buoyant, cheerful person. Though he said nothing and the subject was taboo, the failure of *Jogoro* had shaken him. But now, during our holiday, he was a changed man, full of little quips, and endlessly relating tales of family and county history. I caught some of his enthusiasm, to his great delight. Those shadowy ancestors were coming alive, and no question I asked went unanswered. I marvelled at his boundless knowledge, as it seemed to me, topo-graphical, architectural and genealogical. To him the past was a living pageant. Endowed with an astonishing memory, a gift I gratefully inherited, he walked easily through a labyrinth of names and dates.

When we emerged after breakfast it was a peerless August day promising cloudless sunshine. Our first task was to provide the lunch, we were taking with us. My father was elated by one purchase, two threepenny pork pies. "Melton Mowbray pork pies have no equal anywhere in the world," he declared. Like its Stilton Cheese it enjoyed a national renown. It was nine o'clock when we set forth on our visit to the ancient terrain of the family, on which I had been well primed. We left Market Harborough behind and when we had gone three miles on the road towards Leicester there was a sign 'To the Langtons'. We turned off and at the end of a long road we saw, on a

* In 1867 in an attic lumber room at Lamport Hall there were found, among a pile of mice-eaten volumes, the only two surviving copies of an unknown 1598 edition of Marlowe's *Hero and Leander*, a 1599 edition of *The Passionate Shepherd*, and a 1599 edition of Shakespeare's *Venus and Adonis*. How did they come to be there? "A likely theory is that these little volumes were part of the collection made by young John Isham, a student at Cambridge in the late sixteenth century, who was reputed to be an avid purchaser of books for both himself and to read to his father, 'the blind Squire'"—*In Search of Christopher Marlowe*, by A. D. Wraight and Virginia F. Stern (Macdonald and Co.).

169

rise, a noble tower. It was the tower of St. Peter's Church at Church Langton, our first destination.

I had already been told much about three remarkable rectors of that village. One of them was the Reverend William Hanbury and presently we came to a delightful rectory built by his son about 1795. Young Hanbury had been his own contractor. It was built of red brick with stone facing. A pediment crowned the two-storied front. There were five bays, a Venetian window, a balustrade above the doorway with a fanlight, and a frieze. The eighteenth century can show no rectory more symmetrically beautiful. (Plate p. 225.)

V

There were two other notable rectors of Church Langton who played their part in history long before the astonishing William Hanbury. One of them was Polydore Vergil, an Italian. He was born in Urbino about 1470. His father was in the employment of the magnificent Duke Guidobaldo da Montrefeltro of Urbino. Young Vergil, after completing his studies at the universities of Padua and Bologna, worked as secretary at the court. In 1492 he went to Rome serving as Chamberlain to Pope Alexander VI. He was ordained a priest and in 1498, still in the Pope's service, published his *Proverbiorum Libellus* or *Adagia*, a slim quarto printed in Venice. It was a collection of proverbs and epigrams of famous classical authors. It proved useful to preachers and public speakers wishing to strike a cultural note and rapidly ran into many editions and translations. Unfortunately, it led to a dispute with Erasmus who declared that Vergil had plagiarised his own *Adagia* but eventually the dispute was settled amicably, Erasmus admitting that he had not heard of Vergil's book when he published in 1508 his own. Thereafter they were lifelong friends.*

The year following his first success Vergil published, in Venice, in 1499, *De Inventoribus Rerum*. The first book had been in the nature of an anthology, the second was an original work. It was a resounding success and established his name throughout Europe. Some thirty editions were sold by the time of his death fifty-six years later. It was translated into a dozen languages. Some of its contents offended

* When Erasmus left England in 1500 he was outraged by having to surrender to the Customs at Dover all his earnings. His indignation was expressed in a collection of 'sayings' which became the basis of his *Adagia*. The rapacity of English taxation is no novelty.

the Church and it was put on the Index, which caused a censored edition to be published but nothing stopped its triumphant march. It was almost encyclopaedic in its scope, a long book of five hundred pages, with some singular statements such as that Abraham invented mathematics and geometry, etc., but its reception was universal. It ran through three editions in the first year. An English edition appeared in 1546.

Vergil came into the service of Pope Alexander VI probably through the influence of his kinsman, Adrian di Castelli, who had been sent in 1488 as Papal Nuncio to England, where he became popular with Henry VII. The Pope appointed Castelli the Collector of Peter's Pence, the tribute the English Church sent to the Pope. He also acted as Henry VII's agent in Rome. He was given the see of Hereford and on his return to Rome received a cardinal's hat, becoming Cardinal da Corneto.* Castelli employed Vergil on several missions and in 1502 sent him to England as his Deputy-Collector of Peter's Pence.

At that time Castelli's star was in the ascendant. He enjoyed the confidence of Henry VII. His recommendation of Polydore Vergil to the English Court carried great weight. Agreeable, urbane, clever, an established author at thirty, the young Deputy-Collector was soon in favour with the King. In 1503 he was presented to the living of Church Langton. He became a man of many affairs. Agent at the English Court for Castelli, he looked after his patron's interests, and when in 1504 Castelli was translated from Hereford to the see of Bath and Wells, Vergil acted as his proxy at the enthronement. He soon had fingers in many pies. He obtained a Bull for the foundation by Lady Margaret Beaufort, mother of Henry VII, of St. John's College, Cambridge, and he bought English horses for the Marquess

* The English visitor to Rome has cause to recall Cardinal da Corneto. When going down the Via della Conciliazione he passes the noble Palazzo Torlonia. It was built for the cardinal in 1496. It was here that he gave the supper party that had such tragic results. On August 17th, 1503, he entertained Pope Alexander VI and his son Caesar Borgia. The guests drank poisoned wine, as well as the host. The Pope died. The cardinal and Caesar Borgia recovered. It was believed that the latter, sending the cardinal a present of wine, had sought to poison him, but the plot went awry. Some years later Corneto was involved in a plot to dispose of Leo X. He presented his palace to Henry VIII for an English Embassy and Wolsey spent great sums on it. Early in the nineteenth century Prince Torlonia, the banker, acquired it and gave sumptuous balls there. Thackeray, a guest, used it for *Vanity Fair*, with Becky Sharp attending a reception.

of Mantua. It would seem that some of his transactions were question-
able in the eyes of the law. On June 13th, 1504, he was prosecuted
by the Barons of the Exchequer for dealings in the black market,
having done some exchange business at his lodging on behalf of
Florentine merchants. He had also cashed a bill for 2,000 gold ducats
drawn upon London, paying out £450, an infringement of the
exchange regulations that has a familiar ring to-day. The case against
him dragged on until 1509 but he was a man of some importance,
had 'a friend at Court', and secured the King's pardon.

His Deputy-Collectorship of Peter's Pence was no sinecure. He
was to be the last of them in England. He also had to arrange for
Bulls, Indulgences, marriage decrees and the collection of the much
disputed Pence, which Rome insisted upon but which England
increasingly opposed. "No one wants to pay it. I can't send you what
I don't receive," he wrote to Castelli in 1515. It may not have been a
very remunerative post but it carried with it great prestige. Those
wanting anything from Rome found Vergil their man.

Alas, in 1508 Julius II appointed another Collector but Vergil was
not going to be deprived of his post without a fight. A very firm
letter from the Pope ordered him to relinquish his office to another
and on April 19th, 1509, before the Archbishop of Canterbury, the
rector of Church Langton gave it up. Three years later he succeeded
in getting it back again and held it until Henry VIII's break with
Rome, when it was abolished. Meanwhile, he had not been doing
badly for himself. In 1507 he obtained prebends both in Hereford
and Lincoln Cathedrals, and in 1508, on Castelli's urging, he was
installed as Archdeacon of Wells with a prebend in the same cathedral. He presented hangings for the choir walls bearing his arms, 'a
laurel tree vert, on ground argent, supported by two lizards proper'.
In 1510 he became naturalised, being excused the usual subsidy
demanded of foreigners. In 1513 he obtained a prebend at St. Paul's.
This was most convenient for he lived in a house near the Churchyard.* It is not likely that Church Langton saw much of its rector.

* St. Paul's Churchyard was then the centre of printers, publishers and
booksellers, their shops and stalls displaying trade signs. It was the cultural
centre of the city and continued so into the seventeenth century, a haunt
of the Elizabethan wits and dramatists, known to Marlowe, Jonson, Shakespeare and their aristocratic patrons. In Vergil's day the old cathedral had a
spire, demolished by lightning in 1562. The aisles were a meeting-place
and thoroughfare for merchants and gossips, and a favourite route down to
the river for the hire of boatmen.

The early clash with the Exchequer notwithstanding, he enjoyed a high reputation for his probity, at a time when scandal touched many of the clergy; nor were his enemies, ecclesiastical and literary, able to destroy his character. Throughout all this period he was hard at work on his *History of England*, and his title to fame resides not in the offices he collected but in the pioneer work he achieved as an historian. He broke new ground and blazed a trail for many followers. He had begun his great work soon after his arrival in England, encouraged by Henry VII, who was not disinterested in having the advent of the Tudor reign creditably put on record. Vergil closed his *History* with the reign of Henry VIII. Begun in 1506 it reached completion in manuscript, in its first form, in 1513, being written in Latin and entitled *Anglicae Historiae*. It proved to be a highly influential work and represented a new fashion in Humanistic Latin as practised by Italian scholars who endorsed the doctrine of the sanctity of kings, and God's care of just princes. In this spirit the immigrant Vergil set the fashion for all subsequent Tudor historians and their successors. Henry VII was presented as an upright king under God's providence. England had become the blessed isle. Shakespeare, at second-hand, was one of Vergil's heirs. In his historical plays he accepted the acid portraits of Richard III and Cardinal Wolsey, at times exercising poetic licence to show princes as appointed by Providence to lead their subjects.

In 1514 Vergil made a visit to Rome. He carried with him a letter of commendation from Henry VIII to Pope Leo. Apart from his desire after twelve years of absence to see his family in Urbino he had other objects. He played some part in obtaining the bestowal later of a cardinal's hat for Wolsey. After paying his respects to the Pope he visited his native Urbino in August. He had brought the manuscript of his *History* with him and arranged for the duke's librarian, Veterani, a renowned copyist, to make a copy of his book, his purpose being to present it to Henry VIII. It would seem this was never done, for there is no record of the King ever having received a copy nor of its presence in England. If it was made it went into other hands. Vergil gave his brother Francesco six hundred florins for the endowment of a chapel in the cathedral, and then departed, leaving his manuscript with Veterani. He was back in England in February, 1515. Two months later he was a prisoner in the Tower. Something had gone seriously wrong. A letter he had written from England to Castelli, containing indiscreet references to Wolsey, whom he disliked, had been intercepted. The news of his imprisonment created a sensation in Rome. His house had been sealed and his goods confiscated. But he had staunch and powerful friends. Pope Leo X, Cardinal de' Medici and the University of Oxford appealed for his release. In September Wolsey got his cardinal's hat, which may have mitigated his ire. Vergil was released on Christmas Eve in the same year. He became a determined enemy of Wolsey, and took his revenge when he came to write in his *History* about the cardinal. Its bitter tone influenced English historians in their estimate of Wolsey for over three hundred years.

Henry VIII and the Pope were still on good terms, the Pope appointing the King 'Defender of the Faith', a title to which he stuck even after the break with Rome, and which we still boast on our coinage. Soon after his release Vergil was summoned to Rome again. He was back in England within eighteen months. He had retrieved from Veterani the manuscript of his *History*. He must have been deeply concerned about it owing to events in Urbino. One holds breath at the thought of the hazards of that manuscript's journey across Europe, by horseback, with the chances of theft and murder in an Italy constantly subjected to remorseless *condottieri*. In 1502, soon after Vergil had arrived in England for the first time, the city of Urbino had been sacked by Caesar Borgia. Then again, in the spring of 1516, the city was besieged by papal troops, and at the end of May capitulated. Vergil visited Italy soon after this invasion. He would have lost in the rape of Urbino the manuscript of his *History* but for Veterani's astuteness. The duke's librarian had deposited it for safekeeping with the nuns of St. Clare in Urbino. Vergil brought it back with him to England in December, 1517, and there it remained until 1533 when, lengthened and dedicated to Henry VIII, he took it to Basle for printing.

It is interesting to follow the subsequent history of this manuscript. In 1613 it was presented by Vergil's grand-nephew, Marc Antonio, to the sixth Duke of Urbino, Francesco Maria II. This duke, the last of the great house of Montefeltro, whose most splendid figure, Federigo, the *condottiere* with the broken nose, was immortalised by Piero della Francesca's brush, had a dismal history. He was educated in Spain and returned to his duchy, haughty, piously superstitious, pettily punctilious in etiquette and morose in character. He had fought in the battle of Lepanto with his friend Don John of Austria. Deserted by his wife, Lucrezia d'Este, he married again having a worthless son for whom he virtually abdicated. The youth was a rake and a buffoon. He squandered the ducal wealth and filled the palace with harlots, dying of apoplexy when only eighteen, in 1623. His father, stunned, returned to his duchy but the next year, under pressure from a covetous Pope, abdicated. When he died, seven years later, in 1631, his duchy was added to the papal states. The ducal library, with other treasures, went into the possession of the Vatican and is known now as the Urbino Collection.* There in 1966, four hundred and thirteen years after it had left England finally, I was permitted to examine the autograph manuscript.

Professor Denys Hays in his learned study of Polydore Vergil has completely demolished subsequent statements that the script is in the hand of Veterani, and not of Vergil as his grand-nephew certified. It is in two folio parts, which are bound in three volumes, weighing about twenty pounds. The first volume has three hundred pages, on vellum sheets each holding some three hundred words, written in black ink in monkish latin script, on level lines. This volume has a frontispiece, with a sketch of the duke's arms at the top and of Vergil's arms, a tree with two lizard supporters, at the bottom. There is a six-page prefatory note by the grand-nephew, dated 1613. There follows a six-page preface by Polydore Vergil addressed to Henry VIII. Then he begins his *History*. At the top of every vellum sheet, on both sides, there is written the name of the Virgin Mother, following the sign *IHS*.

The second volume also has a frontispiece, with the grand-nephew's introduction. Vergil begins again at page 1 and goes to page 300. This manuscript is bound in two parts. It carries marginal notes, as in the first volume, made by the duke's librarian, Veterani, possibly for the copyist or, at Vergil's request, for the printer. It was a moving experience to turn the pages of this manuscript on a bright Roman spring morning of 1966, and see the long dead author's beautiful hand-writing. (Plates pp. 160, 161.)

In 1517 Vergil's patron, Castelli, was again in trouble. He had been involved in a conspiracy against the Pope. He extricated himself and fled to Venice, disguised as a fool. He was deprived of his cardinalate, and Wolsey, who hated him, took his see of Bath and Wells for himself. Castelli remained in Venice, the home of all anti-papal exiles, until the death of Leo X in 1521. Then, a new Pope on the throne, he set out for Rome but was murdered on the way. Thus

* Appendix I.

175

ended the life of a man of taste and letters, a renowned humanist and always a true friend of his protégé, Polydore Vergil.

In 1522 Vergil was back in full favour at the English Court, but storms gathered on the horizon. He avoided taking the Oath of Supremacy. He kept quietly at work. Treading neutral ground, he added a preface to a new edition of his second book, flattering the King and Wolsey. Throughout the ensuing storm, when Henry broke with Rome, and Wolsey fell into disgrace, Vergil showed himself to be an adept mariner. He sailed safely into the era of Edward VI, enjoying his favour. He lived to see the ascension to the throne of 'Bloody Mary'. His *History*, the work of twenty-eight years, had been published in Basle in 1534, in its Latin version. This was still the language of the scholars of Europe; the vernacular, rapidly growing, had not yet invaded the field of learning. Vergil, a stylist, had written in the revised classical Latin of the Humanists. It influenced the English prose of those who translated his work.

The first edition of the *History* covered events up to 1509, which saw the opening of Henry VIII's reign. Vergil informed his readers that he had performed the task in order not to waste his leisure, as if the rector of Church Langton had ever known such a thing! He spent six months collecting his material before he began to write. He was tolerant and seems to have been impressed by the character of the English people. He remarked on their piety—"I believe no nation to-day so devoutly and diligently observes all matters that have to do with worship . . . They are the most Christian, most religious."

Vergil's work was not without its sharp critics, especially following the break with Rome, when any Italian was suspect. He was charged with "the Romish blasphemy", and called "the most rascal dogge knave in the worlde". A scurrilous epigram contrasted the two Vergils:

> Maro and Polydore bore Vergil's name:
> One reaps a poet's, one a liar's fame.

They even charged that he had deliberately burned the old records in order that his errors should not be brought to light. But his work was too great an innovation to be displaced by abuse.* Moreover, his character, while not without blemish, was sound. He had risen

* Appendix II.

from a mere priest to an archdeacon in a foreign land and became the trusted friend of kings. His literary achievement was considerable and he had proved himself to be a very reliable man of affairs. He was a Londoner, with a club, Doctors' Commons in Knightrider Street, and a house by St. Paul's Churchyard, near the bookshops and the printers. He knew everybody, from the Venetian ambassadors to the wandering scholars, who all made a point of calling on him. He must have been acquainted with Raphael, also born in Urbino, whom he mentioned in his work with high praise, and who was his junior by thirteen years, and with the celebrated Prince of Courtiers, Baldassare Castiglione, whom the Duke of Urbino sent to Henry VII, in 1505, to receive by proxy the Order of the Garter.

Around 1546 Vergil began to think about a return to his own country, that he might die there in his old age. He started making preparations. They treated him well, even generously considering that he was a Catholic of the old Faith now under suppression. He received a grant for life of the archdeaconry of Wells, to enjoy its rents and profits without fear of forfeiture, a favour granted by Edward VI, who now came to the throne, for his services to Henry VII and Henry VIII. He received in 1550 a warrant permitting him to depart. It warmly recorded his "long, painful and acceptable service". The next year he was given one hundred marks due to him and three hundred crowns of the royal bounty for travelling expenses. But his affairs still delayed him and it was not until March, 1553, that he departed from England, in ferment over Lord Northumberland's bid for the throne. In May he reached his native Urbino. From there he wrote his last known letter to the new Queen Mary who ascended to the throne on July 6th. Dated August 5th, 1553, it is an old man's letter to the Queen, full of political wisdom and hope for a happy reign. He could not foresee that within two years of her succession the Queen would have burnt at the stake, as a heretic, his successor in the Church Langton living. Vergil died in Urbino on April 18th, 1555, at the ripe age of eighty-five, receiving full funeral honours from the reigning duke. He was laid to rest in the cathedral. A new edition of his *Anglicae Historiae* was published that year at Basle. He had been able to bring it down to 1538, describing most of the tremendous events of Henry VIII's reign.

For more than three centuries Vergil's pioneer work was quarried by English historians. One wonders what gave him the most pleasure in his long industrious life, the comfortable sinecures including the

Church Langton living, his friendship with three English kings, his archdeacon's stall in Wells Cathedral or his prebend at St. Paul's. Perhaps it was none of these. In 1526 he had made a present of a white horse to Erasmus, as had his friend Thomas More before him. In return he received the dedication of a new work by Erasmus. It must have given him great pleasure and scholastic kudos. It read: "To the accomplished and learned patron of scholarship, Polydore Vergil of Urbino". Thus across Europe one scholar saluted another.

VI

Vergil was succeeded as rector of Church Langton by Lawrence Saunders in 1535. Following the break with Rome the clergy were called upon to recognise Henry VIII as supreme head of the English Church. Sir Thomas More was beheaded for his refusal, in 1535. Almost miraculously Vergil survived this upheaval but he lost the living of Church Langton. The new rector was the son of Thomas Saunders, a family that had resided at nearby Shangton for a couple of centuries. His brother, Sir Edward, became Chief Baron of the Exchequer. Saunders was educated at Eton and King's College. After Cambridge he was apprenticed to Sir William Chester, a London merchant, but it soon became evident that he had no vocation for business. The young man's desire was to enter the Church. Chester generously returned his indentures and he took up the study of Hebrew and Greek to prepare himself for the priesthood. He was ordained and appointed to the living of Church Langton. He resided at the rectory with his wife and was much beloved by his parishioners.

The living of All Hallows, Bread Street, London, was also given to him in 1553. Conscientiously opposed to pluralities, he would have declined this second living but about that time Edward VI died and Mary, a Catholic, came to the throne. The Church was now threatened by the ascendancy of the Romanists. In order to frustrate any attempt on their part to obtain All Hallows, Saunders decided to administer both parishes. This involved frequent journeys between Church Langton and London. Zealous and fearless, he was soon marked down by the Papists. One Saturday, on entering London, he was accosted by Sir John Mordaunt, a Queen's Councillor, who demanded where he was going. "To my cure in London, to instruct my people according to my duty," he replied. He was warned against proceeding and advised not to preach in his church. Saunders ignored the warning and the next morning preached provocatively against the Church of Rome, comparing its dogmas with the voice of the serpent. His challenge was taken up. On entering the church again the same day he was arrested. He proved obdurate during his examination, denouncing papacy. "Take away this frenzied fool to prison!" cried Gardiner, the Lord Chancellor.

He was in the Marshalsea prison for fifteen months. No friends were allowed to see him. A gaoler, touched by his condition, one day took the baby from the arms of Saunder's wife and carried it to its father in his cell. He was greatly moved and declared he would rather own such a boy than have two thousand pounds given to him. Towards the end of his imprisonment he was allowed to write to Cranmer, Ridley and Latimer, prisoners of the Crown in Oxford. "In my humble wise I salute you, most reverend fathers in Jesus Christ our Lord. Immortal thanks and everlasting praises be given unto our Father of mercies who has made us meet to be partakers of the inheritance of the saints in Light." Just before his execution he wrote to his wife—"Dear wife, rejoice in the mercies of our Christ, and ye also my dear friends. Pray for us, everybody. We are shortly to be despatched hence."

He was condemned to be burnt at Coventry and was taken there by the Queen's Guard. Throughout the whole journey he was in a state of religious ecstasy. On the way to the stake, outside the town, he threw himself on the ground to pray, and when the Sheriff charged him with being a heretic, he replied, "I hold no heresies but the blessed gospel of Christ. That hold I, that believe I, that I have taught, and that I will never revoke." On coming to the stake and about to be chained, he embraced it and kissed it. "Welcome cross of Christ! Welcome everlasting life!" he cried.

Foxe recorded in his *Book of Martyrs*, "With that, being fastened to it and fire put to him, full sweetly he slept in the Lord." The Christians of another ilk, to increase his torture by prolonging it, burnt him with green and smouldering wood. This happened on February 8th, 1555, the year of Vergil's death. One wonders whether in far away Urbino he heard of the burning of his successor at Church Langton. Three years later Queen Mary was dead and Queen Elizabeth was on the throne. Cardinal Pole, Archbishop of Canterbury and Papal Legate, fled. It was now the turn of the other Christians to do some burning, hanging and quartering of their victims, in an equal state of ecstasy.

179

CHAPTER TEN

The Visitation: 11. The Amazing Rector

I

HOWEVER REMARKABLE the history of Vergil and Saunders, two of the rectors of Church Langton, that of another, the Rev. William Hanbury, two centuries later, is perhaps even more so. He lived only fifty-two years and filled them with an astonishing achievement, dying in 1778. At an early age he showed a passion for planting and gardening, not exceptional hobbies in a country rector. He came to Church Langton in 1753, buying the manor when he was twenty-seven. America was still a British colony. Society was nicely ordered, with "the rich man in his castle, the poor man at his gate", as a later hymn put it.

Hanbury took up his hobby seriously, consulting seedsmen and nurserymen, learning about layering, grafting and budding. He conceived the idea of raising large sums of money by horticulture, and applying the profits to the building of a great minster on the land at Church Langton. Many thought he was mad but he persevered in his plan, undeterred by criticism. He formulated a bold enterprise and solicited the aid of the surrounding gentry. Some gave it, some branded him a lunatic. Within five years he had created plantations worth £10,000. His scheme for the Minster was worked out to the last detail. The first £1,500 raised from the plantations was to be devoted to the decoration of his church, the support of an organist and schoolmaster, and, if the income reached £4,000, the foundation of a local hospital. With £10,000 in hand he would build schools in Langton and other places. To-day out of Hanbury's Charity Endowment, from an income of some £2,000, there are payments for books, carting water, scholarship grants, an organ account, a library, a hospital grant, a librarian's salary, and for beef vouchers! This is a little that still remains from so much ambitious planning.

Have ever such grandiose ideas come out of a country rectory?
Hanbury had many schemes for raising money. He arranged for
an oratorio to be given at Church Langton on September 26th and
27th, 1759 that would attract people from all the surrounding towns,
thus anticipating the modern craze for music festivals. It was all
most carefully planned. On the first day when the audience was
seated an orchestra would play the Overture of Handel's *Esther*.
This had been composed around 1720 while he was living with the
Duke of Chandos as director of music at his palace at Cannons. He
was the contemporary craze, "Handel is the unapproachable master
of all masters; go to him and learn to produce great effects with little
means," said Beethoven. Handel had only recently died, in April
1759, and been buried in Westminster Abbey. He therefore was a
topical attraction. After the *Esther* Overture the Psalms would be
chanted and the *Gloria Patri* would be performed with full chorus,
instruments and voices. After that the new organ would be opened,
the voluntaries played, and "the variety of stops be showed off by
the Reverend Mr. Felton from Herefordshire". The sermon would
be preached by the Reverend Slaughter Clarke, vicar of Thedding-
worth. Then the Deed of Trust would be delivered, after which a
Grand Hallelujah would be struck off and Handel's *Coronation
Anthem* would conclude the ceremony of the first day. On the second
day the sacred oratorio *Messiah* would be performed.

Did anything of this happen? Indeed it did. Mr. Hanbury
describes the momentous morning of the 26th. It would seem that
neither Salzburg, Edinburgh nor Glyndebourne has known such
frenzy. "Swarms of footmen, horses, chariots, etc., came flocking in
from every point. Neither was the chain transitory, since a person
upon any eminence might see others appear to keep up the thread
winding off; for as fast as a group of a greater body in this chain
advanced, fresh groups at the farthest extent of view would succes-
sively show their heads; noises from every part were heard but
particularly the great turnpike road rattled with the sound of chariots,
horses, etc. The ladies and gentlemen came out of their vehicles of
different sorts, all fully dressed, and a most brilliant appearance was
every minute collating."

The ceremony began by the Reverend Hanbury coming out of his
rectory in full canonicals, attended by his trustees. "We went in
procession to the church by pairs, preceded by two vergers with
white wands. The Overture was struck up by the instruments the

moment we entered the church, and as few there had ever heard anything of the kind by such a band, most of them were struck into seeming statues. Some of the common people were frightened, and hurried out of the church with all speed, for hearing the kettledrums, which they took to be thunder, and the trumpets sounding in the midst of such heavenly noise of instruments, they thought of what had been reported, that the Day of Judgement was really come indeed. But some stayed and their raptures, devotion and amazement were heightened, and they declared it was heaven. The same effect was perceived in the *Anthem* and *The Hundredth Psalm* though they unanimously declared that if one part was more solemn than the other, it was, upon the immediate starting off of the *Grand Chorus*, my delivering of the Deed. The sermon was preached by the Reverend Slaughter Clarke and after that the *Coronation Anthem* was performed and the benediction closed the service."

It had been a triumphant day for Mr. Hanbury, embarking upon the raising of funds to build the minster of his dreams. He records the events of the following day. "The next day being equally fine, company of all sorts flocked in with redoubled force. All were in full dress, and more than two hundred coaches, chariots, landaus and postchaises were counted at Church Langton, a sight which I believe I may safely say never graced a country village before; neither perhaps had any church in England so splendid a congregation that was composed of so many and such fine women, as well as a proportional number of gentlemen; for the number of beautiful ladies was very great, which occasioned the meeting to be afterwards so much talked of. The time of the beginning of the performance being advanced, the Overture was struck off, and then the different parts of that noble oratorio, *Messiah*, succeeded. The music on so solemn a subject, by so good a band, was most affecting, and to see the effect it had on different persons was astonishingly moving. An eye without tears I believe could hardly be found in the whole church, and everyone endeavoured to conceal the emotions of his heart, drooping heads to render the tears unobserved."

Alas, despite so tremendous an effort there were mean spirits about, as he sadly related. "Upon summing up the profits and expenses of the whole meeting they were found nearly to coincide. For although the company was numerous, the second day at crown tickets, and though a collection was made, and we had a benefaction of ten guineas sent a day or two before the meeting, the expenses of so grand a band of performers from different parts of England, together with the charge of erecting temporary galleries, advertising, etc., were so great we had but just enough to make our way clear . . ."

Undeterred, there was a third day's performance. "*Esther* was substituted for *Samson*, parts of the latter being found wanting or incorrect. Alas, the notion prevailed that *Esther* was not worth hearing, so that the audience for the third day amounted to no more than 120 persons. This alteration was a considerable loss to the scheme and, notwithstanding we had three *Oratorios*, summing up our expenses and profits, we gained only fifteen pounds and a few shillings."

Undaunted, Hanbury promoted another music festival in 1762 at Leicester, where he raised one hundred pounds, and the next year at Nottingham, but this proved a failure. He found himself five pounds one shilling out of pocket. Meanwhile the rector had learned something about human nature. After the first performance of *Messiah* the collection at the doors was so small that it was not thought prudent to publish the amount. "It must have been worth something to watch the various manœuvres of those who would not give," wrote a neighbouring clergyman. "Some gave halfpence, one gentleman dropped in a farthing, as a token of his contempt. One lady had had a bad run at cards. A gentleman, whose daughter had lately been married to a lord, came to the front porch, then to the chancel door, and so to the back aisle and the steeple door, but was everywhere repulsed by the apparition of a trustee with a collecting box, so, returning to the south door, he waited till he could burst out with a greater crowd than usual."

The poor rector had also received rebuffs. At Nottingham he had asked in vain for the use of the principal church. "The theatre, however, was very commodious and proper for our purpose, though I cannot but take notice of the goodwill of the Presbyterians who, upon hearing that the chuches were denied to us, convened a body of their elders and with one consent agreed to offer their meeting-house."

There appears to have been something of a panic at the performance in Nottingham. "The doors were no sooner opened than the ladies thronged in very fast and, notwithstanding we had so strong a guard, we found we had difficulty in receiving them fast enough. In less than a minute every lady exerting herself to be first, the crowding at the door was so violent that all order was for the time destroyed.

The constables used their utmost endeavours, by crossing staves, etc., and we were all forced to assist them in repelling what I believe was never heard of before—a powerful, polite female mob of ladies (those who are in the habit of attending the Queen's Drawing Rooms have seen many such since). Our assistance, however, was in vain for in a few seconds, they bore away four constables, with their staves, three or four porters, besides four gentlemen who used all their skill and strength to keep them out."

Mr. Hanbury was sickened of music festivals. He quarrelled with his conductor. His trustees were also getting nervous. The making of great plantations was sensible enough but this vast minster he planned out of the proceedings of the sale of trees, plants and seeds? Well, he had not wholly failed. The music festivals had served one purpose. They advertised the products he had for sale on his plantations. After the first Festival he announced: "Mr. Hanbury's collection being now open for sale, notice is hereby given to the public that forest trees of all sorts, both deciduous and evergreen, American plants, flowering shrubs, greenhouse plants, fruit trees, perennial flowers, roots and seeds of annuals, will be disposed of at very easy and reasonable rates. *N.B.* The curious in the kitchen garden may be supplied with every article in that way."

'The curious in the kitchen garden' came to see. His plantations proved highly remunerative, and the day of his great foundation, the minster church, seemed not far off. For this building he had not overlooked a detail. His trustees were filled with zeal by the early results. On the morning of the first Quarterly Meeting, June 8th, 1767, the deeds deposited and enrolled in Chancery, the day was saluted with an eight-bell peal by the youths of Church Langton, and a flag was hoisted from the tower. At half-past eleven the trustees went in procession to the church, again preceded by two vergers with white wands, and heard a sermon. They then dined with the Founder, and after dinner drew up certain Regulations, three of them being exceedingly wise: that no money should ever be lent to any trustee; that no money should be invested in the Stocks or Public Funds; that the Society would never meddle in Elections.

At other meetings they enlivened the proceedings with an entertainment. On September 16th, 1769, after the sermon, "Miss Hanbury, being then thirteen years, played Voluntaries on the organ and sang a solo anthem." The trustees then dined with the Founder "on venison and game sent from every part." At another meeting Miss Hanbury again performed. This time she was joined by her brother, Master Jackey Hanbury—"Then seven years old, he distinguished himself by his singing in the choruses." At a later meeting Jackey and his sister sang a duet.

Mr. Hanbury's fame began to spread. In 1769 he was offered a thousand pounds for the manuscript copy of his book on planting and gardening, which he refused, this long before the days of rich American institutions with funds questing for employment, and endowed professors desperately seeking themes. He was also given an honorary M.A. by St. Andrew's University.

He now presented his trustees with completed plans for the great minster and public buildings he hoped to found with money derived from the plantations. The minster was to be 600 feet long, the altitude of the middle aisle 153 feet, the lantern tower 430 feet. The floors were to be made of marble as also the pillars—"the windows the grandest that can be devised." The public buildings were to have four great domes over the four entrances into the four quadrangles. He listed the buildings: a Hospital or Convent for poor women, a Library, a Lodging for professors, a Public School, a Museum, a Hall or general dining-room—"In this trustees and professors are to dine together on public days at the Charity's expense." There was to be an Observatory, a Music School, a Writing School, an Infirmary, a Physic Garden, a Printing Office, and a Temple of Religion and Virtue, two hundred yards long.

The Founder then listed the endowments: To Schools forever, £1,000. Organs forever, £1,000. Beef forever, £100. Professors of Grammar, Music, Botany, Mathematics, Antiquity, Poetry, £150 each. Organist's salary, £100. Eight Singing Men, £400. Choristers, £300. Young Maids on their Marriage, £100. Books for the Library, £2000. Pictures for the Temple of Virtue, £2,000. Curiosities for the Museum, £1,285. Trustees monuments, £1,000. Writing Master, £50, a steward, eight porters, four sacrists, £280. Wax candles for the church in winter, £250. If the income from the plantations rose to £42,000 clear money, then there were to be 12 Canons, 24 Fellows, Precentors, Almsmen, a Florist, etc., added to the establishment. The poor women admitted to the Convent were to have their allowance increased by a shilling to three shillings and sixpence a week, 'for comfortable subsistence'.

The services in the minster were also set forth in detail. The vergers must see that nobody chewed tobacco, they should have keys for the locks of different pews, the choristers should be grave and devout and "never accept pay for civilities, as in some cathedrals." The vergers were to be paid 3*d*. for "seeing the Choir and the eastern part of the church", 2*d*. "for going to the top of the lantern tower, and 2*d*. for seeing the great bell."

The rector estimated that the minster could be finished in sixteen years. The wages of sixty-four stonemasons at 12*s*. 6*d*. a week would take £25,000, four mastermasons at 30*s*. a week, £4,800, sixty-four labourers at 15*d*. a day, £19,200. There were to be no false economies. "The trustees must not fear to build grandly." He made a note that Italian blue-veined marble was sold at Millbank, Westminster, in the block at 13*s*. a cubic foot, black Italian marble at 15*s*., Siena marble at 50*s*. and Sicilian jasper at 55*s*. "The flat pavement stones of Corfu are preferable to those of Sandwich."

Commenting on the reverend gentleman's scheme, the vicar of Welford wrote: "Though I must cut his reasoning very short, the rector pointed out that the grand church of the Escurial cost 1,200,000 ducats. This may encourage the trustees who might think the building of so pompous and magnificent a church beyond any estimate, and a thing that could never be accomplished. He instances St. Paul's and gives a very shrewd reason for assuming that a private undertaking could be carried out at a vastly less comparative cost than a public work."

It would seem that Hanbury did not think very highly of St. Paul's, and in building the minster at Langton he could achieve something bigger, better and less costly. He must have been pleased by some verses that were published in his honour by "the very ingenious Mr. Woty, a local clergyman":

On yon proud eminence where Langton stands,
That yields a prospect of the richest lands,
There shall the grand Collegiate Church arise,
A welcome free-will offering to the skies;
Gothic in style and tending to excite
Free-thinkers to a sense of what is right,
With lengthening aisles and windows that impart
A gloomy steady light to cheer the heart,
Such as affects the soul, and which I see
With joy, celestial Westminster! in thee;

Not like St. Paul's, beneath whose ample dome
No thought arises of the life to come,
For though superb, not solemn is the place,
The mind but wanders o'er the distant space,
Where 'stead of thinking on the God, most men
Forget His presence, to remember Wren.

For a time all seemed to be going well with the schemes of the
rector. His plantations grew in size, fame and prosperity. In the old
church he had already installed a splendid new organ. He had built
a large gallery to accommodate such an orchestra as had never been
seen in a village church. But there were adverse critics and slanderers
around. It was rumoured that the rector was going to put on a
performance of *The Last Judgement*. And there was a whiff of
treason—he was going to set up the Pretender! Bonnie Prince Charlie
and the rising of '45, with its memories of Culloden and the Duke of
Cumberland's butchery, were only a few years past. The duke had
been to Langton to see what was going on, for the organ pipes brought
to the church were really artillery and small arms! Also, all this
gathering of crowds was disastrous to the countryside. Provisions
had trebled in price. Market Harborough was so crowded for the
Festival that "dukes and lesser nobles were forced to sleep where
they could instead of where they would." The roads rattled with the
sound of carriages and horses. The flag hoisted on the tower provoked a brisk gale though the weather was fine when it was hoisted.
It was blown to pieces in a few minutes, the painter having loaded it
with seventy-two pounds of paint.

The crowd in the church had been so dense that it was said that "a
boy squeezed up, walked upon the heads of the people, and such an
outcry had been made by the greater part of the rabble that few
could attend to what the band was doing. A young lady came with a
servant on horseback and offered twenty guineas to anyone who could
procure her admission, but in vain." A further nuisance had been the
rockets fired from the top of the tower from seven till eight in the
evening, at intervals of five minutes. In short, there had been bedlam
brought to quiet Church Langton.

But the rector pressed on, modest, industrious, indomitable. He
refused to build himself a less mean rectory. "Let it be said that
when you go to see Hanbury you meet with an old-fashioned
house and a hearty welcome," wrote a friend. A new rectory might

come in due time but not before the new church was completed. Meanwhile Hanbury had got to the stage of marking out in the adjoining fields the site of the new great minster. He firmly believed that the future income from his plantations would support all his grandiose schemes. Alas, there were quarrels with the trustees, and he was involved in litigation, but in the last five years of his short life the capital value of the plantations rose from £10,000 to £14,000. A century after his death the income had risen to a £1,000 a year, and in the year that I visited Church Langton with my father the Hanbury Charity, as it was now called, had an income of £2,000 a year.

With Hanbury's early death all his schemes for the great minster, with the convent, the college, etc., collapsed. Regarding this remarkable man, it would be rash to say that he would not have accomplished all he planned. Even today something remains of the work of that dynamic clergyman. His son was able to build a beautiful new rectory. There are schools, a library, scholarship grants, nursing and hospital grants, an organ account, and also out of that brave adventure 'beef forever' has survived. The annual account of the Charity still shows payment for eleven beef vouchers for the poor to the extent of £30 a year. Also there were funds left sufficient for the restoration of the churches at Church Langton and Thorpe Langton, for a re-built church at Tur Langton, and to provide for the teaching of music in the Hanbury School.

II

Such is the history, as I learned later, of the three rectors of Church Langton. My father and I were now on our way to call on a living rector, in the rectory built by Hanbury's son who had succeeded to the living. We were most warmly received on that sunny August morning and shown over the commodious rectory. We were escorted to the church. I was astonished by its size. Why should the Reverend William have planned to build a vast minster in a village of four hundred inhabitants? In 1650, runs the record, "the rectory of Church Langton, with divers chapels", was returned as "worth £100. One minister sufficient, and one curate insufficient." As £100 in 1650 had the value of some £2,000 to-day it is easy to understand why this living was regarded as one of the best in Leicestershire. There were charges on this income. In 1220 the Abbot of Leicester, who held the patronage, drew a pension of half a mark. In 1314 the rectory was taxed at seventy marks and paid six shillings 'for Peter's Pence.' In 1534 the value of the rectory had been thirty-two pounds. Its value seems to have risen steadily through the next century.

On entering the church and viewing the majestic nave and chancel my father went straight to the south aisle. On the side wall there was an ornamental arch with an inset freestone tomb before which he stopped. Under this arch there had been found, during a seventeenth-century restoration, a coffin cut out of a solid block of stone. The upper part had been hollowed out for the reception of a head. On removing the heavy lid the blackened bones of a rebuilder of the church, Thomas de Langton, were exposed. The teeth in the skull were perfect. He had lived in the time of Edward III. "Probably carried off by the Black Death that left only half the population alive in the Langtons," said my father. It was not this freestone tomb but the effigy on top that interested him: "And here's your ancestor Sir Richard," said my father. I saw the recumbent figure of a knight, with a large ruff, a beard, and hair curling over the neck. His head rested upon a stone pillow whose ends were carved in the form of feathers. This pillow was painted blue, yellow and red. There were traces of paint and gilding on the effigy, faded with time.

Above the old knight there was a shield bearing a coat-of-arms, a lion rampant sable, and a crest, an antelope's head. With some excitement I recognised the family Ju-Ju, and for the first time felt some interest in this heraldic record. Below the arms, on a black marble slab, there was an inscription:

> Here . . . lyeth . . . buri
> ed . . . the . . . Body . . . of
> Sir . . . Richard . . . Rober
> ts . . . Knight . . . aged
> 80 . . . years . . . Oct . . . the . . . 30
> Ann . . . Dom . . . 1644

The lettering was beautiful and clear. The recumbent figure of the old knight was striking, though sadly marred by the amputated arms and feet. "Those Cromwell ruffians again!" observed my father. "The old boy lived into disastrous times. He was seventy-eight when he was named in King Charles's Commission of Array, and when he died England had been locked in Civil war for over two years."*

Sir Richard's son, Sir William, a High Sheriff in 1629—there were five High Sheriffs in the family—with other Leicestershire loyalists, had been present at the raising of the Royal Standard at Nottingham in 1642. He fought with the army at Edgehill and at Newbury, while the old knight was dying. "Luckily the old fellow missed what was to follow, the billeting of Cromwell's troops, the sequestration of his own and his son's estates, and ruinous fines. He must have suffered also from the divisions among relations and friends, for some were for the King and some were Parliamentarians," said my father. He ran his hand over the effigy. "I wish I had the money to do the monument up. Well, perhaps one day if I can't you will. You'll notice Sir Richard's imposed on top of Thomas de Langton's tomb, some three hundred years later. He set a bad example. When you go into Westminster Abbey, in the Poets Corner you'll see that on the top half of Chaucer's tomb a kinsman, John Roberts, is superimposed. Although it's a beautiful medallion monument it's a rather shameful business. His only title to fame was that he was a successful sinecure-hunter and 'faithful secretary' to Henry Pelham, the Chancellor of the Exchequer who created Consols. Now, above Chaucer, he looks down on memorial stones to Tennyson and Browning."

There was one other monument that drew our attention before we left the church. It was a portrait bust in relief of the redoubtable Rev. William Hanbury. He looked alert and energetic. Very fittingly there was rolled up in front of him a representation of the Deed of Trust he had presented "upon the immediate sounding off of the *Grand Chorus*, on that memorable twenty-sixth day of September, 1759."

III

We said goodbye to the rector, one of the successors of Polydore Vergil, Lawrence Saunders and the Reverend William Hanbury.

* "Sir Thomas Burton, Sir George Villiers, Sir Henry Skipwith of Cotes, who entertained King Charles nobly at his house, Sir Richard Halford, Sir John Bale, Sir Erasmus de la Fontaine, Sir William Jones, Sir Richard Roberts, Sir John Skeffington, George Ashby and Thomas Hartopp, esq., are worthy of remembrance for their loyalty: for when the King's Commission of Array was directed to them, they zealously promoted the King's Service, and when a paper loan was sent to them, they joined and gave the King £25,642; and when Sequestrated by Parliament the composition for their estates came together to £20,000; and after they were imprisoned alike."—Burton, *Description of Leicestershire*.

Our destination was now Noseley Hall, the residence of Sir Arthur Hazlerigg. *En route* we called at Thorpe Langton. Here we found a stained glass window in memory of the Reverend Charles Roberts, who died in 1859. He was the last survivor of the line descended from Sir Richard's second son. He had succeeded to the estate that had come into the family by Sir Richard's marriage to Dorothy Jerveis, of a line that had been at Thorpe Langton since the time of Edward III. The Reverend Charles married an heiress and moved to an estate at Thurnby in Northamptonshire. He was the last Roberts to have residence in Thorpe Langton. After his departure the old manor fell into ruin and the estate was bought by another long established local family, the Kendalls, whose descendants are there to-day.

As we cycled along on that lovely August morning, the flat Leicestershire fields smiling to the far horizon, my father traced for me some of the ramifications of the family line. He had all the zest of a hound scenting a trail. "There's a lot of fun and also a lot of humbug in pedigrees," he said. "They're rather like Sherlock Holmes stories, one clue leads to another. They're a good lesson in the slings and arrows of outrageous fortune. The villain often goes unpunished, the virtuous unrewarded, the son of the upright father turns out a scoundrel, the idler who never works gets a succession of legacies and dies in comfort. I know that your mother and brother think I'm a bit cracked on the subject. Well, it's better than backing horses or raising the bottle, and you learn a lot of history, and history is the deposit left by the human race in the stream of Time."

I assured him that I was deeply interested and that I was enjoying the holiday enormously. He looked at me with a twinkle in his eyes, and said, "Then I hope I'm not wasting my time on you." He stopped and dismounted, being a little out of breath. There was a large tree by the wayside and we rested there in the shade. We watched a farm wagon go by, drawn by two powerful horses with plaited manes and fluffy fetlocks. "A grand sight," he said, "which I'm afraid we're not going to see much longer on the roads. There's nothing so beautiful as two horses and a plough on the horizon as it cuts a furrow. That lad sitting in the waggon, thinking of nothing, will be replaced by the bespectacled graduate of an agricultural college— and I don't think he'll be any happier. I'd like to come back in a hundred years to see how involved the human race gets."

The waggon rumbled slowly on. A summer silence settled over the fields. Presently I asked my father what had happened to Sir Richard's descendants. I saw he was pleased by my curiosity. It opened a flood-gate. Like an expert chess-player he knew every move on the family chess-board. When he did not know he said so, when he surmised he was careful to state the fact. How he would have enjoyed and laughed at an experience I had some twenty years later, on a lecture tour in the U.S.A. I was entertained by a lady who rejoiced in the name of Mrs. Tudor. She gave a large lunch party for me at her country house. She was determined that I was a relation of Lord Robert Cecil, a statesman then much in the public eye with his advocacy of the League of Nations. Nothing I said would shake this conviction. I had already suffered from this confusion of our names. On arriving at her house, we entered a large hall. One side from ceiling to floor was covered with a genealogical table, pictorially embellished with battles, castles and knights, that took in most of the kings and queens of England. It began with Edward III and ended with her late husband, Mr. Tudor. As I examined this astonishing and beautifully executed pedigree my hostess said—"Naturally we Tudors are very proud of our descent!" I observed, truthfully, that it was the most remarkable pedigree I had ever seen.

Resting in the pleasant summer morning amid the sunlit Leicestershire fields, my father traced the branches of old Sir Richard's family. He had had four sons and two daughters. The eldest son, William, had inherited the manors of Sutton Cheyney and Barwell from his uncle, Sir William, who had died in 1631. He suffered heavily from the fines inflicted by the Cromwellian Parliament, for having fought with the Royalists.* He married the daughter of Sir John Bale,

---

* HOUSE OF COMMONS JOURNAL. *September 3, 1646.*

"RESOLVED. That this House doth accept the sum of Seven Hundred and Eighty Pounds of William Roberts the younger, son of Sir Richard Roberts, of Sutton Cheyney in the County of Leicestershire, Gentleman, for a Fine for his Delinquency. His offence is, leaving his own house and residing in the Enemies Garrisons.

"His estate is a rent charge of Two Hundred Pounds per annum to him and his heirs: Four Hundred and Fifty Pounds in Reversion: out of which sum the sum of Seven and Twenty Pounds, Six Shillings and Eightpence, per annum forever, is issuing to an hospital.

"An Ordinance for granting a Pardon unto William Roberts the younger, of Sutton Cheyney, in the County of Leicestershire, Gentleman, for his Delinquency, was this day read, and upon the Question, passed, and ordered to be sent unto the Lords for their concurrence.

"*Sabbate. November 21, 1646.* Mr. Holles was appointed to carry to the Lords the Ordinance, including the said William Roberts's."

"whose tomb we have just seen in Carlton Curlieu church," said my father. "He had nine children, of whom the eldest, like his father, became a High Sheriff. His grandson, Charles, married a girl called Sence, after a stream near here. They lived at Thorpe Langton and had five sons and three daughters. Women had a poor time of it in those days. They married early and died young, most of them in childbirth. You get some idea of the infant mortality from the story of Charles and Sence.

They had buried Anna, aged one, in 1712, William, aged two in 1715, Robert, aged two, and his sister, Maria, aged one, in 1718. There was a scandal over the burial of the last two. In that year "a case was brought against a Thomas Ward for unlawfully taking away the bell ropes and the key of the belfry of Church Langton, the Reverend George Alsop being then the rector, to the obstruction of divine service, and the interment of the parishioners, especially of the two infant children of Charles Roberts, Esq., of Thorpe Langton."

"You can imagine the scene!" said my father. "Ward probably had a quarrel with the rector over something, and to spite him, went off with the bell rope and the key. The funeral procession with Charles and Sence and the two small coffins arrived and there was the scandal of no bell being tolled. We aren't told what was done to the culprit. We're now going to follow the history of one of their grandsons. He married the daughter of Sir Arthur Hazlerigg of Noseley—that's why we're going there now. I must tell you a little about them. They are among the oldest families of Leicestershire, with an unbroken succession at Noseley since 1435. It is said that the first of them, Sir Roger, came over with William the Conquerer. He spelt his name Hesilrig then. In 1509 one of them was an Esquire of the Body to Henry VIII, and in 1622, another became a baronet, probably one of King James's wholesale creations. He must have been a sturdy breeder, he had fourteen children. He died in 1629 and the eldest boy fell under the influence of Pym and made history as one of the Five Members whom King Charles failed to arrest. From their action sprang the independence of Parliament, and the end of 'the Divine Right of Kings'. Of course a large number of Hesilrig's Leicestershire neighbours, Royalists like us, were outraged. Sir Richard Halford got himself into trouble for denouncing him and saying 'He has more

---

In to-day's values this fine would be about £20,000. His father. Sir Richard, had already lost the equivalent of £20,000 in subscribing to King Charles's Paper Loan.

will than wit', and was sent to the Tower. We don't know what old Sir Richard Roberts, his neighbour, said about him. It was probably unprintable, for he had two sons and a grandson fighting in the Royal Army. The tragedy of the Civil War was that it divided families and friends. The Royalists suffered terribly. Their property was occupied and looted and they were mercilessly fined. Our family never recovered from the severities of the Parliamentary sequestrators. By the irony of Fate we had a kinsman, Sir William Roberts of Neasden, who got fat fees for the job, and a baronetcy from Cromwell. Even so, Sir Arthur Hesilrig was an honourable and brave man, acting according to his own conscience. He became a great friend of Cromwell but at the end he quarrelled with him and refused to sign King Charles's death warrant. He was Parliamentary Governor of Newcastle, and the colonel of a regiment of cuirassiers known as The Lobsters, fiercely hated for their ruthlessness. Sir Richard Roberts's son, Thomas, died in 1632, leaving a son, Richard, aged eight. When Thomas married in 1624 at St. Clement Danes, London, Sir Richard had settled on him the manor and estate of Thorpe Langton. It was one of Thomas's descendants, Charles, who married the Hesilrig girl in 1784. She was descended from Sir Arthur, who was arrested upon the Restoration, imprisoned in the Tower of London and died there. His estates were sequestrated by the Crown. Fortunately for the Hesilrigs the Duke of Albemarle interceded for Sir Arthur's son and the family estates were restored to him.

"Now we'll go and have a look at them in their chapel at Noseley," said my father. We mounted our cycles. In about three-quarters of an hour we turned off the main road and went down a fine avenue of trees. It led to Noseley Hall and its chapel. There had once been a village of that name but it had disappeared after the first Enclosure Act, so ruinous to the peasantry.*

At the end of the long drive we came to the chapel and the Hall, eighteenth century and Georgian. It looked south over open country. We dismounted from our cycles and found the front door. My father

---

* Luigi Gentili (1801–1848) a Roman priest, went as chaplain to a proselyte Leicestershire squire, de Lisle Phillips, on whose estates be began his first mission among the poor. He was appalled to find that home industries had been ruined and the arable land turned over to pasture. "There were nine ploughs, there are now two," he wrote home. "I have seen nothing in the Papal States which approaches the destitution and wretchedness of Leicestershire."

rang the bell. Nothing happened. He rang again. There was not a soul in sight.

"Do you know Sir Arthur Hazlerigg—is he 'severe'?" I asked, recalling the incident overnight.

"No, I don't know him. In fact I've never seen him but I've no doubt we shall be well received. It's a Hazlerigg tradition. I've heard my grandfather talk of them."

We rang again and were about to turn away when there was the sound of someone behind the hall door. Bolts were withdrawn, then the door opened and a man in shirt sleeves appeared. He was certainly not a butler. He looked at us suspiciously. I believe he thought we had come to try and sell something but my father's manner at once reassured him. He informed us that the family was not living in the house at present. Yes, we could have the key to the chapel. He invited us in while he went to get it. I had a glimpse of a square hall with a staircase rising up to the first floor, and of portraits hanging on the walls. But that was all I was allowed to see for my father, annoyed that I had muddied my shoes in going to drink at a stream, forbade me to enter. I had to wait on the doorstep.

We received the key and walked across a lawn to the chapel. I can vividly remember the great surprise I felt when we opened the door and saw a long vista before us, light, noble, beautiful, with a rich variety of sculptured monuments under the high wooden roof. Here was an English chapel in perfection filled with the exquisite tombs of an old family. It had been built about the thirteenth century, with east and west windows in the perpendicular style. It was obvious that it had never ceased to be cared for. Long, spacious, with nine bays, each carrying pointed windows, the chapel had a wide nave and chancel. I recall my father's delight in the monuments. He had been there twice before and knew what he was going to find. He pointed out to me the fourteenth- and fifteenth-century stained glass, the octagonal font with crocketed gables. How many Hesilrig infants had been baptised there? Looking up at the flattened roof one saw angels surmounting the corbels, carrying heraldic shields.

But it was the effigies we had come to see, painted and brightly gilded. Here was Sir Thomas, dead in 1629, lying with his wife, and their fourteen kneeling children, eight boys and six girls. An inscription told us that "She clothed her family with fine clothe of her owne spinning." How busy she must have been making clothes for sixteen! We came to the alabaster tomb of the unfortunate Sir Arthur, the resolute Roundhead who had died in the Tower.

Here lyse Sir Arthur Hesilrig, Bart, who enjoyed his portion, of this life in ye times of the greatest civil troubles yt ever this nation had. He was a lover of liberty and faithful to his country. He delighted in sober company; and departed this life 7th of January, in England's peaceable year A.D. 1660.

Sir Arthur lay on a table of black marble with his two wives beside him and, below, dutifully kneeling, his three sons and five daughters. Several of the children are carrying skulls because they died before the monument was made. There is not one word on Sir Arthur's death in the Tower. The wording of that inscription must have been a difficult business, the memories of the Civil War still bitter. One son seems to have been a prodigy, and unlucky.

He was of rare endowments and incomparable learning for his age, both in Hebrew, Greek, Latin and French; of singular wit and judgment, of sweet nature and very pious. He died in the twelfth year of his age, 1649.

"I've always had my doubts about those linguistic prodigies," said my father. "There was Queen Elizabeth fluent in five languages at ten years of age—very un-English!"

We passed on. The squires of Noseley lay in line. We came to Sir Thomas, the fortunate son who had his estates restored to him. Then came his son, High Sheriff in 1686, a bachelor and an M.P., who died at 38. An uncle succeeded who had a grandson, Sir Arthur, the seventh baronet.

"Here's where Charles Roberts comes in," said my father. "His father-in-law, Sir Arthur, must have been an interesting fellow. He patronised the fine arts and spent much of his time in Italy, one of those eighteenth century dilettantes who travelled and collected the treasures now in our great houses. They took with them quite a retinue, a chaplain, architect, valet, grooms, cook, bedding, pots and pans. They had a lot of fun and were often eccentric, 'the mad English', but not too mad to pick up, knowingly, pictures and statues for a few pounds whose sale is keeping some of their homes going to-day."

It was this Sir Arthur who rebuilt Noseley. He had a house in

Northamptonshire also, where he preferred to live, and there he met his wife, Hannah Sturges, the beautiful daughter of the High Sheriff of that county. Hannah and her husband had three sons and seven daughters. One of these was Amabel. It was she who married Charles Roberts of Thorpe Langton.

My father searched through his notebook and found the notice of the wedding.

The Gentleman's Magazine. August, 1784. Marriages.
Mr. Charles Roberts of Thorpe Langton, Leicestershire, and Miss Amabel Hesilrige, youngest daughter of the late Sir Arthur Hesilrige, Bart., of Noseley Hall, Leicestershire. Mr. Roberts is a lieutenant in the 56th Regiment of Foot and was at Gibraltar during the whole of the Siege.*

"Young Roberts was in Italy on The Grand Tour when the war with Spain threatened. I haven't been able to find his exact movements about that time but he succeeded in joining his regiment in Gibraltar. After the close of that three-year siege he returned to England and married Amabel Hesilrige. I think it was a love-match this time. I don't suppose you know who Samuel Richardson was? In 1740 he wrote a novel called *Pamela*. It was a tremendous success and he was called 'The Father of the English novel'. Everybody lost his head over it. The model for Pamela, the heroine of the book, was Amabel's mother, Hannah."

We stayed in the chapel for some time. The caretaker at the Hall probably thought we had gone off with the key for he suddenly appeared and was a little sulky. But his face changed when my father tipped him. "He wants his lunch, I expect," he said.

Forty-five years later I returned to Noseley and checked my notes and memory. This time the Hazleriggs were at the Hall and I had a

* In 1779, while Britain was engaged in a struggle with the revolted American colonies, Spain joined with France in an attack on the fortress of Gibraltar. The siege began on June 21st. General Heathfield defended the Rock with a force of 7,000 men, including 1,100 Hanoverians. The fortress was several times on the point of starvation. In July, 1782, the Spaniards were reinforced by the French, and the Duc de Crillon took command, having boats ready to disembark 40,000 men. The allied attack began on September 8th and continued until the 14th, but by means of red-hot balls and incendiary shells the floating batteries were destroyed, with a loss of only 16 men of the heroic garrison. The siege was broken after three years and three months.

warm welcome from young Lady Hazlerigg. Her husband had now become the second Lord Hazlerigg, his father having accepted a peerage. I was shown a miniature of Amabel who had married Charles Roberts but I was shown something more delightful. In a perambulator, placed in a bay window to catch the morning sun, was a baby asleep. He was the son and heir. It was pleasant to know that the long line of the Hazleriggs would continue in their ancient home.

IV

Soon after leaving Noseley we found a place by a copse in which we ate our lunch. It was very hot. The insects hummed loudly. As we sat on the grass we identified eleven different birds and I saw my first woodpecker busy on an ash tree. Having eaten, my father dozed off. I got up and wandered about, coming to a small limpid stream. It was tempting in the hot noonday and there was not a soul in sight. I stripped and splashed about. Then I lay down to dry and dream in the sun. How pleasant it would be to have been born a Leicestershire squire, with woods and cottages, and horses to ride, and at the end of my days join old Sir Richard in Langton Church in the company of my ancestors, like those in the Noseley chapel. What had gone wrong? Why had we lost all this—carelessness, extravagance, ill-luck? Perhaps it was something of all these. 'Mutabilitie' was the theme of Spenser's verse. Ancestors were like shadows, intangible, despite moments when they took shape before fading away again. Somewhere along the journey Fate had defeated us. I thought of my delightful father, for whom money was an elusive thing. More successful, he might not be nearly so lovable. I comprehended that in a sense he was undefeatable. He was a happy man, dispensing happiness. Even so I wanted more than he had.

Lying there in the sunshine I had ambitious dreams. I would work, I would make a fortune, though how I did not know. And I would win fame. Then I would come back to Leicestershire and re-establish the family. I could not foresee that two World Wars would shatter the mould of our civilisation, that the ancient order was doomed, that annihilating taxes and inept politicians throwing away our great Empire, would wipe out the established order, with its responsibilities, traditions, and also its smug exclusiveness. The shape of a strange uneasy world to come cast no shadow on a boy's dream that day by a Leicestershire brook.

I dressed and went back to my father, who was ready to leave. Our destination was now Medbourne, some seven miles away, on the old Roman road, the so-called Via Devana, derived from *Deva Colonia*, the Roman name for Chester, the colony on the Dee. There was a theory that Medbourne had been a half-way station between Colchester and Chester. I asked why we were going to Medbourne. Robertses had been there for two centuries, offshoots from Langton, said my father.

When we came to it the village was tiny but pleasing. Through the middle of it ran a stream, with a water splash near the church. There was a medieval footbridge used when the floods made the splash unnegotiable. It had four arches spanning octagonal brick piers. The church of St. Giles stood on a mound. It looked as if at some time its site had been moated. We went into the churchyard and entered the thirteenth-century church. It was beautifully kept, there seemed to be the hand of a well-to-do person at work. I learned later that this was Sir Bache Cunard, grandson of the founder of the Cunard Shipping Line. Sycamore, beech and oak trees shaded the old church. How peaceful and lovely it was. There was a large stained glass window in the transept and an effigy of a thirteenth-century knight in mail beneath a helmet.

There had been a Roman villa at Medbourne. Roman coins had been found there as also a beautiful tessellated pavement, in a field near the stream. There was a sad story of carelessness connected with it. The pavement had been thrice uncovered, in 1721, 1793, and again in 1871 when a railway line was made. The tesserae were collected by an antiquarian, a London solicitor who was interested in the pavement. These were offered to the South Kensington Museum, which declined them. For years the stones lay in a bag in his London office. He died in 1906 when, with other lumber in the office, the stones were emptied into a dustbin and disappeared! In the vestry there hung an illustration of the lost pavement, made *in situ* in 1871—all that remained to record some unknown Roman's home.

In his notebook my father had a Medbourne pedigree that showed there had been cross-marriages between the Wadlands of this village and the Robertses. Early in the seventeenth century John Roberts had settled there, coming from Thorpe Langton. He married a Wadland girl. There was a memorial to her on a flat stone in the church.

Here lies the body of Ann Roberts, wife of John Roberts of Medbourne, Gent., daughter of John Wadland of the same place, Gent. *Intravit in requiem*. December 18, 1685.

The stone carried the Wadland arms impaled with those of Roberts. How old was she when she died, I wondered; what sort of a life had she, how many children? We know so little of her yet she must have been closely linked with the fate of the Roberts clan; how close is shown by a curious entry in the Medbourne Church Register. The third wife of Sir Richard had come to end her days with her relations in Medbourne, for a Susan Roberts had also married a Wadland. The entry runs—

Lady Roberts, relict of Sir Richard Roberts, buried Oct. 10, 1679. Paid to the poor for not being buried in woollen, £5.

She had outlived the old knight by thirty-five years. But why was £5 paid to the poor because she preferred a linen to a woollen shroud? My father explained. In the reign of Edward III when Flanders was the great headquarters of the manufacturers of wools, the English entered the industry. Flemish woolworkers settled in England, coming from Ghent and Bruges, and taught the English as they had also taught the French, bringing the trade to high perfection. To contribute to the protection of this industry, after a temporary slump following the Civil War, Charles II promulgated a law, in force from 1678 to 1815, that everyone should be buried in a woollen shroud or pay a fine if they insisted on using a linen one. Lady Roberts died a year too late to miss the fine!

My father told me of a curious link between Medbourne and Lord Byron. In medieval times the Chaworth family had owned the village. There was a William Chaworth, Lord of the Manor in 1235, and a grant was made to him by Henry III in 1266 to hold a market and fair in Medbourne. The family resided there until Sir Thomas de Chaworth, who died in 1480, moved to his other estate at Annesley Park in Nottinghamshire, next to the Byrons' home, Newstead Abbey. It was a descendant, Mary Chaworth, who captured young Byron's heart.

Before taking the road to Nevill Holt we went to look at Medbourne Old Hall, described in the seventeenth century as "Taxed for seven hearths." It was here that the widowed Lady Roberts had spent her last years with her relations. The house had been rebuilt in the middle of the seventeenth century so it was a comparatively new home for her after Thorpe Langton Manor. Her last days must have been very pleasant in this house which was so beautifully placed in a leafy corner of a Leicestershire village quite remote from the world.

V

Leaving the Hall we went up the hill to Nevill Holt. We passed the kennels of the Fernie Hunt and the cottages built by the Master, Sir Bache Cunard. Gaining the top of the hill we presently came to a great avenue of limes and chestnuts which led us to the long beautiful façade of the Hall and the adjoining church. The Nevills had been there since the fifteenth century and Palmers before them until the advent of the Cunards. The house had an Early Tudor two-storeyed entrance porch and a bay with oriel windows. The gothic façade was backed by the spire of the church. Sir Bache, a middle-aged bachelor had married a pretty young wife, Miss Maud Burke, an American. They entertained lavishly. He was mad on hunting, she detested horses.

As we left Nevil Holt, taking the road to Market Harborough, on a woodland path near the Hall, we passed a lady and gentleman walking with a girl of about my own age. For over thirty years I was to wonder about them. In 1940 I met in New York Sir Bache's widow, Lady Cunard. She was one of the most remarkable women it has ever been my good fortune to know. Petite, quick as a bird, always exquisitely dressed, she had a rapier wit and a wonderfully stored mind. She seemed to have read everything and to have forgotten nothing. I did not wonder that she had been one of the great hostesses of London at her Cavendish Square house. Statesmen, musicians, artists and authors were all subservient to a superb ring-master. The friend and patron of Sir Thomas Beecham, 'Emerald' Cunard, as she chose to be called, crossed my path like a meteor.

One day, a frequenter of her little salon in her sitting-room at the old Ritz Hotel in New York, I mentioned Church Langton in reference to Handel's *Messiah*, remarking on its performance there, Sir Thomas Beecham having turned the conversation to Handel. "The Langtons!" she cried. "What do you know about the Langtons? I lived at Nevill Holt for sixteen years." I told her that I had been

taken there when a boy of fifteen by my father. After that our friendship was closer than ever, broken only by her death. Later, I discovered, that in the very year and month of my visit to Nevill Holt
George Moore, an unabashed, importuning lover, had been her
guest there. What Sir Bache made of this Irish author, to whom the
critics offered incense at a shrine in Ebury Street, London, I do not
know. Despite his genius he always seemed a flaccid figure to me. It
comes out mercilessly in Max Beerbohm's caricature. Sir Bache may
have been indifferent, contemptuous or amused, the hard shell of the
Master of Foxhounds untroubled by this jellyfish man of letters.

On August 31st, 1907, returning from a visit to Nevill Holt, Moore
wrote to his hostess—"My eyes turn to Leicestershire as a sunflower
to the sun." This was followed by a rhapsody to the adored lady.
"Dear vision, clear and divine, how shall I tell anew the one thing
that seems worth the telling, that all I am capable of concerning
immortality, I see in thee. Other men, it is said, have seen angels,
but I have seen thee and thou art enough. . . . When I think of
Nevill Holt emotions rather than thoughts arise. . . they drift to the
oak gallery . . . it was kind of you to give me a room facing the
schoolroom. I liked my visits to Nancy's school-room and my walks
with her in the woods where the wild flowers grow."*

"And did you once see Shelley plain ?" asked Browning. And did I,
a boy in Nevill Holt woods that August day in 1907, see George
Moore, Lady Cunard and her young daughter Nancy ? I think they
were the trio I saw.

VI

The next morning after breakfast at The Three Swans, my father
made a change of plans. We would not leave that day for Sutton
Cheney. I hid my disappointment suspecting the reason for this
change. My father looked tired and complained of the August heat.
I was aware that he found cycling exhausting, the slightest incline
troubling him. A contrary breeze had sprung up the previous day
on our way from Nevill Holt. He had been compelled to dismount
several times. It was some twenty miles to Sutton Cheney. The day
was going to be hot again. While my father read and wrote I would
cycle and go for a swim. Also I was glad to have time to write up my
diary which more and more interested me.

* George Moore, *Letters to Lady Cunard* (Hart–Davis, 1957).

I went out into the stableyard, fascinated by the life around me. I watched a young stableman, with whom I had become friendly, grooming a horse. He was quick and lithe and had a merry eye. He asked me if I rode. I told him that I had never been on a horse. "Would you like to ride one with me?" he asked. I could not believe my ears. "Very much!" I exclaimed. "All right, in about half an hour we'll go," he said. I rushed in and told my father. He approved at once and came out to watch me mount. The only animal I had ever ridden was the twopenny donkey at Skegness. Now I was a proper Leicestershire lad except that I wore shorts instead of riding breeches. I seemed to be very high up off the ground. The groom adjusted my stirrups. "Don't break his neck!" called my father as we set off. "I'll bring back the pieces, sir!" said my escort. "What's my horse's name?" I asked. "Fluff—she's a three-year-old filly." I did not know what a filly was, and not wishing to expose my ignorance I did not ask. We went through the town and turned off into a side road. We were going to Dingley Grange, said the groom. I thought it a pleasant name, with a touch of Dickens. On the smaller road we began to trot. I bounced about. "Lean forward, keep your hands down, rise in the saddle from your knees—don't pull on the reins," said my tutor. In a few minutes my nervousness began to go. How sad to think this would be my only ride. I would never have a horse of my own.

The groom was going to see his brother who worked at the Grange. He told me he had five horses to care for and exercise every day, two were suffering from 'grass sickness'. His name was Tom Cutts. He hoped to go to America next year with an American who came to hunt with the Fernie. "We're going to be wiped out by those bloody motors, all stink and dust!" he said contemptuously. I asked him what he would do in America. "The same thing, with better pay. He's got a stud farm in Lexington, Kentucky. I know a boy there already. His boss takes him to Paris every year, races at Longchamps. You get around with those Americans."

We got back at noon. I was hot, shaken, but I'd had a glimpse of paradise. '*A horse, a horse, my kingdom for a horse!*' "Would you like to come out tomorrow morning?" Tom asked, as I dismounted. Would I like! I nuzzled Fluff's soft cheek. To have a horse, to be able to ride the Leicestershire lanes—perhaps to follow the Fernie and the Quorn! Incredible vistas of delight opened from that stableyard, with Tom, dark-eyed and trim in his leggings. I told him I would ask my father but we would probably leave in the morning. "I'll be here if you come before ten," said Tom, unbridling Fluff. He had a warm smile and had been very patient instructing me.

My father, reading in the bar parlour, wanted to hear all about my ride. I gave him an excited recital. When I added, tentatively, that Tom had offered to take me out again next morning if we were here— "Splendid!" he said at once. "We can go to Market Bosworth after lunch."

He wanted to post some letters. We went out together and I walked on air. Returning from the Post Office I saw something that left me wide-eyed with wonder and envy. A small girl with a mass of golden hair under a brown velvet cap rode up on a cob, slipped down, tethered it to a railing and went into a bow-fronted house with a white portico. It wasn't the golden hair flowing over her jacket that stunned me, it was her brown riding breeches. They were all of a piece from hip to ankle. "Jodhpurs," said my father, seeing my surprise. "They've come out of India." "Can men wear them?" I asked. "They are for men but girls have borrowed them. They're convenient to slip into," he replied. My filly Fluff, jodhpurs, this grass country, the old house with the white portico and door. I wondered who the lucky girl was. She came out again, mounted lightly and went off on her roan cob, its tawny mane matching her hair.

I was awake with excitement the next morning at six o'clock and down in the stables at seven, to make sure our horses were still there. Tom was at work hay-forking straw, shirtless and belted. He was pleased I could come. Soon after nine we set off. I had brought two lumps of sugar for Fluff. I found I was less easy in the saddle, having stiff muscles and chafed knees but I would have ridden had I been paralysed. We took a much longer ride this time, going through gated fields. I watched how cleverly Tom manoeuvred the gates without dismounting. He told me about the two Hunts he had worked for. Sir Bache spent money like water on horses, stables and kennels— "But the old bastard wouldn't split a sixpence on you for wages," he said. "Now there is Count D'Arco—an Austrian. A pound in your palm for anything you do for him."

Tom's father had been a groom for the Empress Elizabeth of Austria around 1880. "Her that got murdered—beautiful, a mad rider, said my Dad." No, he wasn't married yet. "I like my fillies on the snaffle!" But when he got to America he'd have money for a girl.

It was nearly noon when we returned. I could hardly stand when I dismounted. I was near tears as I kissed Fluff goodbye. Inside the hotel my father astonished me by giving me a half-sovereign. "A tip for Tom," he said. Half a sovereign, a fortune! I hurried off to the stables and gave it to Tom, affecting an air as though I gave half-sovereigns away every day. "Oh no, sir! Oh, thank you, sir!" he cried on my insistence. Sir, Fluff, jodhpurs, groom-tipping with gold. This fairy-tale world would crash soon.

CHAPTER ELEVEN

The Visitation: III. Sutton Cheney

I

WE LEFT Market Harborough at two o'clock. It was a long ride to Market Bosworth, the town nearest to the village of Sutton Cheney, the name taken by Sutton Cheynell sometime in the nineteenth century. My father adhered to the old spelling. We found an inn. A thunderstorm had gathered and it began to rain, the clouds black and heavy. I felt that we had been evicted from Paradise but my father had recovered his spirits and was as lively as a hound scenting a trail. At Sutton Cheney we were on ground from which the family had spread over Leicestershire since the fifteenth century, when it had come out of Shropshire.

That evening, after a miserable dinner, "which I wouldn't give to a cabman," said my father, we sat in a dark parlour, to the sound of heavy rain. I was thoroughly briefed for the morrow. He would not trouble me, he said, with a collateral line established near Willesden, Middlesex, since the fifteenth century, except for an outline of one remarkable character, Sir William Roberts, an adroit lawyer who successfully hunted with the Parliamentarians and the Royalists in turn. He was born in 1604, a twin, whose brother had died young at Eton. When a handsome lad of just twenty he drew the eye of James I, always alert to a pretty youth, who knighted him at Greenwich in 1624. His uncle Edward had married his mother's younger sister, Susan. They were both daughters of Sir William Glover, a rich dyer who "gave to hospitals in and out of London the sum of £200"— some £6,000 to-day. Uncle Edward was well placed with the great Robert Cecil, the King's Minister.*

* *Bishop of London's Marriage Register. May 3rd, 1606*
Edward Roberts, of St. Martin's-in-the-Fields, gent, bachelor; attending upon the Rt. Hon. Earl of Salisbury; about 27; And Susan Glover, maiden, 20, of St. Stephen's, Coleman Street, daughter of Sir William Glover, Knight, alderman of London, deceased; consent of her mother, the Lady Ann Glover; consent also of Francis Roberts Esq, father of the said Edward.

A bright young lawyer, who had entered Gray's Inn at seventeen, Sir William soon picked up remunerative jobs. He sat on a Royal Commission for "compounding with illegal importing of gold and silver thread," and on another "for enforcing the practice of the long-bow." But when the Civil War broke out he went over to the Parliamentary Party, being a friend of Sir Arthur Hesilrig and John Hampden. As Deputy Lieutenant of Middlesex he was ordered to collect money for the defence of Brentford against King Charles when that monarch threatened London. In 1652 he was a member of "The Commission for promoting the sale of Episcopal Crown Lands."

Sir William did well out of these commissions. He bought five Prebendal Manors at Neasden and Harlesden, as well as that owned by the deposed Bishop of Peterborough, and he received £300 a year as Commissioner of Appeals in Excise. He was a member of the 1656 Parliament and was one of the sixty Peers of the House of Lords created by Cromwell, who placed the greatest reliance on him and "had a high idea of his integrity". He might have come to complete disaster at the Restoration, for he had been chosen by the junta of the Army to be one of King Charles's judges, but he was too wily to let himself be involved in such a hazardous proceeding. He sat in the Parliament that gave Cromwell the title of Protector, and built himself a mansion at Willesden where Cromwell visited him.

It is singular that such a dyed-in-the-wool Cromwellian did not perish in the Tower at the Restoration, as others of his kind. It was touch-and-go in the House of Commons. A proposal to exclude him from the Bill of Pardon and Oblivion was barely defeated. The outraged Royalists were after his head. He had to relinquish some of the prebends he had acquired so cheaply. There is no record of what his Sutton Cheynell and Thorpe Langton kinsmen thought of him. It was probably unprintable. Cromwellian M.P. and supporter of the Protector in 1656, one of the Peers in 1657, how did he contrive to gain the favour of Charles II and become a baronet in 1661, the year after the Restoration? "He was a lawyer of great skill, and prudent," said his obituary. He died, aged fifty-eight and was buried in Willesden Church on September 27th, 1662.

One of Sir William's feats was to beget fourteen children, eight boys and six girls, but even so, he did not equal his grandfather, Francis Roberts, who had nine sons and seven daughters. Four daughters of Sir William's family survived and married. His son

William, born in 1638, succeeded to the baronetcy, sat as an M.P. for Middlesex, in three Parliaments, married, and died at fifty, leaving an only son, the third baronet, who never married. On his death in 1700 the baronetcy became extinct.

"I've never had time to investigate this extraordinary side-history," said my father. Some fifty years later I visited Willesden Church. There are brasses of Sir William's great grandfather, Edmund and of a Margaret Roberts, and over the vestry door a beautiful mural tablet of Francis, his grandfather, restored by a descendant, Mr. John W. Roberts of Richmond, Virginia. The church has other, more modern, interests. Lord Aberdeen lent Gladstone Dollis Hill House nearby, and the Prime Minister used to read the lessons in Willesden Church. Mrs. Gladstone gave badly managed garden parties at the house. The place is now a public park called after him. Charles Reade, who wrote *The Cloister and the Hearth*, is buried in the churchyard.

II

When we came down to breakfast the next morning it was fine and the heat had broken. Our destination was the village of Sutton Cheney (new style), a couple of miles away. The road lay alongside a deer park. This was the terrain of the Wolstan Dixie family, descended from a Lord Mayor of London in Queen Elizabeth's time. One of the Dixies had founded the local school. Samuel Johnson, down from Pembroke College, was an usher there. He hated the position, as well as the squire, since he had to act as a kind of domestic chaplain to the family and say grace at meals. He found Sir Wolstan overbearing and dictatorial, perhaps not surprising of one whose family motto was *Quod dixi dixi*. Boswell wrote of that episode—"After suffering for a few months such complicated misery he relinquished a situation which all his life afterwards he recollected with the strongest aversion and even a degree of horror." But the Dixies have their own story about the uncouth usher. They dismissed him because he was dirty in his habits and attire, they said. They wholly missed the greatness that was latent in him. Dr. Johnson has long gone from Market Bosworth, the Wolstan Dixies are still there and full of spirit. "In the seventeenth century we married into that family," said my father, "and a son was called Wolstan Roberts. He was living nearby at Earl Shilton in 1740."

Sir William Roberts of Sutton Cheynell (1554–1633) and his two wives, (1) Katherine Elkington, widow of Robert Jerveis of Thorpe Langton, (2) Elizabeth Hartopp, widow of George Bale of Carlton Curlieu

Sir William Roberts' "Hospital for six poore men" 1612

The Hall, Sutton Cheney

We came to Sutton Cheney. It consisted of a few houses, a church and an inn, situated on the edge of what is called Bosworth Field, the scene of the battle in 1485. It was to this village that Thomas Roberts came in the early part of the fifteenth century, out of Shropshire. The village church is of Saxon origin, squat and plain, with a square tower. It has a Norman arch and font, and in the interior there are circular piers and arches, probably thirteenth century. In the tower four bells are variously inscribed. *God Save the King, 1635; God Save This Church; Richard Roberts, Richard Swinfen, 1593, Rector and Churchwarden;* and, *IHS Nazarenus Rex Ivdeorum, fili Dei, miserere, W. Mathews, C'warden 1675.*

In the choir of the church we found the alabaster effigy of Sir William Roberts, the elder brother of Sir Richard of Thorpe Langton. He lies clad in mail armour, his hands joined in prayer. The head is handsome above the elaborate ruff. The figure seems to have been ornamented with gold and blue paint which has faded. One end of the tomb-chest carries his coat-of-arms. On the long side there is an inscription cut into the marble slab.

Here lyeth interred the body of Sir William Roberts, Knight, who in his lifetime, being devoted both to hospitality and charity, among other memorable works, erected, out of a pious mind, an hospital for six poore men, adjoining this church-yard, and endowed it with 30 pounds land yearly, for their mainten-ance forever.

"I like the boldness of that 'forever'," said my father. "The old boy was right. The income for the 'hospital', as he politely called it, is still coming in."

We found on the other side of the monument another inscription—

This Sir William Roberts was sonne of Thomas Roberts, Gent., and married to his first wife Katherine, daughter of Richard Elkington, Gent., and to his second wife, Elizabeth, daughter of Valentine Hartopp, Gent., but by neither had issue. He lived 79 years, and died Anno Domini, 1633, February 24.

Above the old knight, on a wall panel, is the memorial to his two wives. They kneel at a *prie-dieu*, facing each other. "The old boy seems to have had a taste for widows," said my father. "His first wife, Katherine was the widow of Robert Jerveis of Thorpe Langton. His second wife, Elizabeth, was the widow of George Bale of Carlton Curlieu. Now we'll go and have a look at the hospital."

It was situated just across the churchyard, its façade making a long low line of one-storey stone cottages with mullion windows. The east end was most curiously honeycombed, as if intended for a dovecote. In the centre, over an archway, there was an inset tablet with the inscription *W 1612 R*, the donor's initials and the date of the foundation.

Burton in his *Description of Leicestershire* tells us that the annuity is derived from a farm at Barwell, a family property, and that a steward "paid to several hospital men at Sutton their annual allowance of £2. 16. 0. each." Among these poor men in 1704 were Mr. Roberts and Captain Talbot who each had an extra allowance of 16/– for a gown and 10/– for coal money.

"I've always wondered about that poor almsman, Mr. Roberts, and the Captain," said my father. "It looks as if they had come down in the world. It must have been embarrassing for the Robertses to have a relation living in the family's almshouse!"

We halted before one of the houses, its window bright with a flower-box, and tapped on the door. An old woman greeted us and asked us in. There was a hob grate on which she was cooking, and a large black cat lay in the armchair. The small single room had cross-lighting and was clean and cheerful. The cat was turned out of the chair for my father. The old woman was 78 and had lived there for ten years. Yes, it would be nice to have water laid on, it came from a tap in the yard. She had a married grandson who was in the army in India, and showed us his photograph. She had not seen him for ten years. We refused a cup of tea and wished her Good Morning. Outside there was a flagged path between the 'hospital' and the church yard wall. The whole front was gay with flowerboxes.

We walked towards the village and came to a large stone-built house on an elevated site. It had Tudor windows and a great gable, visible over a high wall enclosing a garden. There was a wide drive leading to the house, with a farmyard on one side of it. The old Hall is described in Nichol's *History of Leicestershire*. The antiquarian wrote of a visit he had made to Sutton Cheynell on June 17th, 1789.

"Could a more exquisite point of time have been selected? I see at this moment the waving corn through which we walked to Sutton church; the mantling ivy on the mouldering gateway of the Hall-house, once the residence of the respectable family of Roberts, the curious devices, particularly the well-shaped roses, embossed on the walls of the building now hastening to decay."

"I like the 'respectable family of Roberts!'" commented my father, "but you must remember that in 1789 'respectable', like 'esquire' really meant something. If you were 'respectable' you were of good social standing. Both words have been debased in use."

The property, he said, was bought in 1785 by the Countess of Bute whose son, the Hon. Dr. Stuart, Primate of Ireland, held it in 1809, but Robertses had continued to live there until 1805. I asked how the family came to lose the house after more than three centuries. "That's something I have never been able to find out exactly. The Civil War and the heavy fines imposed on them by Parliament ruined them. There were forced sales, and as with all old families the property got split up with legacies and with mismanagement—and sheer ill-luck. We were never a lucky line. There was nothing left after 1785 of the Sutton estate, except the Barwell part that was endowed for the income of the almshouse. Our line went on, at Thorpe Langton and Scalford, but much reduced."

The "ivy mantled gateway" seen by Nichols had vanished utterly. The embossed stone roses were probably Tudor emblems commemorating the victory of Henry VII that closed the long Wars of the Roses. Nichols also mentioned the 'crest of the Prince of Wales', possibly in reference to the family's Welsh allegiance, and also two figures of Hercules and Minerva by the door. They had all vanished. But the end gable of the house, carrying a plaque with the inscription *W R 1613 K R*, the initials of Sir William and his first wife, was as Nichols saw it. He wrote also of having seen the arms of Sir William, impaling those of his wife in the kitchen (?) window. This had disappeared.

It would seem that at the beginning of the seventeenth century Sir William embarked on building operations. In 1612 he had built the 'hospital'. In 1613 he had finished, as the tablet indicated, the reconstruction of the old family mansion. This work had been undertaken less than one hundred and thirty years after the Battle of Bosworth Field. Did he seek by embossing the royal roses on the house to emphasise his loyalty? King James seems not to have doubted it for he knighted him. "We shouldn't put too much store on that," said my father. "He may have been forced to purchase his knighthood. The King, and Charles I after him, did a roaring business with knighthoods and baronetcies. Queen Elizabeth had been parsimonious about them, and they had to be earned, but James I in 1604, then at the beginning of his reign, being very short of money, created 1100 of them, at a price. On one occasion at Belvoir Castle he created forty-six knights before breakfast. He became confused and forgot the name of one of them—"Prithee, rise up and call thyself Sir What-thou-wilt!" he said."*

What a lot of history this old house had seen! The previous evening my father had told me of a legend concerning it—that when the Battle of Bosworth Field was fought the family watched it from the roof. There were also legends about King Richard, recounted by people whose ancestors had lived in the vicinity. "Some are quick to dismiss them as old wives' tales. I wouldn't lightly do that," he said, "There's generally a substratum of truth for them but of course there is no direct proof."

There was a legend concerning Richard III's reputed natural son. The scene was not Nottingham Castle, as in another version, but Bosworth Field. It was said that before the battle Richard sent for him. Wherever it may have been, the story, according to Peck's *Desiderata Curiosa*, was that the King took leave of the boy and made provision for him to be brought up as the son of a poor shoemaker, if things went badly. In that humble disguise he would have a better chance of survival. He lived and worked as a stonemason in Eastwell, Kent, and when he died there, aged eighty-one, he was entered in the burial register, on December 22nd, 1550, under the name of V. Richard Plantagenet, the letter V prefixed being put before the name of every person of noble family mentioned in it.

We waited some time after ringing the door bell, and looked around. The old Hall had been converted into a farmhouse. There was a farmyard with barns, a platform for milk churns, and much mud. The fabric of the house looked very sound. It had wide mullion windows. Presently the door was opened by a maid. We were shown into a room whose windows looked over a terraced garden. The ceiling was high. It was obvious that the room had been partitioned off and had been part of a large hall. After a time a pleasant-faced woman came in. My father explained who he was and that the vicar

* In the fifteenth century it was costly to refuse a knighthood. Every man who owned land worth £20 a year was compelled to accept, with the obligation of providing a quota of servants as soldiers. If he refused the penalties were heavy. In 1564 the dreaded Star Chamber fined one delinquent £5,000. (About £100,000 to-day.)

with whom he had corresponded had given him their name. He had been there twenty years before when the house had another occupant. While we talked her husband came in. Yes, they knew the legend about the battle having been seen from the roof. They had never been up on it but the house was near enough to the battlefield for it to have been seen. They had found a piece of coloured armorial glass in a kitchen cupboard. The farmer's wife went to get it. It looked like a fragment of an heraldic shield which had been set in a leaded window.

An odour drifting in warned us that the mid-day meal was being cooked. After making a tour of the garden, observing the solid mullioned windows on that side of the house, we left, thanking them. They had been very hospitable but obviously they had little historical sense and no thought of the family that had lived there for four centuries. They probably wondered why we bothered about them, dead such a long time. "When you have to battle with weather, get in crops and milk cows, you can't bother about ancient history!" observed my father, as we went back to our cycles. Yet the place seemed full of ghosts. Through those mullion windows, down the years, Thomas, Richard, William, Charles, Wolstan, and their wives Katherine, Dorothy, Elizabeth, Jocosa and Susan had looked out. There were rumours of wars then as now. Soldiers who had been at Bosworth, Edgehill, Naseby, had come courting there. The last occupant bearing the family name, John Roberts, had gone out of the old home in 1805, moving to Scalford, near Melton Mowbray, where a branch of the family had been long established, and where my father was born.*

III

We had shopped for our lunch in Market Bosworth and we ate it on the battlefield, probably sitting over the bones of Tudor lads who died "for something nobody cares a damn about to-day," said my

---

* My father's notebook had an entry concerning them, taken from the Scalford Church *Marriage Register*.
March 16. *1755*. Charles Roberts and Anna Hand.
This marriage was stopped by Richard Roberts, the father of the said Charles.
March 31. *1755*. Charles Roberts, a minor, with consent of parents: and Anna Hand.
So young Charles got his way after a fortnight.

father. We were on a small hill, with the site of the battlefield before us. My father was familiar with the topography of the place. He produced a plan from Hutton's *The Battle of Bosworth Field*. We sat and lunched in sunshine, the sky having cleared. We were on a spot called Ambion Hill, above the flat meadow, part of it bogland on which the two armies had clashed. We looked across to Ambion Wood, where Henry had brought up his army from its overnight camp at Shenton. To our right was Sutton Heath on which the gallant and ill-starred Duke of Norfolk had camped.

"The names of these villages are connected with another eve-of-the-battle legend," said my father. "In moving to Ambion Hill, where he harangued his army, King Richard was fulfilling a prophecy. He'd been told by a witch that he would come to great distress if ever he was surrounded by places ending in 'ton', and that he would lose his life if he lodged in a place beginning and ending in 'an'. Well, here he was on the even of battle with the villages of Shenton, Sutton, Stapleton and Dadlington surrounding him. The early spelling of Ambion was Ambien, so the prophecy tied every cord round his throat."

As we sat there eating our lunch my father reconstructed the battle that had been fought in these fields on August 22nd, 1485. King Richard had marched from Nottingham with an army of seven thousand men. He entered Leicester wearing his crown. He seemed invincible but he was surrounded by spies and traitors, one in particular being Earl Stanley who, unknown to the King, had had a secret meeting with Henry Richmond, his son-in-law. Henry had hoped that Stanley would go over to him openly before the battle. Stanley demurred. The King suspicious, held his son, Lord Strange, as a hostage. Stanley said he would choose an auspicious moment to go over to Henry's side. Wary, he was not willing to risk anything until he knew who was going to win. There must have been many followers in Richard's army who had a true assessment of Stanley. Someone warned the Duke of Norfolk, the King's strongest captain, pinning on his tent overnight the lines—

Jock of Norfolk be not too bold!
For Dickon, thy master, is bought and sold.

In addition to the witch's prophecy it was said later that the King in his tent had been troubled by a vision of those whom he had murdered in his climb to the throne, including the two young princes. This vision the King narrated to his companions the next morning. But Polydore Vergil in his *History* gave the story no credence. He said it was the King's own guilty conscience that had troubled him. "Verum id credo nonfuit somnium, sed conscientia scelerum," he wrote.

The king's challenger, Henry Richmond, had set sail from Harfleur with a mixed army and landed at Milford Haven on August 6th. He marched rapidly through Wales, recruiting the Welsh captains and their retainers, Griffith, Morgan, Herbert, ap-Thomas and Blount. To these he added the English captains, Byron, Digby, Hardwick and Talbot. His army, including two hundred Frenchmen, was only six thousand men but many of these were experienced warriors. Richard had now collected ten thousand men.

On August 21st the armies encamped within sight of each other. The next morning they moved to the attack. The King occupied rising ground, with Sutton Cheynell behind him. Henry's army moved into the position facing, by Ambion Wood. The King's army was drawn up in impressive length, the archers in front, under the command of the Duke of Norfolk and his son, the foot soldiers and horsemen to the rear. Henry's archers, also in front, were led by the Earl of Oxford, with horse and foot behind. The King, uneasy, sent word to Stanley to bring his men closer but he received an answer from the Earl that he would come at a convenient moment. The King replied—"I command your immediate attendance or by God, your son shall instantly die!" Stanley still delayed. He had sent word to Richmond urging him to begin the attack. He seemed to have given up his son, Lord Strange, as lost. Enraged at Stanley's tactics, Richard gave orders for the youth's immediate execution. The block and axe were prepared and the youth was brought from the tent where he had been kept under guard. But some among the King's officers, Lord Ferrers in particular, were revolted by this threat of summary execution. They pointed out that the youth was innocent, that it would only bring disgrace on their arms and the King's character. Moreover, Stanley had not yet declared against them. The King ordered the execution to be delayed.

Henry advanced his men up the hill. Cautious, some said cowardly, he kept himself in the rear. The two armies engaged so swiftly, sword to sword, that the bowmen were frustrated. Confusion and then tumult marked the field. It soon became clear that the King's army, with little enthusiasm for their cause, fought with no passion, whereas Henry's men, largely volunteers, were strong in their cause. At this stage the treacherous Stanley joined Richmond's right, coming over Radmore Plain, to the anger and dismay of the Royalists. Norfolk, on his ensign a star with rays, came face to face with Oxford bearing his ensign of a silver lion. Members of the same family, one attacked the other, shedding allied blood, as throughout the long Wars of the Roses. Oxford hewed the beaver from Norfolk's helmet, bringing him to the ground. Declining to strike against an unguarded man, he drew back when an arrow pierced the Duke's brain. The prophetic warning pinned on his tent had been fulfilled.

"Since you chose to be born in Nottingham," said my father, with a playful remonstrance he could never forego, "you'll be interested to know that two Nottinghamshire soldiers, Sir John Byron and Sir Gervase Clifton were in the battle. Related, and neighbours, they were now in opposite camps. The ancestor of the poet fought under Henry's banner, Clifton under Richard's."

They had made an oath that if either of them was vanquished the other should intercede with the conqueror, so that the estate of the loser might not be forfeited but be retained by his family. There was chivalry threading the cruelty of civil war. Clifton, fighting, was struck down. Byron seeing this, quitted the ranks and went to the relief of Clifton, guarding him with his shield and urging him to surrender. Clifton thinking all was over begged him to remember the pact between them. But Clifton did not die. He lived until 1491, when he joined his ancestors in Clifton church. "As you know," said my father, "the Clifton descendants are still at Clifton while the Byrons have gone forever from Newstead."*

The battle raged for over an hour, neither side having the vantage. A scout informed the King that Henry was just behind the hill. He spurred his horse in that direction calling on his captains to follow him. Lord Lovell, Lord Ferrers, Sir Richard Radcliffe, Sir Robert Brackenbury and Sir William Catesby rode with him towards the hill. Betrayed by Stanley the King felt he must make a decisive blow; he would conquer or go down fighting. Impeded by a bog in which his horse floundered, he dismounted, called for another, remounted, and rode on furiously towards where Henry stood. He challenged his company, struck down the standard bearer, unhorsed Sir John Cheney, and went forward in battle fury, his crown upon his head,

* Appendix III.

determined to reach Henry. At this point the treacherous Stanley threw in his men to aid Henry, cutting off the King from his followers. All Richard's courage was unavailing. He was unhorsed, and under a multitude of blows went down, bludgeoned to death. The crown falling from his head, rolled under a gorse bush, his helmet pierced like a colander. His end was heroic, whatever his character.

A soldier found the crown and brought it to Sir William Stanley, brother of the traitorous Earl, who placed it on Henry's head, crowning him King on the battlefield. Richard's body, stripped naked, was flung over a horse, the head, arms and legs dangling. In this degrading manner he was carried back to Leicester. Crossing a bridge, the dangling head hit the parapet. Bloody, covered with dirt, the body lay exposed in Leicester for two days and was then buried like a dog's. To-day the Bow Bridge carries a plaque marking where Richard crossed, a king, and recrossed, a corpse.

"There was a strange quirk of Fate in the king's end," observed my father. "He had been crowned by the Duke of Buckingham, whom he beheaded later. Sir William Stanley put the retrieved crown, once worn by Richard over his helmet, on Henry's head, crowning him King Henry VII. The king, in turn, ten years later, beheaded Stanley."

With King Henry's ascent to the throne the sanguinary Wars of the Roses, which had butchered over one hundred thousand men, came to an end. The victory presaged a new age, with Henry VII, Henry VIII and Queen Elizabeth leading the kingdom to a greatness it had never known before.[*]

I asked whether Richard was really a villain. "Yes, but then nearly all of them were," answered my father. "They all had murders on their hands. Young and brave as Richard was, followed on the throne by one whose claim was no better than his, England could not stomach the murder of the two young princes in the Tower, as well as other crimes. He remains among the damned, despite all attempts to rehabilitate him. And whatever the historians say, Shakespeare has pilloried him forever in the first forty lines of *Richard III*— 'Now is the winter of our discontent . . . I am determined to prove a villain,' etc."

[*] The term "Wars of the Roses" is somewhat erroneous but now too well-established to be demolished. It was invented by Sir Walter Scott in his novel *Anne of Geierstein*. The red and white roses were only two of many tokens adopted by the contesting Houses of Lancaster and York.

Our lunch finished, we recovered our cycles and went along a road that had been made across the scene of the battle, with enclosed fields on either side. The battle had ended at two o'clock in the afternoon. Richard had lost a thousand men, Richmond only a hundred. We came to a spot in the field marked by a well called Dickon's Well, since the king was said to have drunk there. We found a swamp, possibly the site of the bog where the king had had to abandon his floundering horse and call for another—"A horse! a horse! my kingdom for a horse!" in Shakespeare's words. Ambion Wood had disappeared. It was now ploughed land.*

IV

That evening at our inn my father read to me a story about the Hall, narrated in Hutton's book, dated June 17th, 1789.

"In the house of Mr. Roberts of Sutton, in pulling down an old wainscoat, there was discovered a large quantity of writings which were found to contain an account of the Battle of Bosworth Field; but as no particular notice was taken of the MSS. or value put upon them, they were all actually destroyed by the cook for culinary purposes. It is said that there were four or five quires of them. I preserve this anecdote as the tradition of the neighbourhood, without giving much credit to the importance of the MSS. supposed to have been destroyed; which possibly may have been a copy from some old chronicles, perhaps only some common black-letter book. The tradition, however, was confirmed to me in 1793 by the following letter from a friend at Bosworth—'Mrs. Dixie (née Susan Roberts, married to Wolstan Dixie) has many times stated that she could remember reading the papers alluded to, and that she recollected something about the King stopping at the Well, and about his natural son being placed on a hill, and of the King being set fast in a bog; how another man gave him his horse and the King mounted a second time; likewise the King cleaving Sir Richard Brandon, the standard bearer, down the head at one blow. She mentioned that she read of Henry being quite in the rear, who seemed a coward to the King, and that the King, being on a hill, declared he was betrayed but that he would die a hero, or wash his hands in Henry's blood, etc. I have heard her talk of it several times, and she had a great deal to say about it; she thought it was the only true copy'."

* Appendix IV.

An old wives' tale? Perhaps so, perhaps not. The cook destroyed the evidence. To this story I can add a note of comedy in my own experience. In July, 1951, motoring in Leicestershire, I made a visit to Sutton Cheney. I called on the occupants of the Hall-farm and then I went on to the church to look at the monument to Sir William Roberts which I had seen forty-four years earlier. While studying the alabaster figure I noticed that the knight's nose, broken off, had fallen into a crevice in his ruff. I picked it out and placed it back on the face. Resuming my journey, I thought, as I neared Rugby, how foolish it was of me to have left the nose loose in that manner. Someone, dusting, could easily sweep it away and it might not again be preserved in the ruff. Coming to Rugby, I went into a post-office and sent a telegram to the rector of Sutton Cheney—*Please fasten Sir William Roberts' nose on his face.* The woman who took the telegram looked at it and then at me. "Is it correct?" she asked. "Correct," I replied. Her eyes followed me to the door. Obviously a lunatic was loose. A few days later the obliging rector replied—"I have shown your telegram to the Church Warden who tells me he has three times fixed on the nose of your ancestor!—once with plaster of Paris, and twice with other preparations but unfortunately it has come loose again."

In 1965 I was again in Sutton Cheney. I had a definite purpose in view. One day, a learned friend of mine surprised me by showing me the manuscript of a book he had just written on the Battle of Bosworth Field. I said that I could tell him something of interest concerning it, that there had come down through my family a legend that my ancestors had witnessed the battle from the roof of their home nearby. "You can't believe a preposterous story like that!" he said. "You mustn't repeat such nonsense!" Scolded, I did not contest the point. It occurred to me that I had never verified whether it had been possible to witness the battle from the roof of the Hall. Arriving at Sutton Cheney, I went to the rector's house, a modern one at nearby Cadeby, for he had charge of two parishes. The Reverend Edward Boston proved to be a very jolly and hospitable young clergyman who heartily greeted me and my friend. A bassoon and a flageolet stood against the fireplace of his sitting-room, a recorder lay on a side table along with sheets of music. In and out of these objects on the table ran the rails of a model train.

Oh yes, he played the instruments. He picked up the bassoon and recorder in turn and played some Purcell airs on them very skilfully.

As for the model train, trains were his hobby. We must come out into the grounds, he would show us his real trains. We followed him out and to our astonishment there we found a traction engine (1927) with nameplate, and a shining four-coupled locomotive, built in 1919. Three or four times a year he got steam up and took passengers on a journey on rails laid round the rectory grounds, raising money for the church. He presented us with little printed railway tickets for "The Cadeby Light Railway." On one occasion he had astonished his bishop by arriving at a Diocesan Conference in his traction engine ahead of the bishop in his automobile.

Mr. Boston next took us into a large shed and to our amazement we found an immense model of villages, fields, hills, woods, tunnels, bridges, railway junctions and stations. Around the perimeter of this great tableland there was a double railwaytrack. The line was electric, and from a switchboard the rector sent the trains running in and out · of stations and tunnels, with signals and points all working.

After this entertaining interlude we returned to the rectory and I asked him if he knew the occupant of the Hall-farm at Sutton Cheney, mentioning my desire to go up on the roof and verify if it was possible to see the battlefield from there. Yes, he knew Mr. Burgess. We set out by car, going first to see the church. I was glad to find this time that Sir William's nose was firmly fixed on his face. We then visited the almshouse and talked to an old woman nursing her husband in front of a hob fire. At the Hall-farm the genial farmer said there was no way of getting on to the roof except by a very long ladder and he hadn't one. But there was a large attic, with a window in the west gable. We might be able to see the battlefield from it. We mounted a wide oak staircase of ancient timber winding round a newel post and came to the attic door. The long room immediately under the roof was lit by a window on the west gable. The farmer's wife brushed the cobwebs away from the old rusted lattice frame and opened the small window. Below us were the church and the almshouse. Beyond, not a quarter of a mile away, lay the whole valley of the battlefield! I was satisfied. How old was the house, I asked. The first one was probably late fourteenth or early fifteenth century, stone built. At the beginning of the seventeenth century Sir William Roberts had made alterations and added his initials and the date, 1613, on the west gable. Obviously this attic gable had been super-imposed on the former flat roof, as the chimney shows.

The rector suggested that we should lunch at the rectory. "We've nothing in but I can get some sausages if you don't mind a scrap meal," he said. We demurred. He insisted. We found a butcher's shop in Market Bosworth but instead of the proposed sausages the butcher urged on us a splendid pork pie. "Melton Mowbray?" I asked. "No, sir! Market Bosworth, home-made in this shop!" We bought it and it feared no rival. Never have I known a merrier lunch. The bachelor rector was looked after by the old family governess, Miss Parfitt, an active eighty-nine, who cooked and sat down with us. Every now and then our host jumped up to play a few bars of Mozart on a virginal to illustrate our music talk, or took up the flageolet and gave us a passage of Purcell. We left feeling that we had met a rare soul. After this 1965 diversion let us return to 1907.

V

On the last day of our holiday my father and I turned homewards. We had made the Visitation. The weather was glorious again. In Market Bosworth we passed the fine old mansion of the Wolstan Dixies, built around 1700, and then went on our way to Leicester. Before we reached there I knew that all was not well with my father. The slightest incline bothered him. He made no complaint but stopped frequently. All the time he talked informatively of the places through which we passed. In the village of Kirkby Mallory Lady Byron's father lived, the local squire. After a tempestuous year with Byron she came here in January 1816, with her infant daughter Ada. From the Hall she wrote him a letter—"Dearest Duck. . . . If I were not always looking about for Byron I should be a great deal better for the country air!" It was her last letter to him. When the parents realised the dreadful manner in which he had treated their daughter, half-convinced he was insane, they wrote a letter informing him that their daughter would not return to him and that she would take steps for a separation. Following this wreckage of his marriage, Byron left England, never to return. Lady Byron outlived her daughter Ada, who died in 1852, and was buried in the Byron vault at Hucknall Torkard, along with her father. Lady Byron died eight years later and was buried alone, in a London cemetery. Near the Hall my father showed me a monument she raised to the memory of her daughter.

During a rest, when nearing Leicester, he said to me, "I think we'll take the train to Nottingham. Don't tell your mother I got tired." I obeyed the injunction. One evening, two days later, when I showed him my completed diary, some of it written up from his notebook, he smiled and said, "Well, I think you know a bit more about the family now and you've learned a little history." I had, and I began to understand his obsession with the past. But I had begun to realise something else. I had the future in hand. I was young and the first stirring of ambition told me that all these dead ancestors of the Visitation, however interesting, could contribute nothing to my immediate purpose—to win fame or fortune, or both, or, failing these, at least to enjoy a life of independence and fulfilment in an exciting world.

CHAPTER TWELVE

Tragedy

I

THAT AUTUMN I began a new life. The solicitor's office in which I worked was in a quiet courtyard with trees in it. On the ground floor was the head clerk's office. It had a long high desk with a brass railing that cut it off from the part of the room where clients came. We sat on high leather-covered backless stools, at the sloping desk. Behind was a smaller room, used as a store and a kitchen, where the teapot, jug and kettle were enthroned on a gas stove. At the back of the front office there was a heavy metal letter-press with a revolving screw. In this I had to place letters for copying, written in a special ink. There was no typewriter, no filing cabinet. An old clock, enamel-faced, made in Derby, solemnly ticked on the wall above a Law Almanac with a portrait of a Lord Chancellor in his robes. I also had the task of keeping the postage book. Every outgoing letter had to be listed. I had to be at the office at a-quarter-to-nine. I had an hour-and-a-half for lunch. I left at six o'clock. The office was always very quiet. Upstairs there were two rooms. The front room, overlooking the court, furnished with a large flat-topped desk and leather chairs, had a thick carpet, and an ormolu clock on the mantelpiece. This was the solicitor's private room for receiving clients. There were engravings of famous judges in full-bottom wigs. They all had grim tight mouths. The room behind had steel racks on which were tiers of black tin deed boxes. On these were printed in white paint the names of the owners.

The head clerk, who was very amiable to me, was like a character out of Dickens. He always arrived in a bowler hat, wearing black kid gloves, rather like an undertaker. He was a midget, almost to the degree of being deformed. He had thick black eyebrows and greying hair. He was very formal in speech and manner. He saw everybody, he ran the whole office. There was also a middle-aged clerk, a sad-faced man who wore a flat starched collar and black bow that made him look like a nonconformist minister. The elbows of his dark jacket were patched with black leather. He alone wrote with a quill pen with which he could make wonderful flourishes. The head clerk and I used pens, as also the solicitor, for I had to see that there was ink in the porcelain wells in the silver inkstand in his room, and that the pens had clean nibs. As events turned out, this service was a make-believe. The head clerk was an old bachelor; the clerk had a blind wife and a daughter.

Throughout the whole of the first week the solicitor did not appear. He was absent at the end of the second week. I assumed he was away on holiday. Then I became aware of an air of mystery in the office. People came and asked for the solicitor. The head clerk would go out from behind the rail, take them aside and hold a conversation, *sotto voce*. He would come back to his desk when they had gone and look perturbed. There was a number of elderly ladies among these callers. Sometimes a loud-spoken client arrived and would be hurried upstairs. But the solicitor was still away. On his flat desk there were no papers.

A series of conferences was held upstairs. I heard raised voices. Then one day the mystery was solved. The solicitor would never again sit at that desk with the silver inkstand in the upstairs room. He had blown out his brains in the garden of his house. There were anxious clients pressing for information. The little head clerk was very calm. He had worked there forty years, the other clerk twenty. "I do not know what is going to happen," said the head clerk. "They are trying to find someone to take over the practice. Who could have believed it! I had not the slightest suspicion. I think you had better look for another position." I went home and reported this lamentable news. It was not only the loss of five shillings a week. It was also the loss of the promised articles. I was not going to become a solicitor. I dared not confess it to my worried parents, but I was immensely relieved. I had never wanted to become a solicitor. I wanted to be an author, I had dreams of fame. I saw my name in all the bookshops. Like Dickens, I would give readings and go on an American lecture tour. Beautiful girls would ask for my autograph. My wife would hold receptions in a crowded salon.

Dreams do not make bread and butter. I was earthbound by necessity. There was a tentative proposal to make me a bank clerk.

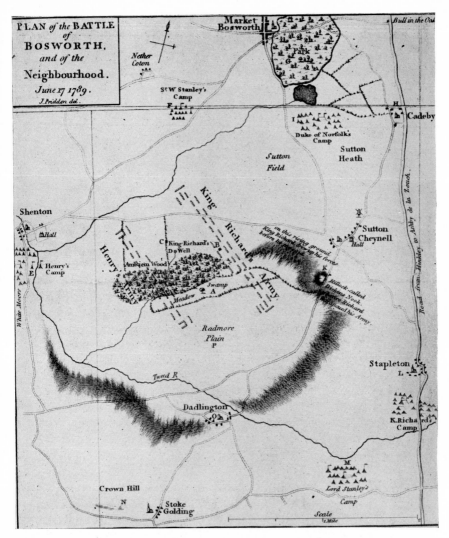

Plan of the Battle of Bosworth Field, showing location of the Church and Hall,
Sutton Cheynell

The Rectory, Rempstone

The Rectory, Church Langton

I was rejected by a severe-looking old fellow. All seemed to have gone well at the first interview. Then I was sent for and asked if it was true I wrote poetry. "Oh, yes," I said eagerly. "I've written a long narrative poem about the ghost at the Friary, and a number of lyrics." I offered to produce them. He declined my offer. Two days later I was informed there was no opening for me. When, later, my father met the manager, as he deposited his firm's money there, he told him that he was sorry he could not take me. "Anyone who writes poetry shows a temperament that is unsuitable to banking." How right he was! Years later, whenever I descended from the manager's office at Lloyds Bank in Pall Mall, and looked down in that main hall on all the young men without 'temperament' destined to sit out their lives on stools, I offered up a little prayer to the memory of that stuffy old manager frightened by poetry. What he had saved me from!

II

It is an obsession with parents to find for their young a position that will be safe, something with the prospect of a pension at sixty. My own parents were not free of this obsession. My mother thought that perhaps Donald's father would come to our aid. He was an M.P., influential, and they did not like bothering Lord Henry again. They suggested I should seek Mr. Richardson's aid when next I went to the Friary, but I recoiled from the idea. I was sensitive about trading on friendship or hospitality. Then one day, greatly to my surprise, my mother said she had been to see Mr. Richardson. "He couldn't have been nicer, and he will try to do something for you," she said.

One evening, I was summoned to supper at the Friary. All the family were there, also a thin, quiet, bespectacled young man who was courting a Richardson relation. It was a merry party, with Dorothy and I fencing as usual. Then some days later I was asked to call at a Nottingham Corporation office buried under the old Exchange, adjacent to the dark smelly Shambles. To my surprise I found myself being cross-examined by the spectacled young man whose name was Austin. Despite his lack of years he carried office under two titles, he was Clerk to the Markets and Fairs Department, and Chief Inspector of Weights and Measures under the Board of Trade. He offered me a career, if I duly passed the examinations, as a future Inspector of Weights and Measures. The starting salary was eight shillings. He seemed in no way deterred by the fact that I wrote poetry, of which he was well aware.

My parents were delighted. I was a Corporation employee, with a foot half in the Board of Trade. I was safe for life, with a pension in view. Nothing except drink or theft could throw me out of employment. The first surprising thing when I reported for work the following Monday morning was the discovery that on the very corner opposite the office there was a butcher's shop with a plaque over it saying that in 1785 Henry Kirke White, Poet, had been born there. The plaque had been placed there only a year previous to mark the centenary of his death in 1806. At the same time a fund had been raised for an annual Henry Kirke White Prize Poem, awarded by the Nottingham University College. In 1912 I won the Prize with a long poem, *The Trent*. Strange how that ill-omened young poet, Kirke White, haunted me. I had begun by writing at fourteen a centenary profile of him in my school magazine, and now, within a year, from my office I looked out on his birthplace.

The office was a dismal place. It had been crushed in between two high foundation walls of the Exchange. It was lit all day by electric bulbs, as it received no daylight. Down the alley in which it was situated came smells from the butchers' stalls in the bloody Shambles, from a penny public lavatory and also from the open stalls in The Poultry, an adjoining street, so-called, a place of plucked poultry and cooped hens.

At first I was sent out with an inspector of weights and measures and his two assistants, in a van. We made tours of the shops, pouncing on unsuspecting tradesmen to see if they were cheating with improper weights. We were received with open repugnance. We were 'snoopers'. Sometimes there were unpleasant scenes. A poor old woman in a miserable shop, whose weights had got worn or had had bits of lead fall out of them, would think she faced prosecution and ruin, and would burst into tears. Deliberate cheats there were, of course, but mostly it was carelessness. I hated the whole business. After a miserable month I could not endure it, and I told my chief so. It was my luck that he was a sympathetic and discerning young man. He moved me to the indoor staff. I had to register the shopkeepers who brought their weights and measures for an annual check, I also kept the ledger of the rents paid for stalls in the great Market Place. Two collectors visited the stalls each Wednesday and Saturday. As October approached there was great excitement in the office. We controlled the letting of sites for shows and round-abouts in the great Goose Fair. At six a.m. on the previous Sunday morning we marked with tapes, brushes and buckets of whitewash, the sites rented out, the largest being that for Bostock and Womb-wells' travelling zoo. Poor Mrs. Capocci, with her ice-cream barrow, was moved to another site to make place for the barred cages of the animals.

My fellow workers in the office were hostile. They derided my speech, my manners and dress. They called me The Duke. I certainly did nothing to placate their ignorance and prejudices. I flung passages of Gibbon, Coleridge, Wordsworth, Keats, Shelley and Oliver Wendell Holmes at them. Little by little I subdued them. Scared of my quick repartee, they were utterly mystified by the odd world in which I lived. Then little by little they found I was an entertainment, and became friendly, though I maintained my individuality. My lynx-eyed chief missed nothing of this. Sometimes he called me in and lectured me. Looking back, I see what a kind and understanding fellow he was. As an office boy I was preposterous. Anyone else would have crushed me or have got rid of me. I was quite unpredictable, and ready to take up a cause. My chief was plagued by a bombastic, ignorant City councillor who sat on his committee. I wrote a rhymed skit on him, and left it on my chief's desk. He called me in. "You must not write such things. It can get you into great trouble, and me also." I asked him if it wasn't true to life. "Yes, it's wickedly true, but you simply must not do it. You are an employee here." I promised to behave. Even so, I knew he had enjoyed it. I heard later that it had been read out to his friends.

III

Four months passed. I began to accommodate myself to this prison house, although my wings still beat against its bars. There were assets to be found in its location. The office was so near to my father's that I could walk home with him to lunch and back every day. I did not know then that on a corner of the Market Place we were passing a legend in banking history. A brass plate on a building said "The Union Bank Incorporating Smiths' Bank." The soft sandstone rock that underlies the town from earliest times was honeycombed with passages, caves and cellars, a veritable labyrinth. In 1653 Thomas

Smith, a draper, kept a shop built over one of these deep sandstone cellars which he converted into a strongroom. He offered to local tradesmen and farmers coming into the town a safe deposit for their money. In times when highwaymen and footpads abounded it was a wise precaution. Soon more and more traders availed themselves of Smith's strongroom. He began to discount bills and handle cash and soon was operating over a wide area. Thus the first county bank was founded. After a time the drapery business was discarded and the shop over the cellar became solely a bank. Later the business was moved from a three-storeyed gable-end shop to premises commanding a fine view of the Market Place. The bank's safety was reinforced by two seventeenth-century brass muzzle-loading blunderbusses which are still on display. The bank amalgamated in 1918 with the National Provincial Bank. Thomas Smith, dying in 1699, passed on his business to his two sons, and an Abel Smith was sent to open a London branch, first in Coleman Street and then at No. 1 Lombard Street, where it still exists.

Thus began the great dynasty of the 'Banking Smiths'. There is no knowing where and in what rôle one of these Smiths, descended from Thomas of the sandstone cellar, will turn up. They have married into the Royal Family, gone into the House of Lords, the House of Commons, the Bank of England, the City, the Navy and the Army. They have become Governors, and directors of great financial administrations, exercising power and fame that match the renown of the Medicis and Fuggers of old. The Abel Smiths are a close clan. In 1960 seventeen descendants of the cellar-owner held between them eighty-eight directorships in seventy-nine companies. Every year they hold the lunch of the Smith Family Club, in a room in Fishmongers Hall, London. Everyone present must have descent from Thomas Smith.

I knew nothing of this history when, a boy of fifteen, going to my office I used to see the brass plate on the corner building. One never heard of the Abel Smiths, one never saw them. They neither appeared in public nor were associated with the city's life, unlike the Portlands, the Players, the Boots, Birkins and Bowdens, local Mæcenases. Over forty years were to elapse before I saw an Abel Smith in the flesh. He was a fellow luncheon guest of Prince Filippo Doria Pamphili in his vast *palazzo* in Rome. He did not look like a banker. He was in fact a naval officer, destined to become a Vice-Admiral and Flag Officer of the Royal Yachts. He was somewhat surprised when I asked him if he was one of the Abel Smith dynasty out of Nottingham. How would I know that? "Well, I walked past your family bank a thousand times a year for five years, to my office a hundred yards away." I wanted to ask him whether at the annual lunch they had a piece of sandstone rock on the table as the symbol of their banking foundation, but I refrained.

There were other places of interest near my office. One was a Boots Chemist's shop with a Lending Library in it. I often slipped out for half an hour to browse on the riches of those shelves of new books. I was not a subscriber, but a very tolerant librarian pretended she did not see me. One day I left a bunch of roses on her desk and after that she smiled at me. Bless you, dear unknown lady who so kindly let a boy trespass on your shelves! It is sad to think that no boy to-day will have the opportunity and pleasure that Boots Subscription Library gave me. On February 5th, 1966, their library closed down forever. It had been founded in 1899 and its cessation marks a dying tradition of subscription libraries throughout the Kingdom that had lasted almost two hundred and fifty years. Sheridan knew of them and made Lucy, a maid in *The Rivals* say "I don't believe there's a circulating library in Bath I ha'nt been at." Boots Library was founded by Jesse Boot's wife, who was the daughter of a Jersey bookseller. It was her idea that if the lending libraries were placed at the back of each shop the subscribers visiting them, passing the counters, would be induced to buy goods. The libraries were a great success and by 1930 there were some 450 of them, excellently run. The subscription was low. An additional book could be borrowed for 2d. The Library had another great merit. It sold off its books from time to time and issued an exciting catalogue of books at reduced prices. There were many, including myself, who thus built up an excellent library at low cost. Authors benefited of course. My publisher was assured of a good order of any new book by me, as a 'favourite author'. Boots had half a million subscribers in 1934, in 1944 they rose to a million and the library bought half a million books a year. The lesser author was helped also as orders from Boots, Smith's, Mudie's, etc., helped to cover the initial costs of a publisher issuing a book by a new author. Alas, after the Second World War these subscription libraries were doomed. The high cost of books, television, the paperback, the improved service of public libraries, the vanishing of 'snobbism' against their use, all contributed to their death. Mudie's went, Smith's went, the Times

Book Club went, even the new crop of Twopenny Libraries folded up. It is a matter for lament. Literature was well served by them. The nearness of Boots Subscription Library was an asset in my private enterprise as an author. There was also another—the office typewriter. I soon learned to operate it, and typed out my poems and articles, often staying late in the empty office. I had no hesitation about making the Corporation of Nottingham subsidise Literature. Who knew what the future held? Perhaps one day they would be proud of having nurtured genius in their basement premises!

At home I had embarked on a new enterprise. I had seen in a magazine called *Hobbies* the design for a home-made bureau-bookshelf. It had a drop-lid writing desk, with four shelves above. My growing library badly needed housing. Also my manuscripts and papers wanted a permanent home. The dressing-table with a swing mirror upstairs was too uncomfortable for literary work. With a few pence it was possible to buy used boxes from the local grocer. This supplied the necessary wood. The grocer knew me well. For some years I had accompanied my mother, with her string bag and veiled hat, on her Saturday morning shopping tour. The grocer often had cheap lines of broken biscuits which I bought. At one end of his counter he kept displays of butter and cheese. He was a genial tubby little man. He lived behind his shop and looked into it through a little window from his sitting-room. When the shop door opened the bell went 'Ping!' and he would pop out like one of those figures on a Swiss chalet weather-guide. There was an absurd little comedy between him and my mother in which I always delighted. She would ask him if the butter was fresh. "Mother, do you expect he would ever say 'No, madam, it is rancid'?" I asked. The butter and other things purchased, she moved on to the cheeses, all colours and smells, standing in a row like undisciplined soldiers, drawn from many places, Cheshire, Cheddar, Stilton, Gorgonzola, Gruyère, and Holland, very glossy and red, and good plain American. My mother at this moment took off her right-hand glove and raised the spotted veil above her nose. "Perhaps . . ." she would say, whereupon the grocer produced a long thin knife like a rapier, delicately thrust it at a cheese, and held for her sampling a small piece on the end. Then came my expected moment. There would be a second thrust—"And the little man?" he would say, offering me my morsel. I solemnly swallowed it, looked at my mother, and nodded, confirming a purchase.

One day I quoted to him some lines à la Omar Khayyám, whom I had just discovered—

I often wonder what the grocer buys
One half as precious as the thing he sells.

"Is that yours?" he asked, "I must write it down and learn it." "No, it is a slightly altered version of a translation by Mr. Fitzgerald. It's a long poem called *The Rubáiyát of Omar Khayyám*, a twelfth-century Persian poet," I replied. 'Now, how would you know that?" he asked. "My father knows it off by heart," I answered. Then I dictated the lines of my version while he wrote them down on a piece of wrapping paper. He opened the glass front of the biscuit tin and gave me a macaroon. It was this grocer from whom I bought six boxes for my bookcase.

I began with sandpapering and planing the wood. It was a long task and, as I had hoped, I drew my father into it. He was clever with his hands and could never resist a job in which he loved to show his skill. There was a protest from my mother. Every night for two weeks we monopolized the kitchen after seven o'clock. I was allowed to work in it on condition that I swept up the mess before going to bed. Little by little the bookcase-secretaire grew. At long last it was completed. We bought a bottle of walnut stain which gave it a crowning finish. At ten o'clock on Friday, February 21st, 1908, I went to bed in a state of excitement. I could hardly wait for the stain to dry before putting my books on the shelves.

The bookcase was dry the next day. I put in the books. It looked magnificent. All that evening I sat at the desk feeling a real author, with dear Dr. Annandale next to the Bible and Philip's Atlas on the bottom shelf. My father was late coming home that night. He often stayed to complete his account books at the end of the week. Shortly after ten o'clock my mother went to bed. About half an hour later I heard her call and went into the hall. She was standing on the landing. "Is your father there?" she asked. I told her that he had not yet come in. "How very strange! I was sure I had heard him call me!" She returned to bed and I to my secretaire. In a short time she called me again. "I'm very worried. It's nearly eleven. Your father is never as late as this," she said. I replied that I would go up the Grove to meet him, he must be here any minute now.

It was a wild February night. A gale of wind shook the trees

violently. The street was dark and empty. At the end of the Grove I
saw a small group of persons discussing something. They looked at
me strangely. I asked them if anything had happened. Yes, the police
ambulance had just been to take away to the mortuary someone
who had fallen dead. He was a tall, thin gentleman. My heart stopped
with apprehension. I knew then it was my father.

The mortuary had been pointed out to me as a grim place near to
which we had gone from school for our woodwork class once a week.
It was about a mile away. I set out in the blustery night along the
empty streets. When I came to the mortuary I saw a light in the
police station next door. I went in. There was a police superintendent
in charge. He looked up from his desk. I think he guessed who I was.
I asked if a tall man had been brought to the mortuary. He said
"Yes, is your name Roberts?" I nodded. He took from a drawer a
leather wallet, a gold watch and chain, a pipe, a tobacco pouch and a
small flask with some liquid in it. The wallet was my father's. In it,
along with his visiting cards, were two newspaper cuttings. One was a
letter by me, published in the local newspaper, the other was the
report of a legal case in which a witness had pertly said he was a
gentleman. The judge replied "The term is very loosely used. A man
is only entitled to call himself a gentleman if he or his father has held
a coat-of-arms."* The bottle had a label on which my father had
written in his bold hand *Brandy. For Emergency.* It was characteristic
for he did not wish to be taken for a tippler. It showed that he was
conscious of his critical heart condition.

The superintendent said that he was just about to send an officer
to my home. He asked if I was willing to identify my father. I said I
was. He put a hand on my shoulder kindly, and led me to a heavy
iron-sheeted door. It opened into a large blank room lit only by a
single pendant electric bulb. The walls were whitewashed, the floor
was concrete. It was cold and grim. There were four marble slabs.
On one of these lay a figure under a tarpaulin. We approached and he
turned down the sheet exposing my father's face. The skin on his
nose was slightly broken, apparently from his fall. After a moment or
two the superintendent put back the sheet and we returned to the
office. He gave me my father's belongings, and asked if I would like

* In 1596 Shakespeare applied to the Heralds for confirmation of a coat-
of-arms said to have been granted to his father while Bailiff of Stratford-on-
Avon. The arms being granted, William Shakespeare in his Will signed
himself 'Gent'.

an officer to accompany me home. I said "No, thank you." He took
me to the door and wished me Goodnight. I set off down the long
silent street. I was incredibly calm. It was as if I were playing a rôle
in some drama that was only make-believe. I must remain calm. Soon
I would have to break the news to my mother.

I entered the house very stealthily, put my father's things on the
table and went upstairs. In my mother's bedroom the light was
turned low, she was not asleep. She sat up, her long beautiful hair
falling down over her lace-frilled nightgown. I think she knew the
moment she saw my face. I went to her and put my arms around her.
"I've seen him. He died at the top of the Grove. They took him to the
mortuary," I said, choking. Then we cried, holding each other. After
a time she said I must go to bed. I kissed her goodnight and went to
my room. There would be a lot to do tomorrow. I turned out the
light and, exhausted, fell asleep. When I woke it was daylight. For
a moment I thought I had had a bad nightmare. Then my tumbled
clothing, not folded as usual, told me the truth, as also another very
strange thing. In my agitation I had not put on my pyjamas and had
got into bed naked.

IV

The next four days are strangely indefinite in my memory. I
went to inform my brother and the doctor. We were able to avoid an
inquest as he had been attending my father and knew his cardiac
history. It was thought that battling against a high wind had been
fatal to him. I went to the shop on Long Row. The manager of the
Northamptonshire company that owned the business was deeply
moved when I told him my story. He took my face between his hands
and tears filled his eyes. "I can't tell you what we feel about your
father. He was a very dear and remarkable man. We talked together
such a lot in this office—not business always. Only the other day he
told me with great pleasure that your brother's wife is expecting a
baby. He knew so many things and was always so trustworthy and
had such perfect manners. You know how very proud he was of you.
He would say—'What do you think my boy's been doing now?' and
would show me your letters and articles."

Going home I reflected that my father had never said a word to
me about my writing. "He didn't wish you to become conceited,"
said my mother.

In the afternoon I took the doctor's certificate to the Registrar's office. When I got back they had brought my father home. He lay in a trestle-borne coffin in the drawing-room. There was the smell of new varnish. He had a bruise on his nose, otherwise he looked very calm and distinguished. I noticed that his long fingers bore traces of the walnut stain we had used on the bookcase. Somehow I still thought that he would get up and look at our work. He had never seen how splendid it was with the books along its shelves.

V

The day after the funeral there was a knock on the door. It was Mr. Ellis, the insurance agent, dapper as usual but fittingly solemn on this occasion. "Ah, my poor dear boy! What sad, sad news!" he exclaimed, stepping in. "And your dear mother—I hope . . ." My mother appeared. He put down his little bag as soon as he was in the sitting-room and took her hands in his. "Alas, Mrs. Ellis and I were away visiting this week-end. What a shock! Very personal to me, I had such an admiration for him. Now, I have hurried because I know that at a time like this money is necessary—all the dreadful expenses."

He opened his bag, took out some papers and put on his *pince-nez*. "Now, there is due to you on Mr. Roberts's Life Policy fifty-eight pounds five shillings," he said, opening a little linen bag and pouring out the sovereigns.

"But is that all, Mr. Ellis? The policy was for three hundred pounds," said my mother.

"Yes, it was, but unhappily Mr. Roberts drew on the Policy—he needed money for his invention, I believe."

There was a silence. "So that is all that is left?" asked my mother quietly.

"Alas it is. It is most unfortunate," replied Mr. Ellis, fingering papers and putting the gold sovereigns in small piles.

I had never seen so much money. My mother signed a receipt. It was a new Mr. Ellis. All his cheery bounce gone. No sixpence for me. No funny story. He closed his bag, took off his *pince-nez* and stood up. He was sure that the All-seeing Father would look after us—"He defendeth the fatherless and the widow." He turned to me and prophesied that I should be a great help. My mother, very quiet, hardly replied. I heard him at the door say, "Be of good heart, my dear Mrs. Roberts. Mrs. Ellis and I are very grieved about this."

My mother came back to the sitting-room, opened the cashbox and put the sovereigns into the tray. When she had closed it she sat down with the box in her lap. "I just don't know what we are going to do—all that gone in the *Jogoro* business," she said. "I knew that something was gnawing at your father." She got up and began to lay the table. I remember seeing a cat walk along the top of the garden wall in the half-light.

The next day a letter came from the Manager asking my mother to call at the shop. I went with her. The company in Northampton was giving her three months of my father's salary in appreciation of his work. He had been with them twelve years. When we got home the money went into the cashbox. It was nineteen pounds ten shillings, being thirteen weeks at thirty shillings a week. There were no debts to settle. After the funeral expenses were paid there was a net sum of fifty-six pounds. With that we faced the future. I was my mother's sole support, earning eight shillings a week. In those days there was no widow's pension, no children's allowance, no health service. They were talking about an old-age pension of five shillings a week at seventy. My mother was fifty-two, my father had died at forty-nine, I was three months short of sixteen years. My brother, expecting his first child, did not feel he could contribute. I never asked him. At the next meeting of the Markets and Fairs Committee they increased my wages of eight shillings to seventeen, on compassionate grounds. Let this be recorded of them for righteousness.

VI

It was clear that we could not go on living in the same house, the rent was twelve shillings a week and rates. It was also too large. It was then by good luck that the crippled scholar, Erasmus Horsley and his dictionary-loving wife, Mrs. Horsley, of 'commanding port', as Pope said, came with the news that one of the villas where they lived, set back at right angles to the Grove, with a tiny front garden and an open aspect, was going to be vacant. It was quiet and with-drawn in a corner. A laburnum tree grew before the bay window. It had a scullery, sitting-room, front room, two bedrooms on the first floor, an attic bedroom and lavatory. The rent was eight shillings a week. All the rooms were small but light.

I came to love that little house, it was a nest that nourished my dreams. The neighbourhood had not then become a depressed area, as fifty years later, when a flood of foreign immigrants created a progressive deterioration. My mother's plan was to let off the two front rooms, furnished. That left us with a sitting-room, a back bed-room and the attic. Within a month we had moved in. Some furniture had to be sold, including the piano but my precious secretaire-bookcase was retained, as also my dog Ruff, the Skye terrier, the recipient of my eloquence and companion of those walks along the Trent Embankment where I declaimed the the works of Milton, Wordsworth, Keats, Shelley—and Cecil Roberts.

Despite the terrible shock I had received and the grim outlook, I was buoyant with youth. But I came more and more to realise that in my father I had lost a wonderful companion, together with the richness of his mind ever devoted to my well-being. Ten days before our migration, while washing my dog, I fainted, with no warning. My mother in great consternation, sent for the doctor. He was not my beloved Dr. Harrison, but his successor, heavily built, fat-fingered, ponderously kind. He tapped me. Breathe in. Breathe out. As usual that old cardiac eccentricity puzzled him. Yes, overgrown, or probably delayed shock or . . . he did not say so but he knew I was suspect, following my father's medical history. But I was up and as alert as ever the next morning.

The furniture movers came. They are endowed with an easy irreverence for things. With personal care I carried the coat-of-arms, dear for my father's sake, whose successor I now felt myself. By right it was my elder brother's. He was very disdainful when I acknowledged his claim. "You can have the thing—and all the manors and lands that go with it!" he said. A baby was due. That was all that concerned him.

By sheer good luck the secretaire-bookcase just fitted into the living-room recess. The coat-of-arms went up into the attic. *Pro aris et focis.* There was no hearth or fireplace in my attic bedroom. I hung it between portraits of Keats and Byron, above my writing-table. There was no gas in the room but I had a paraffin lamp with a rose-coloured shade that my mother made for me, and a chintz-covered easy chair. To her dismay I sawed off the wooden foot and headboard of the bed and turned it into a divan. "Where's the hookah?" asked my brother. But he gave me a green carpet he could spare. I fixed a long bookshelf on the end wall. Lit up at night, I thought my den enchanting. My mother came up sometimes and sat in the easy chair while I read my latest creation to her.

I was worried about the future occupant of the two front rooms. It was a blow to one's independence and pride, an infringement of privacy. There was a music-hall song—

Our lodger's such a nice young man,
A nice young man is he,
So good, so kind, to all the family.

However good and kind, he would be an intrusion. The Robertses might have had Cromwell's soldiers billeted upon them. That was in a Royal cause. This was sheer dispiriting poverty. To my dismay my mother thought they might be a married couple who would take the rooms. And so it transpired. An advertisement in the 'Furnished apartments to let' column of the newspaper brought successive viewers. My mother weeded them out. Finally a very young couple moved in. I regarded them critically. She was a pretty girl, little over twenty. He looked equally young. I disliked him on sight. He was thin, slight, spotty, with a receding chin and mousy eyes. He was assertive and had a high-pitched voice. My mother had noticed the ring on her finger. They were three months married. "Almost a pair of children," she commented. They would pay eight shillings a week for the rooms, light extra. That covered our rent. On my seventeen shillings and a little from 'the fund' we had to live. We did and kept our heads high.

The tenants were a disaster. They quarrelled, or, rather, the chin-less husband bullied his girl-wife. He brought with him a horrible gramophone that he wanted to play after midnight. My mother vetoed that. At the end of the second week they both came in very late and noisy. Then they began to quarrel loudly and it sounded as if they were fighting. My mother and I went to their bedroom. The little lout had been drinking and the girl looked scared. They made no reply when my mother told them they would have to leave at the end of the week. She would not tolerate scenes. My mother went back to her bedroom. She sat down and I was alarmed to see her burst into tears. She was always so self-controlled, but in a few moments she was her usual self again. She saw me shivering in my pyjamas. "Go to bed," she said. "We will deal with this in the morning."

I lay awake in my room. The humiliation of it! One thing was unchallengeably clear to me. Without money you could be trampled on. The world was not governed by the law of merit. To lack money was to lack independence, and without independence the slings and arrows of outrageous fortune assailed one. I had no inheritance of any kind except my character and brains. In three days, on May 18th, I would be sixteen years old. No legacies would come my way to mellow the passage of time. Lying in the darkness of my attic room I made a vow that before I was thirty-five, the half-way of our mortal journey, I would be independent of any man's will. In what manner I would achieve this I did not know. I would try every door until I found the exit to freedom.

I got out of bed, lit my lamp and took down my diary. Under the date May 18th, 1908, I wrote firmly, "On May 18th, 1927, I will be independent. I will have saved £10,000." In some manner the resolution calmed my nerves. It was my Declaration of Independence. I put out the light and got into bed. In the morning, on waking, when I looked at what I had written the resolution did not seem at all preposterous. I was of the same mind still.

Downstairs my mother had already taken action. She had given the couple a clear week's notice. The timorous wife came to see my mother. She burst into tears. She was expecting a baby. Her husband, aged twenty-two, had no work. He was living on what he could extract from an indulgent grandmother. The father, well-to-do, had washed his hands of him and would not receive his wife. "Poor foolish child," said my mother.

They left at the end of the week. It was a setback. It meant the cost of another advertisement and the rooms unlet for a time. In ten more days we had a new tenant. "He looks like a gentleman," said my mother. He was a man of about fifty. His brother was a clergyman. He proved to be a slight thin man, rather shy and reserved. He came and went quietly. One thing disconcerted my mother. He did not go to work. He took his meals out. "It looks to me as if Mr. Hartley doesn't get enough to eat," said my mother. Twice she sent me in with something she had cooked. He accepted it rather diffidently and she wondered if she had offended him but he thanked her gracefully. He talked a little with me, discovering I was an avid reader. He paid his rent promptly for three weeks. Then he announced that he was going away for the week-end to stay with his brother at the Rectory. When my mother asked where the Rectory was, he said

"Near Loughborough." This was some twelve miles away. He did not tell her the name of the Rectory. He took a little portmanteau with him. He always wore gloves and a bowler hat.

He did not return on Monday, or Tuesday. My mother was uneasy. When she looked in his wardrobe there was little there. All he had left behind was a very worn pair of shoes, and a pair of pyjamas of which the jacket was torn. The book left on the mantelpiece was from the City Library. He had never received any letters. "I don't think we shall see him again," said my mother.

A week passed and he did not return. We began to think of another advertisement. "And yet, somehow, I felt sure he was a gentleman," said my mother. In the middle of the second week there was a postcard saying he would be back early next week. The postcard had no address. The postmark was Rempstone. He had said the rectory was near Loughborough. But was it a rectory? He now owed two weeks rent. I went to the Public Library and looked in the *Clerical Directory*. Yes, the rector's name was Hartley. He was an M.A. The 'living' was in the gift of Sidney Sussex College, Cambridge, worth £350.

We felt relieved. But on Monday there was no Mr. Hartley. He did not come on Tuesday or Wednesday. On Thursday my mother decided to write to him at Rempstone Rectory. "If he is a fraud the rector will reply," said my mother. I went out to post the letter, and just as I turned into the Grove, there was Mr. Hartley coming towards me! He was carrying a small portmanteau. He smiled and walked up the path towards the house. I returned by the back door with the letter unposted. A little later my mother came into the room, smiling. "It's all right, he's just paid me. He says he had so much to do in the garden he couldn't get away."

In the next six years Mr. Hartley, who happily stayed with us, demure as a mouse, often repeated his disappearing act. Once he stayed away two whole months, with no sign of life and the rent unpaid. He then sent a cheque made out by his brother. There was so much to do in the garden, he wrote, but he hoped to come soon. We became very curious about that garden. In the course of time we learned a little about life in the Rectory. There was the rector's wife, and a daughter, Dorothy, who went to boarding school.

I was soon on friendly terms with Mr. Hartley. He invited me to sit down and talk. He was well-read and one day he excited me by telling me that Rempstone appeared in Shakespeare's *Richard II*. It transpired that among the company named by Northumberland in

239

Act II. Scene 1. as coming out of Brittany, was Sir Thomas de Rempstone to help Bolingbroke to take the throne from Richard:

Sir Thomas Erpingham, Sir John Ramston,
Sir John Norbery, Sir Robert Waterton and Francis Quoint,
All these well-furnish'd by the Duke of Bretagne
With eight tall ships, three thousand men of war.

'Thomas' and 'John' were changed for the metre.

Bolingbroke, now Henry IV, rewarded his followers. Sir Thomas was made Constable of the Tower, which held Richard II, whose abdication deed he had witnessed. He was a Privy Councillor, Admiral of the Fleet and Knight of the Garter. In 1406 when crossing the Thames he had the misfortune to be captured by French pirates. He was soon released but on returning and taking ship on the Thames he was drowned. He had a gallant son, Thomas, who fought at Agincourt where he was taken prisoner. He was ransomed for a large sum. He now lies buried with his father and mother only ten miles from Rempstone, in the church of Bingham where the family had another estate.

Mr. Hartley was also well-read in Roman history. I mentioned one day that I regretted I had not learnt Latin at school. He looked at me and said quietly. "If you really wish to, I'll teach you." Thus it began. On three evenings a week I had a lesson. He took me through Caesar's *Gallic Wars*. Then, excitingly, the incomparable Horace and Virgil. Unhappily there were gaps when he was away, working in the Rectory garden.

One August day, in the second year, he invited me to stay a weekend at the Rectory. "I shall enjoy your company—the family's away and we'll have to get our own meals," he said. "I work in the garden a great deal." I avowed I would love to work in the garden with him. So at last I saw Rempstone Rectory. It was a four-mile walk from Loughborough, the nearest station, and just in Nottinghamshire, on the very edge of Leicestershire. Nearing the Rectory I was amazed to find myself back on that little brick bridge over the King's Brook, where, on that memorable day, my father had described the passing of King Richard's army.

The Rectory had a forecourt and stables as you entered from the village. It was a black-and-white timbered house. I pulled a rusty bell by a Gothic porch. Presently I heard footsteps, the door opened and there was Mr. Hartley, in old flannel trousers and brown pullover. He welcomed me into a small hall. I looked into a garden. The vista made me breathless. There was a very long wide lawn divided by a path. At the far end of the lawn there was a row of great elm trees. Through those one caught a glimpse of the Charnwood Forest. There was a profusion of flowers in the herbaceous borders. My host took me up to a little bedroom. "This is my niece Dorothy's room," he said. It had a view over the lawn, also it had shelves filled with books. She was away with the family. The drawing-room had a very large bay window facing the long lawn and its leafy screen of elms. Next to it there was the rector's study-library, very untidy but a real den with books all over the place, and a flat-topped desk with masses of papers. There were photographs of college groups, a dozen pipes on the mantelpiece, and some easy chairs, well-worn. How lovely to be a rector, to live here amid flowers and books!

When I went outside on the great lawn and looked back at the long low Rectory, with its black-and-white timber and bay windows, it was oddly familiar. And then I knew. Surely this was the home of the Vicar of Wakefield—

> A man he was to all the country dear
> And passing rich with forty pounds a year.

However poor one was, this would seem heaven—to hear the birds sing, the wind in the elms, and see the shadow on the lawn, from a window seat in the bay—

> How happy he who crowns, in shades like these,
> A youth of labour with an age of ease.

I discovered there was little ease for Mr. Hartley. How he laboured in that garden! The rector had no gardener, his brother filled the rôle. It explained his long absences from Grove Villas. I began to speculate. Was my gentle host the poor brother, of very slender means, possibly a remittance-man, who toiled in the garden? I mowed the lawn to a point of exhaustion (the lovely smell of mown grass), I picked gooseberries and raspberries and dug up fresh potatoes and cut celery and rhubarb. Each morning a woman came in from the village and cooked lunch and cleaned a little. We got our own breakfasts, teas and cold suppers. No one ever called. We lived in a leafy bird-voiced oasis with crimson sunsets and the moon large and yellow coming up behind the elms.

We never left the grounds, and in all the visits I made through five years I never once met the rector, his wife or daughter. I was invited when they were away. I speculated about the girl whose room I occupied. She must be about my age. You can usually learn much about a person from his books, but all these books gave me no clue, they were so varied in subject. She seemed interested in everything. Thirty years later I received for review *The Countryman's England* by Dorothy Hartley. "In speaking of the countryside that lies between the Rivers Nen and Trent," she wrote, "I know of no other part of England where one may travel so far in any direction, so comfortably, without any great adventure, but with a day full of pleasantness." I wondered. Was it possible that this schoolgirl whose bedroom I had occupied when we were so very young, had turned author? The Rivers Nen and Trent fitted the picture, and at the Rectory every day had been a day of pleasantness. Another twenty years passed and the name again appeared with a delightful country article in *The Manchester Guardian*, and I had no doubt. The rectory she mentioned must be Rempstone. So I wrote to her and back came a letter from her small cottage in North Wales. Yes, she knew I had occupied her room. Uncle Dick often spoke of me. So two budding young authors had occupied that rectory bedroom fifty years earlier! Then came a second letter, in April 1966, with the news that she had been awarded a Civil List Pension in recognition of her work in difficult circumstances. "It would be fun to see you when you come back to England. You have slept in my bed but we have never met! To me you are still 'Uncle Dick's clever boy friend' and Mother's 'nice little laddie'. She was delighted with *Scissors*, your novel bringing in the rectory."

Fifty-eight years after I had first occupied her bedroom, at the rectory, we met. We were both visiting London and we lunched together. She was the image of her uncle and astonished me by telling me that he had possessed a fine tenor voice when a young man and had toured with the D'Oyly Carte Opera Company!

Through those years at Grove Villas when Richard Austin Hartley lodged with us and gave me my Latin lessons, I made repeated visits to the rectory. It never lost its enchantment. When in 1920 I began to write *Scissors* the rectory appeared as Renstone Vicarage, the home of the gay young Marsh and his family. I drew a portrait of them: gentle Mrs. Marsh in a large straw hat with leather gardening gloves and clipping basket, who took the orphaned young Scissors to her heart, and of the Vicar, called The Skipper, with his pipe, who annoyed the local squire by reading the radical *Nation*. I placed a Bechstein piano in the drawing room in order that Mrs. Marsh could play Liszt and Bach, and make Scissors sing *Who is Sylvia?* to her accompaniment. The description of the house still stands but the characters I put into it are largely imaginary.

When I came to the rectory again, fifty years later, nothing had changed except the human element. The house had passed into private ownership, and the owners knew at once who I was when I rang the bell. *Scissors* had brought visitors down the years, and like myself they were most hospitably received. In the house and on the long lawn I evoked those happy days of my boyhood. Then I went across to the churchyard and found three graves, that of the rector, who died in May, 1923, aged 75, his wife in May, 1932, aged 79, and, placed at their feet by the entrance porch of the church, Richard Austin Hartley, my kindly tutor, October, 1932, aged 80. They had enjoyed long and tranquil lives in that old rectory looking on the distant Charnwood Forest. The ghost of my boyhood haunts the place.

The end of the first volume of this Autobiography.

Appendix I

Federigo of Montefeltro (1444–1482) Duke of Urbino (father of Guido-baldo I), the famous *condottiere*, kept a brilliant Court. The Library, now part of the Vatican Library, was founded by him. When only a boy he began collecting books and later employed some forty 'scrittori' or learned copyists. It was one of the great libraries of the Renaissance. The Urbino library contained catalogues of the Vatican, of St. Mark's Florence, of the Visconti of Pavia, and of the library at Oxford. It had no rivals in its richness and variety. The collection contained works on [medicine as well as theology, with a complete Thomas Aquinas, Albertus Magnus and Bonaventura. All the great writers of the fourteenth century were represented, the complete works of Dante and Boccaccio occupying the first place. There were collections of the works of twenty-five humanists, with both Latin and Italian texts. There was a large collection of Greek manuscripts covering the Fathers of the Church, as well as the works of Sophocles, Pindar and Menander. There was a continuous acquisition, at great cost, of ancient manuscripts. These volumes were mostly bound in crimson velvet with silver clasps. Professional copyists who were Greek scholars had the highest rank and were known as 'scrittori', an honourable title. They were limited in number and they received high remuneration. Under them worked ordinary copyists, clerks, schoolmasters and poor men of learning who were welcomed to the Court. The librarian, Veterani, followed in a long tradition of learned librarians and copyists. The books were mostly inscribed in the beautiful Italian handwriting of the day, on vellum, and great honour was shown to the contents of a book by the beauty of its presentation. The innovation of printed books was frowned upon for some time, especially by Duke Federigo "who would have been ashamed to own a printed book". This was the library with which Polydore Vergil, his father, and Baldassare Castiglione, were familiar.

Appendix II

Polydore Vergil's style and power of assessment is well demonstrated in the closing pages in which he ends his survey of the reign of his patron Henry VII, after his death in 1509, when his son Henry VIII succeeded to the throne. The translation from the Latin of *Anglicae Historiae* is by Denys Hay. (Camden Series, 1950, Royal Historical Society.)—

Henry reigned thirty-three years and seven months. He lived for fifty-two years. By his wife Elizabeth he was the father of eight children, four boys and as many girls. He left three surviving children and an only son Henry prince of Wales, and two daughters, Margaret married to James, King of Scotland, and Mary, betrothed to Charles, prince of Castile. His body was slender but well built and strong; his height above the average. His appearance was remarkably attractive and his face was cheerful, especially when speaking; his eyes were small and blue, his teeth few, poor and blackish; his hair was thin and white; his complexion sallow. His spirit was distinguished, wise and prudent; his mind was brave and resolute and never, even at moments of the greatest danger, deserted him. He had a most pertinacious memory. Withal he was not devoid of scholarship. In government he was shrewd and prudent, so that no one dared to get the better of him through deceit or guile. He was gracious and kind and was as attentive to his visitors as he was easy of access. His hospitality was splendidly generous; he was fond of having foreigners at his court and he freely conferred favours on them. But those of his subjects who were indebted to him or who did not pay him due honour or who were generous only with promises, he treated with harsh severity. He well knew how to maintain his royal majesty and all which appertains to kingship at every time and place. He was most fortunate in war, although he was constitutionally more inclined to peace than to war. He cherished justice above all things; as a result he vigorously punished violence, manslaughter and every other kind of wickedness whatsoever. Consequently he was greatly regretted on that account by all his subjects, who had been able to conduct their lives peaceably, far removed from the assaults and evil doing of scoundrels. He was the most ardent supporter of our faith, and daily participated with great piety in religious services. To those whom he considered to be worthy priests, he often secretly gave alms so that they should pray for his salvation. He was particularly fond of those Franciscan friars whom they call Observants, for whom he founded many convents, so that with his help their rule should continually flourish in his kingdom. But all these virtues were obscured latterly only by avarice . . . This avarice is surely bad enough in a private individual, whom it forever torments; in a monarch indeed it may be considered the worst vice, since it is harmful to everyone, and distorts those qualities of truthfulness, justice and integrity by which the State must be governed.

Blessed be our Lord God Jesus Christ
Mary mother of God
Pray for us all
Amen.

Appendix III

The story of the death in battle of Sir Gervase Clifton at Bosworth Field, having obtained a promise from Sir John Byron that he would intercede for him with Henry VII, so that his children would not lose the family estate, is a myth. He is commemorated in a brass in Clifton Church, having died in 1491 and been buried with his ancestors. He was created a Knight of the Bath at the coronation of Richard III, who gave him large attainted estates, and he received favours from Henry VII, who pardoned him. The myth was perpetuated in a long poem written by Sir John Beaumont, called *The Battle of Bosworth Field*. It was published posthumously by his son who sent it to Ben Jonson, who wrote a poem *On receiving the Poem of His Honor'd Friend Sir John Beaumont*. The first line is 'This Book will live, it hath a genius . . .' It was a flattering prophecy never fulfilled.

Appendix IV

The Battle of Bosworth Field is still being waged by the adherents of King Richard III and Henry VII. *The Times*, August 22nd, 1965, printed the following letter from Mr. Brinley Evans, founder of the Bosworth Society:

"On the very day of the anniversary of the Battle of Bosworth (Aug. 22. 1485) may I appeal for a complete cessation of hostilities in the Wars of the Roses? It will no doubt surprise most people to know that the Yorkist King Richard III is still defended on Bosworth Field by members of The King Richard III Society (the Fellowship of the White Boar), who cherish an obelisk erected there to commemorate his death, upon which the Welshman, Henry Tudor (King Henry VII), the victorious champion of the House of Lancaster, is described as 'the usurper'. No respectable historian will deny that the merits of the claims of both Richard and Henry to the throne of England can be debated *ad infinitum*; but it is monstrous that the strife of long ago should be perpetuated in a partisan, revengeful, and slanderous 'graven image' of a British monarch about whom Sir Winston Churchill wrote: 'He magnified the Crown without losing the cooperation of the Commons. He identified prosperity with monarchy. Among the princes of Renaissance Europe he is not surpassed in achievement and fame by Louis XI of France or Ferdinand of Spain. Such was the architect of Tudor monarchy, which was to lead England out of medieval disorder into greater strength and broader times'."

Index

251